THE ENGLISH CONQUEST
OF IRELAND

THE ENGLISH CONQUEST
OF IRELAND

FOUNDED ON THE *EXPUGNACIO HIBERNICA* OF
GIRALDUS CAMBRENSIS

HASKELL HOUSE PUBLISHERS LTD.
Publishers of Scarce Scholarly Books
NEW YORK. N. Y. 10012
1969

First Published **1896**

HASKELL HOUSE PUBLISHERS Ltd.
Publishers of Scarce Scholarly Books
280 LAFAYETTE STREET
NEW YORK. N. Y. 10012

Library of Congress Catalog Card Number: **68-25237**

Standard Book Number 8383-0947-X

Printed in the United States of America

A PARALLEL TEXT

FROM TWO MSS., I. AB. 1425 A.D.   MS. TRIN. COLL., DUBLIN, E. 2. 31;

II. AB. 1440 A.D.   MS. RAWLINSON B. 490, BODLEIAN LIBRARY, OXFORD

THE ENGLISH CONQUEST OF IRELAND

FOUNDED ON

GIRALDUS CAMBRENSIS.

(*MS. Trin. Coll., Dublin*, E. 2. 31.)

[CHAPTER I.]

[Fol. 1 a.]

When Henry II reigned in England, Dermot Macmurgh ruled over Leinster, A.D. 1135–71.

His folk hated him ;

[¹ &, an, a].
[² heart].

but the wife of King Rory of Meath loved him,

and sent for him when Rory was away.

He took her to Leinster, A.D. 1152,

YN the tym that the kynge henry, þat was the kynges fadyr Richard & the kynges fadyr Iohṅ, regned in englaundʼ well, & ¹ heighe maṅ in Irlandʼ, þat het dermod Macmorgh, princes of leynyster, that is I-toldʼ þe fifte parte of Irland. That dermodʼ, 4 from the tyṁ that he was lordʼ of londʼ, & foll sholdʼ gouerne, he went amonge his heighe meṅ, andʼ so hardʼ haṁ biladde þat þay casten grete hat to hyṁ, andʼ myche thay wax hyṁ ageyṅ in herth², þegh þey ne durst nat oppenly shewe. Whaṅ he hade 8 longe whill þus biladʼ hyṁ amonge his meṅ, bettidde an aduenture that turnede hyṁ þer-aftyr to mych harme ; ffor in mythe was a kynge that hegth Rowry, & a well fayr wommaṅ to wif ; andʼ as meṅ tellede oft, andʼ soth it is I-foundʼ, that soṁ of heme ben 12 to vnstable of herth², wher-throgh many harmes ben oþer-whill, þat ne beṅ nat now al to rekne. This Rouryes wif worthen to þe loue of Macmurgh mor þan hyr owṅ lordʼ, and he hir also, & this was longe ; bot to-giddre ne myghtyṅ þei nat coṁ as 16 the woldʼ ; for hit betidʼ a tyṁ þat hir lordʼ went owt of his contrey in-to fer londes, for grete nedes þat he hade to doṅ. his wif a-waitede full well, & aspiedʼ þat hir lordʼ most longe be owt of londʼ, sendʼ to Macmurgh, & bade hyṁ, þat if he euer woldʼ his 20 will hawe of hir, that he sholdʼ coṁ to hyr, for sho was redy to do all þat hyṁ likede. ❡ Macmorgh name power with hyṁ, andʼ went thar this lady was ; & as hit be-spoke was, he name hir, & broght hir out of myth into leynestr, and hell hir that to 24

OF THE CONQUESTE OF IRLAND
BY ENGLYSH MEÑ.

(*MS. Rawl.* B. 490, *Bodl. Libr.*)

[CHAPTER I.]

IN the tyme that Kynge Henry, that was the kynges Fadyr [Fol. 1 a.]
Rychard and the kynges Fadyr Ihoñ, regned in Englanď, Capitulum
was an hey man in Irland, whos name was callyď Dermot Mac- Iᵐ.
murgħ, Prince of leynystre, that is y-tolde the fyfte Parte of Leinster
Irlande. That Dermot, from the tyme that he was lorde of lond, *and* is a fifth
folke sholde goveriñ, he werret cruely amonge his hey men, *and* so Ireland.
harde hame lade, that thay castyn grete hate to hy*m*, *and* muche
they we*re* ayennes hym in herte, theght they ne dvrste nat opynly
shewe. Whan he hadd thus longe tyme lade hym amonge hys
men, be-felle an aduenture that turned hym ther-aftyr to mycħ
harme; For in myth was a kynge, whos name was Roury, *and* Tiernan
hadď a wel fayre woman to wyffe; and as men tellyth ofte, and sith O'Rourke,
hit is y-founď, that some of them ben vnstabill of hert, wherfore Breifny.
many harmys ben ofte-tymes, that ben nat now all to reherse //

This Rouries wyfe lowyd more Macmurgh than hyr owyn lorde ; ' Varium
and he hyr also, and this was longe; but to-giddyr ne myght they et mutabile
not come as they wolde ; for hit be-felle in a tyme, that hyr lord femina'
went out of his contrey into fere londys, for grete neddes that he (Virg.Aen.
hadde to done. His wyfe be-thoght hyr ful well, and, Supposynge iv. 569).
that hyr lord moste longe be out of londe, Sche sente to Macmurgħ, and sayde to hym, that yf he eu*er* wolde his wille haue of
hyr, that he sholde cvme to hyr, for she was redy to do al that
hym lykyď //   A. D. 1152.

Macmurgħ toke wyth hym many men, and went the*re* this lady O'Rourke's
was. and as hit was be-for spoke be-tweiñ them both, he toke hyr wife
wyth hym out of myth into leynestere, and helde hyr there to hys carried off.

A.D. 1152.
and kept
her there. his wiɫɫ. Nat for-þaŋ sho grad and cried, as thogh he naṁ hiꝛ agaynes hiꝛ wiɫɫ, as hit nas nat so. Than hir lord hit herde, he was theꝛ-of tened swith stronge, and mych moꝛ of the shamme

Rory and
his ally,
the King
of Con-
naught, þat to hyṁ was doŋ, þan of the harme; aɫɫ that he mygth do, 4 he didde, for to awreke hyṁ; he sent afteꝛ his owŋ poweꝛ, ande eke aɫɫ þat he myght of other; and the kynge of Connagth, þat was that tyṁ lorde of Irlandꞇ, coṁ to hyṁ with his poweꝛ:

march into
Leinster. he gadrede so moch folke(?) þat noŋ endꞇ nas, and coṁ into 8 leynestꝛ for to wreke hyṁ of his shame. Tho Macmorgh this herdꞇ, he sent to his meŋ þat þay sholde hyṁ helppe ayeyŋ his fomeŋ þat þus wereŋ commyng toward hyṁ. They bethoghten

Mac-
murgh's
men refuse
to help
him; haṁ of the teŋ & the traysoŋ þat they haṁ hade ydoŋ þer- 12 to-fore | andꞇ forsoke, al out of dout, þat þay nogth woɫɫ hyṁ helpe; andꞇ many of haṁ openly turnedꞇ to his fomeŋ ayeyns hyṁ, ffor to wreke haṁ of the iniurie þat he haṁ hadꞇ doŋ. Macmorgh saw þat poweꝛ hyṁ failledꞇ, & euerich half he was amyde his 16 fomeŋ beset. he was maŋ of hegh hert; and with þe litiɫɫ poweꝛ þat he hadꞇ, he werrede as long as he myght; bot he ne myght nat aɫɫ-way aɫɫ-oŋ ayeyns aɫɫ the lande folke | he was so narowe biladꞇ þat nedes he most thoɫɫ deth, otheꝛ þe londꞇ leue; he saw 20 þat noŋ oþer remedy was: he went to the see, andꞇ fondꞇ shippe

so he sails
to Eng-
land, A.D.
1166, redy, andꞇ wynde at wiɫɫ, & passede oure into englandꞇ, with weɫɫ fewꝛ with hyṁ; andꞇ on this maneꝛ he sawit his lif, & lefte londꞇ & lede & aɫɫ his otheꝛ goodꞇ. Hereby þat meŋ may witte, þat 24 be a maŋ of neueꝛ so mych power, bettꝛe hym is þat hys men hym loue þane hate. ❡ Whane Macmorgh was thus icome in-to england, al hys thoght was how he myght hym best worck of the schame þat hyme was done, & of þat þat he was so vilich out of 28 hys kynd lond I-dryue, he nyst of whom he myght bettꝛe besech

[*Fol.1b.]
and then
to France,
to ask
Henry II's
aid. help þane of þe kynge. And þe kynge was þane fer in the realme of fraunce for grete nedes þat he hade to done. Macmorgh passed oueꝛ to hym. þe kynge fayr hym vndrefynge, *& with mych 32 mane shipe. and whan had he tolde hyme the enchesoun of hys comynge to hym, and whar-for he was out of hys londe ibanshed, þe kynge was swyth wo therfor, & good hert hadde hym to helpe, naꝛ oþer grete nedes þat he hade to done. Whane he ne myght 36

wylle. And ther-for*e* she Cryed, and mad moche sorow and lemen- A.D. 1152.
tacioñ, as thogh he toke hyr ayeynnes hir wyll: As hit was not So /

Than hyr lorde hit herd, he was ther-of full stronge a-greued, and O'Rourke
mych mor*e* of the shame that to hym was don, than for the harme. is wroth at
the shame
Al that he myght do, he dyd, forto be wroke on hym. he Sente done him,
aftyr his owyn men, and eke al that he myght of othyr; and the and
kynge of Connaght, that In that tyme was lorde of Irlande, come to
hym wyth his Power. And he gaderid so myche Pepyll, that they invades
were vnnvmerable, Comynge Into leynystr*e*, forto be vengyd of his Leinster.
shame //

Tho Macmurgh her[de ther]of, he Sent to his men, that thay Mac-
sholde hym helpe ayeynes his foe-men, that thus weryn comynge murgh's
to-warde hym.

Thay bethoghten them of cruelte and the traysouñ that to ham
he hadd done therto-for*e*, And forsoke al out of dowte that thay
wolde noght hym helpe. And many of them opynly turned to his
Ennemys ayeynes hym, ffor to wroke tham of the Iniury that he
to them hadd done //

Macmurgh sawe that his men failled hym; and on Euche halwe men fail
he was amyd his ennemys besegyd. He was a man of hey herte; him,
and wyth the fewe Pepill that he hadd, he werrid as longe as he
myght; but he ne * myght not alway dure ayennes the Londe folke. [*Fol.1b.]
He was so narow bylade, that nedys he mvste suffyr deth, or the
londe leue. he saw that non othyr remedy was. He went to the
see, and fovnde shippe redy, and wynde at wyll, *and* passyd owyr so he
into Englañd, wi*th* wel fewe wi*th* hym; *and* on this maner he sauyd crosses to
England,
his lyfe, *and* lefte lond and lede, and al othyr good// Here-by men A.D. 1166,
may witte that, be a mañ neu*er* of so mych Powere, bettyr hit is to
hym, that his men hym loue, than hate // Whan Macmurgh̄ was
thus y-come Into Englañd, al his thoght was, how he myght hym
best wreke of the shame that hym was y-doñ, and of that that he
was so shamfully out of his kynde londe I-dryue. He wyst not of
whoñ he myght bettyr beseke helpe *and* sokovr*e*, than of the
kynge. And the kyng*e* was then fer in the reame of Fraunce, for and then
to France,
gret nedys that he hadd to doñ. Macmurgh̄ passyd ou*er* to hym. where
the kynge fayr*e* hym vndyrfonge, *and* wi*th* mych vyrchipp. And Hen. II
welcomes
when he hadde tolde hym the cause of hys comynge to hym, *and* him.
the cause wher*e*-for he was out of his Land y-baneshyd, the kynge
was sory therfor, *and* good-will hym hadd to helpe, ner*e* othyr grete
nedys that he hadde to doñ. Whan he ne myght nat ellis do, he

A. D.
1166–7.

Henry
appeals to
his sub-
jects to
help Mac-
murgh,

who
returns to
Bristol,

and agrees
to give
his
daughter
and Lein-
ster to
Earl
Strugoill,
in return
for aid.

Macmurgh
goes to
South
Wales,
A.D. 1167,

where Rys
is prince.

nat elles do, he name of hym homage, & othes, & lete hyme mak
hys lettres, that thus mych ben to vndrestond: 'Henry, throgh
gode-is grace kynge of englond, duc of normandy & of Acquitayne,
& erl of angoy, to al hys liegemen, englyssh, normannes, Walshe, 4
Scottes, and to al oþer that to hym ben subiect, sendeth gretynge.
Whan þese lettres to yow ben i-com, witte ye þat we, dermot,
prince of leynester, in our grace and in our goode will hawe
receyuet; wharfore þat all þay that hym as our lawfull man 8
hell[pe] willeth, into his lond hym to restore, our grace and our goode
leue haue þay þer-to.' Whan Macmorgh hade the kynges lettres
thus y-purchasede—þe kynge hym yaf also richely þat hym nedet
of his tresour—he nam leue of the kynge, & wentt in-to englond 12
& com to Bristow, & soiourned thar a whill; & so mych the
blethelier, for þer com oft shippes theder out of Irland, & men,
þat he myght hir tythynge of the lond & of his folkis, for his hert
was mych there-to. The whill þat he ther was, well oft he let rede 16
þe kynges wrytte to-for the peple; & largely he beheght londes and
rentes, & Rich yiftes, if any wer that hym helpe wold. Bot he ne
fond noon with-all, that such tynge wolde ne durst vndirtake,
till þat the erle of Strugoill, Richard þe Erles son Gilbert, com 20
to hym. Ther was þe parlement so longe y-dryue betwen ham,
& sekiritesse y-makyd, þat the Erle shold hym helpe with all
his power þe next somer þer-after, and he shold yeue þe Erle
his doghtre, with all þe lond of leynestre. ⁋ Whane this was on 24
this maner ypu[rueied, for the grete] talent þat Macmorogh had
to ben neer his lond—as man tynke [no place so ¹] mery lyghtly, as
in his kynd stidde,—he went hym thennes in-to south walys, to
seynt dauyes toun, vp-on þe see; & mych hit gladet his hert, 28
thogh he stronghly mourned, þat he myght in fayr weder haue
somdell syght of his lond.

⁋ In that tym was prince in wales, Rys, Gryffynes son, onþer ²
the kyng of england; & a swith good man bisshoppe of seynt 32
dauy, and was his nam, 'ahon dauy'; & both þe prince & eke þe

---

¹ Dermitius, desiderio visendae patriae plurimum accensus, eaque dulcedine,
qua natale solum cunctos ducere solet, amplius allectus.—Gir. Camb., *Expugnacio Hibernica*, cap. ii, *Op.* v. 228, Rolls Series.   ² under.

toke of hym homage *and* othis, *and* lette hym make his letter*es*,   A.D.
1166-7.
that thus myche ben*e* to vndyrstond̄ // 'Henry, throw goddys   The
grace, kynge of England, Duke of Normandy and of acquytanye,   Kyngys
and Erle of angoy, to al his lege men, Englyssħ, normannes, Walshe,   letter*es*
Scotes, and to al othyr that to hym ben subiecte / Sendyth gretynge.
Whan this *let*tres ben to yow y-come, witte y*e* that we, Dermot   in favour of
Prince of Leynystre, in our*e* grace *and* in our*e* goode-wyll, haue   Murrough,
receuet ; wherfor that al thay that hym / as our*e* laufull man he[l]pe
will, Into his londe hym to restore, our*e* grace and our*e* good̄-wyll
haue they therto' // 'When Macmurgħ hadd̄ the kynges Letter*es*
thus y-Purchasyd̄, (the kyng hym yafe also rychely, that hym nedyd̄
of his tresour*e*,) He toke Leue at the kynge, *and* went into England̄,   who comes
and come to Brystow, *and* soyorned̄ ther awhyle ; *and* myche radyr,   back to
for ther come oft shippis thedyr out of Irland̄, *and* men, that he   England,
myght hyr thythynge of the Londe *and* of his Pepyll ; for his hert
was mych therto // The whyle that he ther*e* was, well oft he made
to be redd̄ the kynges *let*tres to-for the Pepyll ; and largely he
promysyd̄ londys, and rentis, *and* othyr ryche yeftys, to them that
hym wolde he[l]pe. But he ne found̄ none, wyth al that, that Suche
thyng wolde ne druste vndyrtake, tyll that the Erle of Strugoill,   and is
Richarde, the Erlis Sonn*e* Gylbert [1], come to hym.   Ther was the   promist
Parlement [2] so longe y-dryue be-twen ham, and̄ sekyrnesse y-makyd̄,   help by
that the Erle sholde hym helpe w*ith* al his Power*e* the nexte   Richard,
somer*e* ther-aftyr, And he sholde yeue the Erle his doghtyr, w*ith*   Earl of
al the lond̄ of leynystre // Whan this was on this maner purueyed̄ [3],   Striguil.
For grete affeccion that M*a*cmurgħ had̄ to ben neer*e* his londe, (as
man thynkyth no Place so Myrry lyghtly as in his Kynd̄ * Place,)   [*Fol. 2 a.]
he went fro thens Into Suthe Walis, to Seynt Dauyes toun vp-on
the see ; *and* mych hit gladdyd̄ his herte, thegh he strongly mornyd̄,
that he myght in fayr*e* weddyr haue somdel Syght of his lond /
In that tyme was prynce in walis, Rys, Gryfynes Sonn*e*, vndyr the
kynge of England̄, And a wyrshipphul man, Bishope of Seynte
Dauy, *and* also his name was dauy [4]. And̄ both the P*ri*nce *and* also

---

[1] Camden adds 'dictus Strengbow, *fortis arcus*.'—D.   [2] Colloquium.
[3] His itaque seriatim hoc ordine completis.   [4] Davidque secundo
Meneviae praesidente.

A.D. 1167. bisshop̄ wełł wẏrshipfully vndrefẏnge Macmorgħ, & mycħ reut
had of his enemyte, & of his mycħ lostes, & of þe mycħ shamme
þat hym̄ was i-doñe.

[CHAPTER II.]

Rys has in
prison a
Sir Robert
Fitz-
stephen,
once
Constable
of South
Wales.

In the tẏm̄e þat this was so, was in prisoñ with þe prince 4
of wales, a knygħt þat heght Robert Stefenes-soñ, þat som̄
tym̄ had y-be constable of ałł south walys, & many il turnes had
idoñe vpoñ þe princes meñ whañ þay any thẏnge mysdedeñ ; &
progħ traisoñ of his owñe meñ he was I-take & delyuered̄ to 8
the prince ; & þre yeř he was I-hold̄ in prisonñe ar Macmorgħ
theder cam̄. Oft þe prince hym̄ profred̄ to delyuer hym̄ out of
prisoñ, so þat he wold̄ be his helppe to werry vp-oñ þe kynge ;
bot Robert was a trew mañ, & for no tynge wold̄ do thynge 12
wher-of he mygħt be þer-after I-wyted̄ of wntrowth. Thañ—þrogħ

[*Fol.2 a.]
He sets
Robert
free, on
condition
that he
and his
half-
brother
Maurice
Fitz-
gerald
help Mac-
murgh.
[1 MS.
kyng.]

besechẏnge of * þe bisshope & of Moryce fitz-Geraud, þat wereñ
Robertes two brethereñ on his moþer half,—he was delyuered̄ owt
of prisoñ on this manere : þat he & Morice his brother shold̄, þe 16
next somer, wend̄ in-to Irland̄, with ar poweř to helppe Macmorgħ ;
& he shold̄ hym yeue þe toñ of weysford̄, with þe twey next
cantredes ; & of this was good sekernes Imaked on etheř half.
❡ Whañ this thyng [1] was ałł thus bespokene, Macmorgħ ne mygħt 20
no lengere suffre þat he ne most to his land̄ wend̄, thegħ he ne fond
nat þe aduentures þat he sogħt, such as hẏme lif weř, ne non

Macmurgh
sails to
Ireland,
and
winters at
Ferns.

other poweř he ne brogħt with hym̄ than he out ladde. He had
shippe redy, and̄ good̄ wynd̄, and passed̄ ouer in-to Irland̄, & boldly 24
arẏued in lond þer he had many fomeñ and fewe frendes. from̄ þe
see he went to fernes ; and wełł simply he lyued̄ þer ałł þe wynttyř
with the Clergie of þe chirch, wiche wełł fayř hym̄ vndrefynge,
and by hare poweř to hym̄ & to his, fondeñ þat hame was nede. 28

A.D. 1169.
Fitz-
stephen
collects
30 knights,
60 squires,
and 300
foot-men

[CHAPTER III.]

Vnder that tyme, Robert Steunes-soñ hym̄ dyght to
wend in-to Irland, as a mañ þat on ałł maner wold̄ hold̄
lawfully his trowthe and̄ his behest . he hade purueied hym̄ of
xxxti knyghtes and̄ lx skyers, & ccc of foot-meñ with bowes and 32
arowes ; and̄ knyghtes and þe skyers wełł I-horsed̄ and wełł
y-wepened̄, ałł of his owñ kyne and of his owne nurtuř. Thay

the Byshope wel wyrchipphully vndyrfonge Macmurgh, and myche A.D. 1167.
Pite hadd of his Enemyte and of his mych Lostys, And of the mych
shame that hym was done.

[CHAPTER II.]

IN the tyme that this was so, was in Prisonne wyth the Prince Capitulum
   of Walys, a knyght, whos Name was Robert Steues-Sonne, 2ᵐ.
that sometyme hadd y-be constabill of al Suthe Walis, and many Ea tempes-
yll tvrnys hadd y-done vp-on the Princes men, when thay eny tate Rober-
thyng mysdedyn; and throgh traysoun of his owyn men, he was tus filius
y-take and delyuerid to the Prince. And thre yere he was holde qui apud
in prison, are Macmurgh thedyr come. Oft the Prince hym Kereticae
proferyd to delyuer hym out of pryson, So that he wolde be his caput, &c.
helpe to wer vp-on the kynge; but Robert was a trew man, and for
nothyng wold do thynge wher-of he myght be ther-aftyr reprovid
of vntrowth //

    Than,—throgh be-sechynge of the Byshope and of Moryce fiz- Interveni-
Geraud, that weryn Robertys two bretheryn on his Modyr syde,—he igitur
was delyueryd out of Pryson on this manere: That he and Morice uterinis
his brodyr sholde, the nexte Somyr, wende Into Irland, with har fratribus,
Powere, to helpe Macmurgh; and he sholde hym yeue the toun of &c.
weysford, with the twey nexte cantredes: and of this was good
swrte y-fondyd on euery syde. / Whan this was al thus Spokyn,
Macmurgh myght not lengyr Suffyr that he ne mvste to his Lond
wende, thegh he ne found nat the aduentures that he Soght, suche
as hym lykyd, ne none othyr Powere he ne broght wyth hym, than
he out-ladd. / he had shipe redy, and good wynd, and Passyd ouer A clero
into Irland, and boldely arryued in londe ther-as he hadd many honorifice
Enemys and few frendys. / From the see he went to Fernys; and juxta
wel sympylly he lyued there al the wyntyr, with the Clergy of the facultatis
chyrche, whych wel fayre hym vndyrfonge, and by har Power to hym exhibitus,
and to his, foundyn that ham was nede.   &c.

[CHAPTER III.]   A.D. 1169.

VNder that tyme, Robert Steues-Sonne hym dyght to wende Capitulum
   Into Irland, as a man that on al maner wolde holde lawfully 3ᵐ.
his throuth, and his beheste. He had Purveyed hym of xxxti Nec pro-
knyghtes and lx Squyeris, and ccc of fote-men with bowes and immemor,
arowes; And the knyghtis and the Squyris wel y-horsyd and wel nec fidei
wepenyd, al of his owyn kyn and his owyn nurture. Thay dyddyn tor, &c.

and lands at Banow, c. May 1, 1169.

diddeɳ hame to saiH att send dauyes, and arẏuedeɳ at Banow in Irlaund; weH vnsikere on euery halfe. thay vncharged hare shippes, & made haɱ loges on lond. Thane was fulfilled a prophecie

A prophecy of Merlin was thus fulfild.

þat merlyɳ seid of this commynge: "A knyg̑ht with party armes 4 shaH formost breke þe clos of Irlanḋ." Such armes bare þat Robert. he send soɳ to Dermod Macmorg̑h, and didde hyɱ to witt of his commynge; anḋ þe thedynge spronge fort soɳ into aH þe lonḋ, what folke was to hyɱ Icoɱ. and of þo that to-for hyɱ 8

Macmurgh and Fitz-stephen unite their forces,

hade I-left, and litiH tolḋ by hyɱ, commyn soɳ to hyɱ, so þat he had I-gadereḋ fywe hundreḋ meɳ. he wentt witt this folk to þe Englysse-meɳ; and [when] þay coɱ to-geddr̄, euery of haɱ was the gladder̄ for other. Ther was the forwarḋ meued bethweɳ haɱ, 12 and othes y-swor̄, anḋ sekernesse I-made to conferme aH þe forward, as hit there-by-for was purueied by-for the prince of wales.

[CHAPTER IV.]

and march to Wexford, about twelve miles from Banow.

Whan this sekernesse was thus y-maked, þese twey maner folkes, with ooɳ wiH, and with ooɳ hert, with Baners 16 i-lacet, nam the wey towarḋ weysforḋ. The meɳ of þe self toɳ wereɳ ywar̄ of har̄ commyng, and tok haɱ to rede—for þe tother wereɳ so few, & day so many—that þaẏ wold figt̑h with haɱ in þe

The towns-men at first resolve to meet them in the field, but, on seeing their array, retire within the city.

pleyne felde. They caɱ owt of the toɳ arraieḋ on har maner; bot 20 whan þay sawe the Englismeɳ, with hors I-helleḋ with yreɳ harnes, haɱ-self weH I-wepneḋ with haubergeons, anḋ Bright helmes and sheldes, wich the sawe neuer þer-to-for, they toke a-nother̄ rede, anḋ turneḋ ayeyɳ to toɳ; & aH þat was with-owt þe 24 walles, thay sett a-fyr anḋ brent, & redieḋ haɱ to holḋ haɱ with-yne the waliẏs with streynthe. Robert with his meɳ went strongly for to assayH to toɳ, & sette the bowmeɳ for to wer the

[*Fol.2 b.]

fight of the kernels, and turneḋ the wepneḋ meɳ to fill þe *diches . 28 thay with-yn defendet haɱ stalwarthly with stonnes anḋ stakes, wher-of they wer I-warned, and wer many I-hurt whit-yn anḋ eke

The assault on Wexford is success-fully resisted.

with-out, so that thay with-out mosten nedes leue of the assaut, & withdraw haɱ. Among haɱ was a yong knyght þat het 32

Robert de Barri has a

Robert de Barry, þat drog̑h yong blodes hete, anḋ for hys stalwardnes, reght nat of his lif: as he wold with þe formoste passe ouer the wall, he hent a dynt with a greth stone vpon þe

ham to sayle at Seynt Dauyes, and londyd at the Banow in Irland, A.D. 1169.
wel vnsykyr on euery syde. thay vnchargid har shippis, *and* made
ham logis on londe *. Than was fulfillid a prophesy that Merlyn [*Fol.2b.]
seyde of this comynge : 'A knygh[t] *with* Party armys shall formyst ^{Party per} pale gules
breke the clos of Irland.' Such armys bare that Robert. He sent & ermyn
sone to Dermot Macmurgh, and didde hym to vndyrstand of his a saltyer contre-
comynge; And thythyngis spronge forth sone Into al the londe, what chaunged.
Pepill was to hym come. And many of them that to-forn hym Miles bipartitus
hadd forsake and lefte, *and* lytill seett by hym, comen sone to hym, armis,
So that he hadd gaderid v. C. men. / He went *with* this pepyll to claustra
the Englysh men ; And when thay come to-geddre, eu*ery* of them primus irrumpet.
was the gladdyr for othyr / Ther were the for-sayde conontis
rehersyd *and* mevid betwen tham, and othis sworn, *and* sekyrnesse
made, to conferme all the forsayde, as hit was ther-to-fore Purveyed
be-fore the Prince of Walys.

[CHAPTER IV.]

WHan this sekyrnysse was thus madd, this two maner Cap*itu*lum
Pepyll, wyth on wyll, and *with* oon herte, *with* baners ^{4in.}
lacyd, toke ther wey toward*es* weysford. The men of the toune
weryn y-ware of thare comynge, *and* toke them to consayll,—for the
othyr weryn so few, and thay so many,—that thay wolde figh[t] *with*
ham in the Playn felde. Thay come out of the tou*n* arrayed
on ther man*er*; but when they sawe the Englysh men, *with* hors equestrem turmam
y-hellyd *with* Iryn harneys, ham-Selfe wel wepenyd *with* hauber- loricis et clipeis
geons, and bryght Salletis and sheldys, whych thay sawe neu*er* galeisque
there-to-forn, thay toke anothyr consayll, *and* turned ayayn to fulgenti-
tou*n*; and al that was *with*-out the wallis, thay sette afyre *and* signem ...
brente ; *and* arrayed tham to kepe ham *with*-In the wallis *with*
Streynth. Robert, wyth his men, went Strongly to assaylle the
tou*n*, *and* sette the bowmen forto were the fyght of the propugna-
cornelis, *and* turned the wepenyd men to fill the dichis. thay sagittariis
wythin defendyd ham boldely *with* Stones and Stakys, wher-of eminus observanti-
they wer*e* y-warnyd, [. . . . .] and mosten nedis lewe the assaute, and bus ...
wythdrawe ham / Amonge ham was a yong knyght / whos name
was Robert de barry, that, throgh yonge blodis hette, *and* for his juvenili insultans
boldnys, roght not to lesse the lyfe / As he wolde wyth the fryst calore ...
Passe ou*er* the walle, he hadd a stroke *with* a grette stone vp-on

heueď al with the helme, þat he fel doun yn the grounď of þe dicħ; & vnnethes he was I-draw vp throgħ his felowes, þat mycħ put har lyf in aduentuꝛ for to saw his lif. The cry was well gret on euery syde, for this knyght þat thus was I-hurt. Thay 4 with-drow hañ fro the wallys anď wenten hañ to þe stronď; anď

The assail-
ants of the
town burn
the ships
they find
on the
strand.

all þe shippes þat þay þer fonď, thay settene a-fyre. And . O . shippe þer was, that was I-coñ owt of Brittayne aftyr cheffaꝛ, anď was y-charget with whet & with wynes, anď lay I-ancred in the 8 hauene: the best parte of the englismeñ wenteñ with bottes anď tok his shippe. þe shippmeñ werne many, anď saw that þer weren bot a few englys in the shippe, & the wynď was of þe lond; thay cutte the cable of the ankre, anď þe wynď bare the shippe 12 in towarď the see: her fellowes saw this, anď wenteñ after with bottys; anď vnnethe with rowyng, anď with gret peril of all har lyues, þay come ayeyn to lond. Macmorgħ saw this, & wereñ sore amaied, for thay wenď neuer more þat on [of] ham sholď haw 16 coñ to lonď a-lyue. The assaut was I-left all þat day. A-morowe, whan masse was I-herď, al þe host þay wentene to the assaut wislyere anď warliere þan thay diddeñ the day befor, and strusten

as well to sleght as to streyntħ. The meñ of the toñ sawe ham 20 commyng, and wer right soꝛ aferď that day sholď nat withstond the assaute, and vndrestonden al-so that with wrong day holden ayayn her lorď; thay tok ham to red, and besoghten pees; & drogħ be-sechynge of twe bissoppes, that þat tym weren with-yn 24 the toun, and other possible men al-so with ham, thay yolden hañ al to Macmor[gh]; and four hostages, the best þat he wolď chese, delyuered to hyñ for the pees, and trywly with hym for to holď frome þat tym forward, as har kyndly lord. Macmorgh, 28 as wise & waꝛ, ffor-thy that he wolď that þe out-commyn men sholď haw the bettre hert, and will, hyñ for to serue, he bethoght

Macmurgh
gives
grants
of land to
Maurice
Fitzgerald
and
Hervey of
Mount-
maurice.

þat, of the fyrst good aduentuꝛ þat hym was befall, þay that best weren worthy sholď hawe haꝛ parte, and þe host. Al þe 32 ton of weysford, with twey cantredes aller-next, he yaf to Robert, steuenes sone, and to Morice fitz-Gerauď, as forwarď was to-foꝛ maked; othere thwey cantredes he yaf heruy of Mountmorthy,— neghest thay tweyn on the syd toward Waterford,—a knyght þat 36

the hedde al with the Sallet, that he fell doun to the grovnde of the A.D. 1169.
dyche ; and vnnethis he was vp-rerid' throgh his fellovys, that myche
Put har lyfe in aduenture forto sawe his lyfe. The cry was well
grette on euery syde, for this knyght that thus was y-hurte. Thay
wythdrow ham all from the wallis, and wenten to the stronde ; and A Breton
ship with
al the Chippis that they ther found', thay setten afyre. And oo wheat and
shippe ther was, that was y-come out of Brytayn aftyr cheffare, and wine is
taken by
was y-chargid' with whete and with wynes, and lay y-ancred' in the English
sailors.
Havyn. The beste Parte of the Englysh men wenten wyth botis, The French
and toke this shippe : the Chippmen weryn many, and saw that cut their
cables and
ther weryn but a fewe Englysh men in the shippe, and the wynd set sail;
was on the londe syde ; thay cvtte the Cabilys of the ancre, and the but the
English are
wynd bare the Chippe to-ward the see. Her Fellouys sawe this, and rescued.
wentyn [1] aftyr wyth botis ; and vnnethe with rowyng, and wyth [1 went-
yntyn, MS.]
grette Perill of al there lyues, they come ayeyn to lond'. Macmurgh
saw this, and was sore aferde, for they wende neuer * more that one [*Fol. 3 a.]
of Ham sholde haue come to Londe a-Lyue. The assaute Was The allies
march to
Lefte al that day. A-morrow, whan masse was herd', al the Oste assault
the[n] wenten to the assaute wyslyer and waryr than thay diddyn Wexford
again ;
the day to-fore, and trusten as well to sleght as to streynth. The
men of the toun saw ham comynge, and were ryght sore aferde that
thay ne sholde not wythstonde the assaut, and vndyrstodyn also
that with wronge thay heldyn ayeyn her lorde. thay toke ham to
consayll, and besoghten Pees ; and, throgh besechynge of two Bisshopis
that that tyme weryn wythin the toune, and othir Pesibbill men
also with ham, thay yoldyn ham al to Macmurgh ; and foure but it is
yielded to
Hostagis, the beste that he wolde chese, delyuerid' to hym for the them.
Pees, and trewely wyth hym forto holde from that tyme forward', for
har trew Lorde / Macmurgh, as wysse and ware, For cause that he
wolde that the strangeres sholde haue the bettyr hert and will, hym
forto serwe, he bethoght hym that, of the fryste good' aduenture that
to hym was fall, thay that best weryn worthy, they sholde haue
there Parte, and the hegheste. All the toun of weysford', with It is given
to Fitz-
twey cantredes alther-nexte, he yafe to Robert Steuenes-sone and to Stephen
Moryce fiz-Geraud', as the Promes to-for was made / othyr twey and Fitz-
Gerald.
cantredes he yafe Heruey of Montmvrthy,—nexte to thay two on the

A.D. 1169. com in that same *flote, hym þriddesum of knyghtes, and com
[*Fol.3a.] progh the Erle Richard, more for to spÿe the lond than to fight.

[CHAPTER V.]

The united [1] **V**han this was thus I-don al after haṙ will, they tok with hame
forces
invade   the folk of weysford, and wenten ham toward Ossery, with 4
Ossory, to ferd as mygĥt by tre thousant men; and was than prince of
the prince
of which   Ossory, Macdonenild, a man þat was Macmorogh switĥ lotĥ and
country   all his men, for mych shame that thay had hym i-do. At þe
Macmurgh
was a   begÿnynge, as thay com in-to the contrey, in narrow weys drogĥ 8
bitter
enemy.   woddes and mores, thay fonden the men of the contrey stalwartĥ
             for to defend haṙ lond; & mych tene ham didde, ar that daÿ mygĥt
             [take] the pleyne; and eke into the pleÿn thay folwed ham full
             freslÿ. the horsman saw this, and turned manly vp-on ham, & 12
             anoon slowen right many of ham, & discomfited ham euerychone.

They   And thay þat þe horsmen kest to ground with speres and with
defeat him, swerdes, þe yrisshe fotemen smotene of the heddes. Whan þe
             slagĥt was all I-do, and har enÿmÿes all ouer-comen, thay 16
             broghten well ccc heudes [2], and kesten at Macmorgh feet. he
             be-held ham, & tried euerÿ of ham bÿ ham-self, for to know hame,
             & hild vp his handes and tanked god almygĥtÿ ful Inwardly.

and   Oon hede ther was, a-monge þe otheṙ, of a man that he ouer-dede 20
Macmurgh   and mych hated; he name hit be the heeṙ and by the eers, and
triumphs
in a brutal with girslicĥ bit, as no man ne oweth to done; with his teetĥ
way.   he karue of his nose and botĥ lippes. There-after þeÿ wenten
             fortheṙ into the contrey, slowen, robeden, and branden full manly 24
             al þat hame withstonden, in-to the tÿm the prince of Ossory, by
             consaill of his men, send to ham, & be-soght pees: the pees was
             graunted whan he hit bÿsoght, vp-on good ostages, and othes

Peace is   I-sweṙ, þat he, to his lord Macmorgĥ, shold be trew, and trowth 28
made with
the prince hold, trÿwly serue fro that tÿme forward. in these fightes as in
of Ossory. many othere, thogĥ that in the englishe host noon weṙ bot good

Robert de   and stalward, Robert þe Barṙ and Meiler fiz-henrÿ weren thaÿ
Barri and
Meiler   that best deden. Thaÿ weren both ÿong knyghtes, and Robert 32
Fitzhenry   Steuenes-sonnes neues; the oon his brotheṙ sone, the otheṙ his
fight best.
            susteres sone; of diuerse maners, both [3] of hardnes & of stalworthnes

[1] a small w is inside the V.   [2] heuedes, heads.   [3] but.

syde toward watyrford[1],—a knyght that come in that same flitte, A.D. 1169.
hym thyrdesum of knyghtes, and come throgh the Erle Rychard,   [1] *mari con-*
more forto spy the londe than to fyght.   *terminos.*

[CHAPTER V.]

W han this was thus don al aftyr har will, thay toke with Capi*tul*um
    tham the Pepill of weysford, and wenten ham to-ward Ossory, v[m].
with oste as myght be by thre Ml. men[2]. And was than Prince of [2] cum
Ossory, Macdonenylde, a man that was myche be-hatyd of Mac- exercitu
murgh, for myche shame that thay hadd hym donne. At the quasi
begynnynge, as thay come into the contrey, in narrow weyes throgh trium
woddis and mores, thay foundyn the men of the contrey bolde forto milium.]
defende har londe; and mych sorrow ham didd, ar thay mygh[t]
take the Playne : and when thay come to the Playne, thay folwid
ham ful fresly. the hors-men saw this, and turned boldely vp-on
ham, and anoone slowyn rygh[t] many of ham, and dys-comfited
ham eu*er*ychon.   And thay that the hors-men keste to ground
wyth Sperys and wyth Swerdis, the Iryssh footte-men Smoten of 300 heads
the hedis. Whan the slaght was al y-do, and har ennemys al of foes are
ouer-come, thay broghten wel ccc. hedis, and kesten at Macmurgh brought to
is fete. he behylde ham, and tvrned euery of tham[3] by hym-Selfe murgh.
forto know tham, and hilde vp his handis, and thankyd almyghty [3] than,
god ful Inwardly. Oone hede ther was, amonge the othyr, of a man MS.]
that he gretly dreddid and myche hatid; he toke hit by the heeres He bites
and by the Ers, and grymly hit bitte, as no man sholde haue dou*n* ; off the
wyth his tethe he kutte of his nose and bothe lippis. Ther-aftyr nose and
they wenten fourdyr Into the contrey, kildyn, robedyn and brandyn lips of one.
ful boldely al that ham wythstodyn, into the tyme the Prynce of His men
ossory, by consaylle of his men, sent to ham, and besoght Pees. the kill, rob,
Pees was graunted whan he hit be-soght, vp-on good Ostagis, and and slay,
othis y-Sworñe, * that he, to His Lord Macmurgh, shold be trewe, till Mac-
and trowth Hold, and trewely Serwe fro that tyme forth. In this donough
fyghtes as in many othyr, thoght that in the Englysh hoste noone sues for
were but good and bolde, Robert de barry and Meyler fiz-henry peace.
weryn thay that best diddyn : they wer both yong knyghtes, and [*Fol.3 b.]
Robert Steuenes-sones emys[4] both, the one his brodyr son*n*e, the [4] nevens,
othyr his Systyr Son*n*e ; Of dyuers maners, but of hardynes and nepotes.

A. D. 1169. mostdele al I-lých; ffor Meyler was a maū that ouer mych
desyred to be I-preiscde, and þat men sholden mých speke of
his stalwardnes, and preisen hym. Robert was kyndlye, hardy,

[*Fol.3b.] & stalwarde, *and euer with the forthmost in euery fight and 4
in euery peril, bot he hatede notynge so mych as that me
shold spek of his stalwardnes, ne hyme preiese. The whill the
host was thus in Ossory, befel þat þay wereū a nýght I-loget

A phantom in an old castell, & aboute; and these tweyn, as haᵽ wone was, 8
army at
night   weren both I-hosted to-gedderes: ffeᵽ with-yn nyght come an
creates   host vp-on ham, of so mych folk as thegh hit were fele thousand,
terror
among the on euery side smýtynge vp the host as they wolden in wode
English;   raas ferly ouersaill hame, al, with wepne ryngýnge, speres and 12
sparthes ruthlynge to-geddre, with cryynge so grysly that noon

[¹ MS.   ende was of helf faᵽ, as ¹hoft-sithes was wonet to be-fall in ostynges
host.]
  in Irland; of whiche frightnes the most parte of the oste was so

[² MS.   aferd, that þay flowe ² and hidden haū, some in wodnes, som in 16
slowe.]
but Meiler mores. These twey stalward men henten haᵽ wepene, & lep to
and
de Barri hors, and wenten a-noon to Robertes tentes, (Steucnes sone,) and
manfully   cryed vp-on haᵽ felowes þat day sholden withstond, and tak hert
withstand
the panic. to hame, and defend ham-self; bot few theᵽ weᵽ that so diden, 20
til they saw that this crie and þe noise was all I-left, & nas
bot fantasy. Whan the host hem gaddred ayaýn to-geddre, thaý
weᵽ full soᵽ ashamet that thay so argly put ham to f[l]ight, and
mych speche was amonge ham, and maný, hadden gret enuý, and 24
mých wonder toght of Robert de barᵽ, that whan the host was

Character in so gret frightnes, he was that maū þat stydfastly most hým
of Robert
de Barri. held, and most hým entised for to withstond and fight; and
amonge all the goode thewes that in hym weren, þis inamliche is 28
i-told of hým, that for no violence ne ferly aduentuᵽ þat hym
mýght betid, he was neuer whan-hopefully argh, ne aferd, ne
amayed of hert, ne shamefully ne didde hym to flight, bot euer
moᵽ he was I-lich redy to weppen and to defend hym-self, and 32
to helpen all oþer; he the formost knýght that in this conqueste
of Irland first receyued dýnt and hurtýng in battaill. A wondeᵽ
was of that fantasye: A-morowe whaū hit was daý, I the place,
ther this folk I-seýe smýten vp-on hame, the wedes and the grase 36

boldnys mostdele al y-lyke. For Meyler was a mañ that gretly
desyryd' to be Praysid', and that men shold myche Spèke of his
boldnys, and Preysyn hym. / Robert was kyndly, hardy and bold',
and euer with the fryst in euery fyght / and in euery Perill ; but *nec*
he hatyd' nothynge so myche as that a man sholde speke of his *laudis* *exactor,*
boldnys, ne hym Preyse. / The whyll the hoste was thus in Ossory, *nec aurac* *popularis*
befell that thay weryn a-nyght y-logid' in an olde castell, and aboute. *aucupator.*
And thus two, as they wer wonyd', weryn in one Plase to-gedderis.
Fer with-in nyght, come an hoste vp-on ham of so mych Pepill, as A phantom
they were many thowsandis, on euery syde Smytynge vp the hoste, host
[tanquam
as they woldyn, in wode raas, fersly ouersayle hame al, wyth wepyñ *in impetu* *furoris*
ryngynge, Speris and sparris rutlynge to-giddyr, wyth cryynge so *sui cuncta* *devoran-*
grymly, that none ende was Of elf fare, as ofte-tymes was wonet to *tium]*
befall in hostyngis in Irland'[1]. Of whych ferde, the moste Parte of frightens
the
the Oste was so a-dred', that they flow and hiddyn ham ; somme in English-
woddis, some in mores / This two bolde men token har wepyn, and men, who
run and
lepe to hors, and wentyn anone to Robert Steuenes-sonne, and cried hide ;
on har fellowis that ' they sholdyn wytstond', and take herte to hame,
and defende ham-Selfe ;' but fewe were that so diddyñ, tyll they saw
that this cry and this noyse was al cessid', and nas but a fantasy. but are
much
whan the host them gaderid' ayeyn to-giddyr, they wer ful sore ashamed
asshamyd' that thay so fently Put ham to flyght ; and mych Speche when they
find it was
was amonge hame ; and many haddyn gret enuy, and mych wondyr all fancy.
thoght of Robert de Barry, that Whan the host was in so gret ferde,
he was that man that moste stidfastly hym helde, and moste them
styrrid' to wythstond' and' fyght. / And amonge al the good' dedis
that in hym weryn, this Pryncipaly is of hym tolde, that for no
vyolence ne ferly aduenture that to hym chanssyd', he was neuer in
wanhope sette, ne agaste, ne aferd', ne abassid' of herte, ne shamefully did hym to flyght ; but euer-more he was lyke redy to wepyn,
and' to defend' hym-Selfe, And to helpyn al othyr. he was the
formyst knyght that, in this conqueste of Irland', fryst receyued' *in hac*
Hiberniae
stroke and hurte in bataill // A wondyr was of that fantasy *expugna-*
a-morrow, whan hit was day : In the Playn ther this Pepill y-seye *tione.*

[1] Cujusmodi phantasma in Hibernia circa expeditiones frequens esse solebat.
—*Op.* v. 235.

A.D. 1169. that stoden al euen vp-right, thay lay all I-drow a-doune and I-cast
to grond. [*This grass, &c. only in Harl. MS.* 177. *Op.* v. 236.]

[CHAPTER VI.]

A s this was on this maner I-don, the tythynges sprongen
[*Fol.4a.]   in-to al Irland hwow Macmorgh conquered his lond * vpon 4
his men, and that no man myght hym withstond for out-comen

Roderic   men that he lade with hym. Roryk O'Concowr of Connaght,
O'Conor
tries to   that was that tym kynge of al Irland, vndrestod hym, and toght
raise the   in his hert the gret peril that myght be-fall hym and al the 8
whole
country   lond folk, drogh the owt-comen folk þat was thus in-to the land
against   I-com; he sent his messagers to al the gret men of the lond,
Macmurgh
and the   and in a lityll whill gaddred ham to-geddre to a parlement,
English.   and tok ham to rede that euery on his half shold gaddre al the 12
                 power þat they myght, for to wer vpon Macmorgh. And as
                 hit was purueied, so hit was don ; Thay assemblet so many hostes
                 and so mych folk on euery half, that noon end was, and comen

Many of   to Okensely for to weren vpon Macmorgh. Whan this hostes 16
Mac-
murgh's   weren thus assemblet, the most parte of Macmorghis men, ayeyne
followers   har trowth and ayeyn har othes, some priuely whithdrow hem
desert him,
but Fitz-   that day, nold nat to hym com, some al openly leften hym, and
stephen   wenten to his fomen ayeyn hym ; so that, in his most nede, trew 20
and his
men stand   frendes ne fonde he non, sawe Robert, steuenes son, and his.
by him.   With the lityll folk that thay hadden, thay wenten in-to a place
                 nat fer frome ffernes, a pleyn place bisette about with montaignes
                 and woddes, watres and mores, on euery side il to com [to]. the 24
                 entrees that ther weren, by Robert-is deuice thay setten men for
                 to stopen, in some place with trees I-cast don, and in other

They   places depe diches I-cast. thegh the place wer stronge of kynde,
occupy a
strong   thay maden hit mych stronge[r] with engyn, so that hit was 28
position   I-now seker recet to ham, and [to] her enemyes ful strong to com
not far
from   to, and with litill folke hit myght be I-kept ; & derne weies thay
Ferns.   hadden purueied to ham-self, owt to goo, ayeyn In to com,
                 whan ham liked. Whane the kynge of Connaght, with so many 32
                 hostes, was to ham I-com, he send to Robert by Messangers,
                 and present hym with rych yiftes, and many mo he hym be-het,
                 and fast hym be-soght that, owt of þe Contray, wyche no Right

smytyn vp-on ham, the wedis and̃ the grasse that stodyn al euyn A D. 1169.
vp-ryght, thay lay al y-throw dov͂ne *and* cast to ground̃.

[CHAPTER VI.]

As this was thus donñe, the thythyngis Spronge Into al Capi*tulum*
Irland̃, how Macmurgh conquerid̃ his londe vpon his men, ᵛⱼᵐ.
and that no m̃an myght hym wythstond̃, for strange men that he
ladd̃ wyth * Hym. Roryke Oconghour*e*, of Connaght, that was [*Fol. 4 a.]
that tyme Kyn*ge* of al Irland, vndyrstode hym, and thoght in his
herte the grete Perel that myght be-fall hym *and* al the londe- *tam sibi*
Pepill, throgh the stranger*es* that was thus in-to the lande com͂e. *quam*
He sende his messanger*is* to al the Lordis of the Londe, *and* in a *toti.*
lytyll whylle gaddred̃ ham to-gedre to a parlement, *and* toke ham
to consayll, that eu*e*ry on his Syde sholde gaddyr al the Pepill
that thay myght, forto werr*e* vpon Macmu*r*gh.   And as hit was
Purueyed, so hit was dou*n*.   Thay assemblid̃ so many Hostis, *and*
so mych Pepill on eu*e*ry syde, that were vnnowmmerabill, and
comyn¹ to Okenseley forto werr*e* vp-on Macmu*r*gh / Whan this [¹ comyn.
host is weryn thus assemblet, the moste parte of Macmu*r*gh -ismen, MS.]
ayeyn har*e* trowthe and her*e* othis, Some p*r*iuely wit*h*-drow ham,
that they nolde not to hym come.   Some al opynly leften hym,
and wenten to his ennemys ayey͂n hym ; so that, in his moste nede, *in neces̃si-*
trewe frendis ne fownde he noñe, Sawe Robert Steuenes-Sone *tatis*
and his. wyth the Lytill Pepill that they haddyn, thay wentyn into *articulo*
a place not far*e* frome Fernys, a pleyne place be-sette aboute wit*h*
monttanys and woddis, watris and moris ², on euery Syde il to come ²*paludibus.*
to.   The entrees that ther weryn, by Robert-is deuyce thay setten
me͂n fortc stopyn ; in some Place wit*h* trees y-caste douñe, and in
othir Placis depe dichis y-caste. thegh the Place were stronge of *naturalem*
kynd̃, thay maddy͂n hit mych strongir wit*h* Engyn, So that hit was *difficul-*
sure recette to tham, and̃ to ther ennemys stronge to come to, and *tatem in-*
wit*h* lytill pepill hit myght be kepte.   And Erthe-weyes thay *dustria*
haddyn madd̃ to tham-Selfe, out to goo, and ayey͂n In to come, *plurimum*
when them Plesyd̃.   Whan the kynge of connaght, wit*h* so many *et arte*
hostis, was to tham com*e*, he sende to Robert by Messangers, *and* *municit.*
presentid̃ hym wit*h* rych yeftys, *and* mych more hym Promysyd̃,
and gretly hym besoght that, out of the contrey, whych no ryght

C 2

A.D. 1169. he ne hadde to, ne no chalan*g*e ne myght setten vp-on, he and
his, with pees and lou[e] shold depar*te*. Mich they spek of this,

Roderic and litell thay sped. Ther-aftyr, the messagers turned to Mac-
urges Fitz-
stephen to morgh, and be-soghten hym on the kynges half, OConghour, 4
retire from that he forth, *with* ham, shold turne vp-on the owt-comen folk,
the
country, ham to slee and vndo. And if he so wold, thay wold delyu*er*
[*Fol.4b.] hym al leynestr, and stidfast pees and frend- *shipp*e mak hym
and, failing haue of the kynge and of all other. Many reisons thay shewed, 8
in this,
tries in both for the land & for the land folk ; bot notynge thay ne spedde,
vain to
induce ne noon answar ne hadden, that ham liket. Oconghour saw and
Macmurgh herd of his Messagers that he myght nat in such man*er* spede,
to turn
against the and that he most with streynth do, that he myght nat with fair 12
English.
speche : he tok his wepne grymly, and stod vp a-monge his folk,
O'Conor and thus sayd to ham ; "Mighty men, and stalward in fight for
addresses
his to defende y*our* lond and y*our* franchise! vndrestondeth, ayeyn
followers, whice folk, and for what encheson, ye sholl this battaill tak an 16
hond : al ou*re* enemy, that afor thus was owt of lond I-dryw
for his wykkedne*s*se, In *com*mune confusion of vs all, al be-tak
with owt-comen & wepned folk, is ayayn *com*men for enuy and
harme of vs, & hath I-broght vnked folk vp-on vs, that the harme 20
and de- wich he had no power to don vs hym-self, throgh help*e* of ham &
nounces
the maynten*au*nce, the bett*er* myght brynge to end ; and hath dight
poisonous
Mac- hem to sheden his attyr so wide, that he rechet nat of his own
murgh. deth, bot that al mowen hawe our bale trogh*e* hym, and for 24
noon shold be I-spared, and he ne spared hym-self. Ther-for we
willen *with*stond the begynynge, and þe yuel whil hit is comyn,
ar hit be Iroted ; ffor harme wexet eu*er* *with* longe abiddynge.
Patriam Our lond & our fredom defended we manly ; so that the slaght 28
itaque
tuentes, et of þese fewe be ferdnesse to many ; & be ensample of these, al
libertatem other out-lond men to be adrede, such folies to begyn, and the
[¹ MS. mynd of vs, *with*-out end to rest ¹."
best.]

[CHAPTER VII.]

Macmurgh
harangues
the men of
Leinster.

Macmorgh, on his halue, be-held his men, and saw ham 32
sor amayed : *with* wordes that he myght, he conforted
ham on this man*er* : "Men of leynest*er*, which, sothfast trowth
& stidfaste kynd in al a*d*u*e*ntures, vs hath felawes I-maked,

he hadd' therto, ne no calange ne myght setten vpon, he *and* A.D. 1169.
his, wyth Pees and loue, sholde deperte. Mych[1] they spoke of [¹ Myth,
MS.]
this, and lytyll thay Spede / There-aftyr, the messangers turned'
to M*a*cmurg͡h, and be-soghten hym on the kyngis be-halfe, Oconnoghoure, that he forth, wyth tham, sholde turne vpon the strangere*s*, *ut in*
hame to kyll and vndo. And yf he so wolde, thay wolde delyuyr *exteras
nationes*
hym all leynystere, *and* stydfaste Pees *and* frendshippe make hym *delendas*
haue of the kynge and of al othyr. Many reysonys thay shewid', *simul cum
ipsis arma*
both for the londe and for the lond-pepill ; but nothynge thay ne *conver-
teret.*
spede, ne noone answere hadde, that ham Plesyd'. Oconnoghoure
saw and herde of his messyngers, that he myght nat in suche
maner spede, and that he moste w*ith* streynth do that, that he
myght not w*ith* fayre speche. He toke his wepyn grymly, and
stode vp amonge his pepill, and thus sayde to tham :—" Myghty
men, and bolde in fyght forto defende youre londe and youre *patriae*
fredome ! Vndyrstondyth, ayeyn͞ whych *Pepill, and for whate [*Fol.4 b.]
cause, ye sholde this Bataill take on Honde. Al oure ennemy, *tutores, et
libertatis.*
that afor this was out of londe ydrywe for his wickidnes, In
comynne confusion of vs all, all be-take wyth strangere*s* and
wepened Pepyll, is ayeyn comyn, for Enuy and harme of vs, and *quod,*
hath broght strange Pepill vp-on vs, that the harme whych he *cunctis*
hadde no Powere to don vs hym-selfe, throgh helpe of them and *communi
labe in-*
mayntenavnce, the bettyr myght brynge to ende ; and hath dyght *fectis, ut
nemini*
hym to shedyn his wenym so wyde, that he takyth no fors to dye, *parcatur,*
but that we al mow haue oure [e]will throgh hym, and for none *nec ipse
sibi*
sholde be Sparid', and he ne Sparyth hym-Selfe. There-for we will *pepercit.*
wy[th]stonde the begynnynge, and the Perel whyle hit is comyn, are *exterae
nationes*
hit be rotyd'. For harme wexeth eue*r* wyth longe abydynge. Oure *ab ausu*
londe and oure fredome, defende we manly ; So that the slaght *tam
nefario*
of this fewe be ferde to many ; and by Ensampill of thes, al othyr *imper-
petuum*
strangers sholde be aferde, suche folies to begynne, And the mynde *abstru-*
of vs, wyth-oute ende to abyde." *antur.*

[CHAPTER VII.]

M Acmurg͡h / on his syde, be-held his men, *and* Sawe hame Capitul*um*
sore a-bassyd'. w*ith* wordis that he myght, he confortid' vij^m.
ham on this manere : " Men of leynyster, wych, trusty trouth and *comites*
stydfaste kynde in al aduentures, vs hath fellow*i*s y-made, wyth- *indivisos*

A. D. 1169. *wi*t*h*out any partyng, a-rer we our hertes, styfly vs-self to defend.

The maistre of wreth and of Coueytise, that *with* streynth wold

vs brynge vnderfoot, and ows ayeyn dryue out of lond, other, that
wors is, in the same lond, vs tynken vndo : that god shild! loo, her 4
is I-com vpon our hed, of his mych gaderynge of folke prowt &
hauteyn. be ye well vndrestond, þat nat trogh gret tale of men

ne trogh greth streynth, both drogh *right and trowth that man

hath *with* hym, battailles doth ouercom. We haue for vs, ayeyn 8
har pryd, mekenes ; ayayns har vnryght, right and trouth ; ayeyn
har boldenesse and ouer-truste, mekenesse and maner. Thay
fighten for coueytise, for to get good ; and we, for to flee harme.
with al this we bene in strong place and wel I-warned. The mor 12
that her commeth, the more encombrement we shall do hame, by

lityll folk ham to ouercom, so that we be of on hert, and stifly
withstond.'

[Chapter VIII.]

Whan Macmorghe had his tale I-endeth in his speche, 16
Robert Steuenes-son, spake to his felaws and to his
meigne on this wise : " ffightyng fors, & yongelynges I-corne,
that so many perilles hawe to-geddre I-soffred, and euer in al
aduentures, and of heigh hert ibe ! If we inly vndrestonde wiche 20
men we ben, *with* what lodes-man, and for what thynge we this perille vndre-tok *with* stalwardnesse, as our [wone]ys, we shullen ouercome ; & the grace that ye I-haue i-hadde ar this of god, ne shal vs
nat forlete. Of the folke of Troy we ben kyndlých y-come, on þat 24

oon half, fro þe first begynnyge ; of ffraunce, we haue kynde on
other half. Throgh kynd of Troy, we owe to be hardy ; throgh
kynd of ffraunce, we ben vsed in wepene ; & so as we bene of double
mane kyndly, of good herth & well y-wepned, & well y-lernet yn 28
wepne, ne dout no man, þat such vnwepned rascayll any power

haw ows to wythstond: on that other halue, we come nat yn-to
thys land as hyryng men, ne for no couetyse of gold, ne of syluyr,
ne galyotȝ ne robbers ; bott for to helpe thys heyth man that ys so 32
noble & so fre, &, þrogh hys owne men, lodderly was of lond
y-dryue. we hawe reuth of hys harm ; & helpeth vp þat adoun was
ỳ-broȝthe ; to hys kynd sted, bryngeth hym þat vnkyndly was

out eny p*ar*tyng*e*, arrer*e* we vp our*e* hert*es*, boldely vs to defende. A.D. 1169.
The maystyr of wreth *and* of couetyse, that wyth streynth wolde ¹ the oration
vs bryng*e* vndyrfote, and vs ayeyn dryue out of loned, Othir, that [in a later hand].
wors is, in the same loned Purposyth vs to vndo / that god *quod*
forbedde / be-holde, here is come vp-on our*e* hedd, of his mych *absit*
gadryng*e* of pepill Proute and hauteyn. be ye wel vndyr*s*tond,
that not wyth many men, ne wyth grete Streynth, bot by ryght
and trouth that man hath wyth hym, batalis doth ou*er*come. We
haue for vs, ayeyñ har pryde, mekenys; ayeynes har*e* vnryght, ryght
and trouth; ayeyñ har boldnys *and* ou*er*-truste, mekenesse *and modus et modestia.*
man*er*. thay fyghtyn for couetyse, forto gete good; And we, to
shonne myschefe. wyth all this, we byth in strong*e* Place, and well *tam arte quam*
warnyd. The mor*e* that her*e* comyth, the more encomb*re*ment *natura*
we shal do ham, by lytill folke ham to ou*er*come, So that we be of *munitissimum.*
oñe herte, *and* styfly wystonde."

[CHAPTER VIII.]

WHen M*a*cm*u*rgh hadd his tale y-endyd in his spech*e*, Capit*ulu*m viij*m*.
Robert*e* Steuenes-Soñe spake to his fellowys, *and* to them
in this man*er* Sayde : " Fyghten feris, *and* yonglynges y-know, that *Bellorum socii,*
so many Perelis haue to-geddyr Sofferid, and eu*er* in al aduentures, *adolescentes*
and of hey hert ben! If we Inwardly wndyrstonde what men we *electi.*
ben; wyth what lodes-man, *and* for what thynge, we this Perel
vndirtoke; w*ith* boldnys, as we wer*e* wonyd, we shall ou*er*come; and
the grace that we haue hadd ar this of god, ne shall vs not forsake.
// Of * the folke of Troy we Ben Kynly come, on that one syde, fro [*Fol. 5 a.]
the fryste begyn[i]ng*e*; of Fraunce, we haue kynde on the othyr
halfe. Throgh the kynde of troy, we sholde be bolde; throgh
kynde of Fraunce, we ben wsyd in wepyñ; and so as we ben of
doubil man*er* kyndly, of good herte *and* wel wepenyd, and wel
lernyd in wepyñ,—ne dout no man, that Suche vnwepenyd rascaill *populum inermem.*
any Power*e* haue to vs to wyth-stonde. One that ou*er* syde, we
come not into this loned as wagid men, ne for no couetyse of
golde, ne of Syluyr, ne of galiotʒ, ne robbers ; but forto helpe *Non ergo piratae,*
this goode man that is so nobill and so fre, and, wyth his owyn *non praedones huc*
men, wickydly was out of his loned drywe. We haue Pite of his *advenimus.*
harme ; and helpyth vp that adouñ was caste / to his kynde state,

A.D. 1169.
He has
given us
land.
[¹ MS.
ouer.]

We'll win
the battle
and glory.

O'Conor,
doubtful of
the issue,
makes
terms with
Mac-
murgh,

[*Fol.5 b.]

who, it is
agreed,
shall hold
from
Roderic,
and give
him his
son as a
hostage.

Maurice
Fitzgerald
now
arrives,
with a fol-
lowing, at
Wexford.

ther-of I-bansheth. And he, as largh maɴ & goodͬ prynce, hat
vs yeueɴ wyde londes & ryche townes, & owͬ lond folke wyll
setten & planten stydfastly yn þys lond, nowe & euer¹. Therfor,
men, full [of] streynth & stalwarthnes, such thyngͧ y-magýneth 4
to-day hartly to do, that owͬ kynred ne go nat out of kyndͭ,
& yn thýs, lyuynge oþer dey, we manly wyɴ the pryce, that
euer more torne to whyrshyppe vs & al ouͬ that aftyͬ ws shullen
come." 8

[CHAPTER IX.]

Wythe these wordes, & otheͬ suche, these heghe meɴ
comfortedͭ haͬ folk, for day schuldeɴ hawe the bettyr wyll
well for to fýght. And whaɴ day were oɴ euery half redy for to
smyth to-geddre, OConoȝwýr, be-thoȝghthýng that the aduentuͬ 12
of battaylle ben ofte doutouse & mýche vɴcerteyne, And as the
whysmaɴ seythe 'all tynge me shaĦ assay, ratheͬ thaɴ fyȝth,'
& all-so he & hys doutendeɴ well scre to assemble wíth folke
I-wepnedͭ, On al maner that he myȝght, * He was abowte thame 16
sholde make peas. thane, throgͪ besechyngͧ of goode menͦ
that went betwene, & throgͪ grace of the holy goste, was
the peas y-made, oɴ þis maner ; that thay sholde leve leynester
to Maccmorghowe, & he sholde hiɫt holde of Oconoghouͬ, & 20
hym ꞌknowlech, & suget be to hym as to a kyngc & prynce
of Irlandͭ. And þat thys sholdͭ be stydfastly I-hold, Macmorgh
býtok hým hýs ꞁone to astage, by so, þat yf he goodͭ pees holdͭ,
& trewlý hým helde, Oconghuͬ shold hým yeue hys doghter to 24
wyff. Whaɴ thys was comynly I-shewed & I-knowe, & othes
I-shwerne oɴ euery half, all thýs trewly to hold, Anotheͬ thyng
was bespoke bytwen ham, bott þat preuely, that Macmorgh ne
sholdͭ nomore brynge vnked mon yn-to the lond, & thay that 28
he hade y-broght, as rathe as he had leynestre yɴ good pees,
he sholdͭ anoon send ayenne home, & delyueryd þe lond of ham.

[CHAPTER X.]

Aftyr that þe pees was thys Imaket, þe host departed,
euery oɴ hýs half. Sone þer-after come Moryce, Geraudes 32
soɴ, Robertes brotheͬ, of whom we spokeɴ ar thys, wyth .x. knýghtes
& .xxx. Squyres & ij houndred footmen, & ar[y]ued at weysford ;

bryngyth hym that vnkyndely was therof¹ y-banshet. And he, A.D. 1169.
as large man and good Prince, hath vs yevyꝺ wyde landis and *gentem hic*
iyche townes; *and* oure londe-pepill will setten and Planteꝺ *nostram in*
insula
stydfastly in this londe, nowe and eu*er*. Therfor, men full of *plantare.*
seu vin-
streynth and of boldnes, Suche thyng*e* ymagyneth to-day hertely *cendo seu*
moriendo
to do, that oure kynred ne go not oute of kynde; and in this, *perpetuam*
lywe or dye, we manly wyn*n* the Pryce, that eu*er*-more shall *nobis*
gloriam
tour[n]e to our*e* wyrchippe, and to al oure that aftyr vs schalle *strenuitate*
compa-
come." *remus.*

[CHAPTER IX.]

Wyth this wordis, and othyr Suche, thes good men confortyd Cap*it*ul*um*
hare Pepill, for thay sholdyn haue the bettyr wyll, well ix^m.
forto fyght. And when thay were on eu*er*y halfe redy forto smyte
to-geddre, Oconghour*e* bethoght hym that the aduentu*re* of bataill
ben ofte doutfull *and* mych vncertayn. An[d], as the Wysman Ter. *Eun.*
Seyth, "Althynge we oghte to assay, radyr than fyght" / And also IV. vii. 19.
he and his douteden well sore to fyght wyth Pepill wepenyd. On al
man*er* that he myght, he was besy to haue Pees. Then, by the
besechyng*e* of good men that wente betwen*e*, and throgh grace of
the holy goste, was the Pees mad on this man*er*; that thay sholde
leue leynystere to M*a*cmurg*h*, and he sholde hite holde of Oconghour*e*, and hym knowlech, and Subiecte be to hym as to a kyng*e*
and Prynce of Irland. And that this sholde be stydfastly holde,
M*a*cmurg*h* toke hym his sone to hostage, by So, yf he good Pees *filium*
helde, and trewely hym helde, Oconghour*e* sholde hym yeue his *suum*
Cnu-
doght*e*r to wyfe. whan this was comynly shewyd *and* know, and *churum.*
othis sworꝺ on eu*er*y Syde, al this trewely to kepe, Anothyr thynge
was spokyn be-twen them, bothe that Pryuely, that M*a*cmurg*h* ne
sholde no more stranger*e*s brynge into the londe; And thay that
he hadd broght, as Sone as he hadd leynystere in good Pees, he *statim*
remitteret.
shold Sende them home, and delyuere the londe of hame.

[CHAPTER X.]

Aftyr that the Pees was thus made, the hoste departyd, on Cap*it*ul*um*
his halue. Sone there-aftyr come Morice, Geraudis Son*n*e *, x^m.
[*Fol.5b.]
Robert-is Brodyr, of whom we Spokyn ar this, Wyth x Knyghtis
and xxx^{ti} Squyeris, and two hundred fotemen, and londid at

A.D. 1169.   A man fuł queynt, trow trogħ al thynge, & stalwarth, & stydfast
of word, & of hert symple, & shamffast as a mayd. Waꝺ Macmorgh
& Robert hyt wysten, thay weren ful glad, & bolder þan thay
before were : thay come to ham sone wyth þe oste þat thay had. 4

Macmurgh   Macmorgh be-thoght hyꝳ of the mych vnryght that þe men of
determines
to attack   deuelyng̃ hym hadden done, & hys fader all-so, many sithe :
Dublin ;   he assembled hýs hostes, & redied hym to wend thedere.   Boot
and goes,
accom-   Robert byleft with somdell of þe meýne, fore to rere hym a castell 8
panied by
Fitz-   at a place that me clepeth þe karryke, & ys twey myle out
stephen.   of weysford ; & Moryce went wyth hým.   Macmorgh, as mayster
& leder of the host, & cheuetayn of al.   In lytell whyle, all
þe contreys about dyuelyn, wyth robynge & bernyng & sleýng, 12

[¹ MS.   weren ¹ neght I-broght to nogħt.   The sitezeyns of dyuylyn, whan
wepeu.]   thay thys wysten, thay sentten to ham, & besoghten pees, & yaue
The   ham so mych gold & syluer that non end was at har wylle,
citizens
submit and & good ostages, & othes I-[s]wore that þay sholden to Macmorgh 16
acknow-   trew be, & hým knowleche þan-forward as lord & prynce.   Fro
ledge
Macmurgh   that tyme that thys was y-do, ther was noon Iryshman yn
as their
lord.   leynnester, of hey kyne ne of low, that for seruesse ² of englysse-
[²for ferd-   men ne yeldet hym to Macmorgh, so þat þer was noght of þe 20
nesse?]   londˀ-folke þat all nas subyett to hym, & redy to hys wylle.

[CHAPTER XI.]

O'Conor   IN thys whyle, wax a grett wreth & a grete stryfe betwyx
makes war
on O'Brien   þe kyng̃ of Connaght, & donoll Obreyꝺ, þe kyng [of] lymeryke,
of Limerick & of thomond.   the kyng of connaght, Oconoghur, gadderedˀ hys 24
[*Fol.6a.]   hostes for to weir vpoꝺ Obreen.   Obreen sent *to mamorrowz, for
and sen·ls   allyaunce that was betwen ham, that he shold hym helpe.   he spake
Fitz-   þer-of to Robert & to Moryce, & bad ham that þay sholdˀ go theder
stephen
and   for to helpe Obreen.   Thay name har meꝺ wyth ham, & weuten 28
Maurice to
oppose   ynto thomondˀ, and ffondeꝺ Oconoghur, that stryffly stode ayeyꝺ
him.   ham, & many fyghtes ham yaue.   Bot the dysconfitur turned vpeꝺ
O'Conor is   Oconoghur, & many of hys meꝺ wer I-sleyꝺ, so that wythe shame
defeated,
and   he most turne ayeyꝺ ynto Connaght.   And fro that tym, Obreen 32
O'Brien
becomes   wythdrow hym froꝺ Oconoghur, & neuer after was subyect to hyꝳ
inde-
pendent   as he was thar-by-fore ; & the englysh hoste, wyth grett gettynges
of him.   & with rych yiftes, turned ayeyne yꝺ-to leynestre.

weysford. A man full quent, trew throw al thynge, bolde, and A.D. 1169.
stydfaste of word, *and* of hert sympil, and shamefaste as a mayd //
Whan Macmurgh *and* Robert hadd wyttynge of Morice-is comynge,
they weryn full glad, and boldyr than thay before were.　thay
came to tham Sone wyth the hoste that thay hadde / Macmurgh
bethoght hym of the mych wronge that the men of Deuelyn to hym *grares*
hawydyn done, and his fadyr also, many tymys : he assemblid his *Dubli-*
neusium
hostes, *and* made hym redy thedyr forto goo.　But Robert lefte *injurias.*
wyth some of the meyngne forto rere hym a castel at a Place that
is callid the Karryke, and is two myle out of weysford; And
Morice went wyth hym. Macmurgh as gouernoure and ledere
of the hoste and capytan of all.　In lytell Processe of tyme, al
the contreis about deuelyn, wyth Robynge and brennynge *and*
kyllynge of pepill, weryn al-meste broght to noght // The Citseynys *ad exter-*
of deuelyn, whan thay of this had wyttynge, thay Sendyn *and* *minium*
fere
besoght Pees, and yaue hame so myche golde and Siluyr that none *reducto.*
ende was at har will, and good hostagis, *and* othis Sworne that thay
Sholdyn to Macmurgh be trewe, *and* hym knowlege as lord and
Prynce.　Fro that tyme that this was done / ther was none
Irysh-man in leynystre, of hey kyn ne of low, but that, for fere
of Englysh-men, thay yaue hame to Macmurgh, So that ther was
none of the londe-pepill, that al nas subiecte to hym, and redy
to his wille /

[CHAPTER XI.]

IN this tyme, rose grete debate and wrete be-twyxe the Capit*ul*um
kynge of Connaght, and Donalde Obreyn, the kynge of xj^m.
[Fol. 6 a.]
lymerike, and of thomonde. the kynge of Connaght, Oconghoure,
gaderid his hostes forto werre vp-on obreyn.　Obreyn Sende to
Macmurgh, for allyaunce that was betwen ham, that he sholde hym
helpe.　He Spake therof to Robert *and* to Morice, *and* bade them
that th[a]y sholde go thedyr forto helpe obreyn.　Thay, and har men
wyth hame, *and* wentyn Into thomonde, and foundyn oconghoure,
that styfly stode a-yennes hame, *and* many fightes hame yaue. *post*
But the dis-comfyture turned vp-on oconghoure; *and* many cf his *varios*
conflictus
men were sleyn, So that wyth shame he mvste tvrne into *ubique*
connaght. / And fro that tyme, Obreyn wythdrowe hym from *victoria*
potitus.
oconghoure, and neuer aftyr was subiecte to hym as he was
ther-to-forn.　And the Englysh hoste, wyth grete gettynges *and*
wyth ryche yftis, turned ayen Into Leynystre.

[CHAPTER XII.]

A. D. 1169.
Macmurgh
aspires to
be king of
all Ireland.

Fitz-
stephen
and
Maurice,
whom he
consults,
advise him
to bring
over more
English-
men.

He sends a
letter to
Earl
Richard
urging him
to come
over.

[*Fol.6b.]

Macmoroʒwʒch sawe the englysshe-men so stalwarth that no power myght ham wythstond. he bethoght hym of thynge that was passed, & that sume of hys eldre to-fore hym hadden somtyme the kynge-dome of all Irland, & that al the 4 lond was subyet to hym : he wold, by hys myght, by ryght of hys eldren, brynge hyt yn-to the self state, that al þe lond shold be vnder hys lordshyppe, as hyt was wndre hys eldren to-fore hys tym   Of þys tynge he spak preuely wyth Robert, & wyth 8 Moryce, & besoght har consayll therof ; And þay hym answerd, & seiden, that 'lyghtly that myght be done, yf he wold make come more plente of englyssh men ynto þe lond.' he bad ham well þorwe, that thay sholden yn al manere senden after more of har 12 kyn & frendshype. & for thay shold the bettyre wyll haue ther-to, he profred ham to yeue hys eldest doghtre to on of ham, whych hyre so wold, wyth all hys lond aftyr hys day. bot, fore euery of ham had wyf & I-spoused that tyme, after mych spech, & 16 many dalyaunce ther-of at thys consaylle, thay thoght þat he, to the erle Rychard, (of whom we haue ar thys I-spoke, & to whom he behete the same doghter ther-to-fore at Brystowe,) hys lettres shold send on thys maner : " ❦ Dermot Macmorgh, pryynce of 20 leynestre, to Rychard, Gylbertes son, erle of strugoyl, sendeth grettynge. If þou rekenest the tyme that ys Igoo, as well as we that nede haue, our mone nys ycome to þe no rather than hys tyme. Storkes & swalewes, & oþer somer foules, we haue 24 aftyre I-loked : thay comen, & wyth þe cold north-westre wynd þay ben awey ywent. Bot thy comynge, that we so mych haue desyred & so longe I-loked after, nether estren wyn[d]e, ne noon other, vs ne hath I-send, as thou vs be-hete. þerfor, that thou ne 28 hast y-dene troght some grete lette, hastyly be about to do ; for that wer al our gladnes, that thou hast swyth. If þou stalwardly comest, & wyth good myght, the four partyes of Irland shal sone be turned to þe fyft." Whan the erle had thys I-hard, he was 32 yn many thoghtes ; & aftyr many selcouth * & dyuers redes, at the last he bethoght hym, that so fewe men as weren yn-to the lond I-come ther-to-fore, hadden yn so lytyll whyll so well I-sped of har aduentures : he name to hym the better herte, & thynge 36

Macmurgh sawe the Englysh-men so bolde, that no man *Capitulum*
myght ham wythstond. he be-thoght hym of thynge *xij*ᵐ.
that was passyd, and that some of his eldryn to-fore hym haddyn
some tyme the kyngedome of al Irland, and that al the land was
subiecte to hym. he wolde, by his myght / by ryght of eldryn, *ad avita et*
brynge hit Into the same state, that al the londe sholde be vndyr *antiqua*
his lordshipe, as hit was * Vndyr His eldryn to-fore His tyme. Of [*Fol.6b.] *jura.*
this thynge He Spake wyth Robert *and* wyth Moryce, and be-soghte
har consayle vp-on this. And thay hym answerid, *and* sayd, that
'lyghtly that myght be done, yf he wolde make come more Plente *hoc facile*
of Englysh-men into the londe.' He Prayed ham, that in al haste *fieri posse.*
thay sholde sende aftyr more of hare kyn *and* hare frendis. and
for thay sholde haue the bettyr will therto, he profered hame to
yeue his eldyst doghtyr to one of ham, whych hyr so wolde, w*ith*
al the londe aftyr his day. but, for euery of hame hadd wyfe, and *legitime*
spoused that tyme, Aftyr mych spech, *and* many delyaunce therof *copula*
gaudebat
at this consayle, thay thoght that he, to the erle richard (of whom *uterque.*
we haue ar this spoke, and to whom he promysyd the same
doghtyr there-to-for at Brystowe,) his lette*res* sholde sende on this
manc*re* // " Dermot Macmurgh, P*ri*nce of leynystere, to Richard,
Gylbertes sone, Erle of strugoil, sendyth gretynge. If ye haue *Ovid, Ep.*
rekenyd the tyme that is I-goo, as wel as we that nede haue, oure *Her. ii. 7.*
compleynte is not come to yow no radyr than this tyme. Storkys
and swalewes, and othyr Somyr fowlis, we haue aftyr a-waytid:
thay comyn; and w*ith* the colde north weste wynde thay ben *circio jam*
flante nec
away I-went. But youre comynge, that we so mych haue desyrid, *favonius*
and so longe lokid aftyr, nethyr estryn wynd, ne none othyr, vs ne *nec eurus.*
hath sende, as ye vs promysid. Ther-for [as] ye ne haue this done
but throgh some grete lette, hastely be a-but to do ; for that were al
oure gladnys, that ye haste blywe. Yf ye boldely come, and wyth
good streynth, the foure Parties of Irland shal sone be turned to *de facili*
conver-
the fyfte " // Whan the Erle hadd this hard, he was in many *tentur*
thoghtis ; and aftyr many and dyuers thoghtes, at the laste he
be-thoght hym, that so few men as weryn into the londe y-come
ther-to-fore, haddyn in so lytill tyme so wel y-spede of har
aduentures : he hade the bettyr herte. and thynge that he dowtted

A. D.
1169-70.
The Earl
resolves
on the
enterprise.

that he douted myche ther-by-fore to begyne, he wax tho the
bolder to tak an hond. Fro that tyme, al hýs thoght & all hys
wýlle was, nyghte & day, wyth all hys myȝth to wend in-to Irland.
He went hym to þe kynġ henry, & hym swith be-soght þat he shold 4
delyuer hym hys londes þat sholden be hys by ryght of herytage,
other yeue hym leue to do hym yn adventur, lond to purchace yꝺ
vnked land.

A. D. 1170.   [CHAPTER XIII.]

W̲han the Kynge wyst hys entent, whoder he wold go, 8
he ne yaue hym fully leue, ne fully hym ne warned ; bot
wyth such leue as he had, he dight hym þe wynter tyll the
begynny[n]ge of Maye. He sent to-for hym ynto Irland A knyght

He sends
Reymond
le Gros to
Ireland,
who lands
near
Waterford,
ab. May 1,
1170.

that was I-called Reymond le gras ;—wyth hym, x knytgthes, & 12
fourty Squyers, & four score bowmen ;—A man ful hardy & stalwarde, & well proued yꝺ wepne, Robertis neueu, & Moryces, har
eldest brother, sone.   Thay arryued at a place i-called dun-
doneuile, four myle a south halfe Waterford ; & ther thay arered 16
a dyche, & a feble castel vpon, of yardes and turues[1].   The men
of Watterford, & wyth ham Malaghelyꝺ of olan, thys waren
I-ware that thay y-hadden such neghborhede ful loth, & toke
ham to rede, þat þay wolden vpoꝺ ham, ar mo com to ham. Thay 20
assembled ham togeddre, well thre thousand meꝺ, & wenteꝺ ouer

He is
attackt
by the
Waterford
men and
O'Phelan,

the wattyr of sur, that parteth the twey contres of leynestre
& of mounestre, & setteꝺ ham yꝺ thre hostes, ful boldely for to
assaýlle the englysshe-meꝺ with-In har castell.   Reymond & hys 24
meꝺ—thogh they fewe wer, theý wer nat feýnt—with vneuenlý
host wenteꝺ out & assembled wyth ham.   Bot, as no wonder was, .
so few men ne myght nat all priuely fýghten aýeyꝺ so many,
thay turned haꝺ aye to har recet. the other wenedeꝺ that thay 28
departed yn dýscomfyte ; thaý brakeꝺ har sheld. Iꝺ, & wentteꝺ

and is
forced to
retreat to
his camp.

aftyr : & thay war nat fully wythyꝺ þe yate, that some of haꝺ
neʀ ratheʀ In thaꝺ þe englyssh.   Reymond saw that he & hys
wereꝺ yꝺ gret perylle, & vpon poynt to lese the lýfe. he be-cryed 32
hys felewes, & turned stalwarthly vpoꝺ heʀ formeꝺ[2] ; & þe fyrste
that come yꝺ, he claue hyꝺ the heed, & throgh slaght of that

---

[1] MS. iurues, or inrucs.   [2] men in front.

mych ther-be-for to begyn, he wax than the boldyr to take an A.D. 1169-70.
honde. Fro that tyme, al his thoght and al his will was, nyght *vel in exteris* and day, wyth al his myght to wende into Irlanď. He went then *regionibus* to the kynge, and besoght hym that he shold delyuere hym his *se fatis et fortunae* londis that sholdyn be his by ryght of heritage, othyr yeue hym *commit-tendi* leue to do hym in aduenture, londe for to Purchase in vnkyď *licentiam daret.* lanď.

[CHAPTER XIII.] A.D. 1170.

Whan the kynge vndyrstode his entente, whedyr he wolde *Capitulum xiij^m.* goo, he yaue hym not full leue, ne fully be-name hym not ; *quasi* but with suche leue as he hadď, he dight hym the wyntyr till the *licentia, ironica* begynnynge of may / he Sende to-for hym into Irlanď a knyght that *namque* was calliď[1] Reymond Legras ;—wyth hym, x knyghtis and fourty *magis quam* Squyeris, and foure score bowmen ;—A man ful hardy and bolde *vera.* and wel proueď in wepyn, Robert-is eme [2], and Morices, hare eldyts *[2 eme, uncle, is* brodyr, sone. Thay londyď at a place that is y-calliď Dundonenylď, *'nephew'* foure Mile on the Sowth syde of watyrforď; and there they reriď a *in this MS.]* dyche, and a febill castel vpon, of Iardis and turues *. The men of *[*Fol.6b.]* Watyrford, and wyth ham Malaghelyn Of olan, this waryn y-ware *ex virgis* that thay haddyn such neghboris, that ham were loth [3] ; and toke *et cespite.* ham to consayle, that thay wolde vp-on ham, ar mo come to hame. Thay gaderid ham to-gaddyr, wel iije. Ml. men, and wentyn ouer the watyr of Sure, that partyth the two contreis, that is to Say leynystre and mounestre, And settyn ham in thre hostis, ful boldely forto assayle the Englysh-men with-In har castel. Reymond and his men (thegh thay fewe were, they were not feynte) with few pepill wentyn out, and mete with hame. But, as no woundyr hit was, so few men myght not al plenary fyghteñ ayeyn so many, that *de plano resistere* turned ham to thare recette. the othyr wende that thay depertiď *non potuit.* in descomfite; thay brakyn har sheldrun, and wentyn aftyr. and *intra valvas* thay were not fully wythin the gate, that some of hame nere *vix plene* radyr In than the English. Reymond saw that he and his were *suspensus certatim* in grete Pereil, and on Poynte to lese here lyfe. he cried on his *intrando susce-* fellowis, and tvrned boldely vp-on here enemys. anď the fryst that *perunt.* come In, he clewe his hede. and throgh deth of that o man, al the

---

[1] R. Legras. [3] Exterorum viciniam suspectam habentes, v. 248.

A. D. 1170. maꝺ, all the ost was dyscomfyte, & tok haꝺ to flyght. The

oþer ham folwed yꝺ-to all þe pleyꝺ, & leyd haꝺ oꝺ so, þat yꝺ

lytell whẏll thay slowe of haꝺ fyfe[1] hundred & mo; & þe most parte of þe otheꝛ felleꝺ adoꝺ yꝺ-to þe see, of þe heye rokes, & 4 drent haꝺ-selfe. In thys fyght, was a knyght that hete Wyllyaꝺ ferand, that dydde ouer-weħ & aboue all otheꝛ: he was a maꝺ that hade semblant as thoght he weꝛ oꝺ the mich yuell, & þer-foꝛ

he put hyꝺ-selue[2] alwey theꝛ *the most perille was; ffor he ne 8

raght thegh deth come betwene hyꝺ & hẏs ẏuell, ar hyt waꝛ to mẏch I-smẏt vpoꝺ hyꝺ. Heꝛ þe pryd of waterford felle; heꝛ aħ hẏs mẏght went to noght; heꝛ-of come the Englysshe hope & comfort; & to the Iresshe, dred & wanhope; ffor hẏt was neuer 12 theꝛ-to-for I-herd, that of so fewe men, so grett a slaght was done. Bot lyder consaylle thay dẏddeꝺ þer-after, that turned ham to mẏch cruelte; ffor whaꝺ the maẏstrẏ was al har, & al har fomeꝺ ouercome, In þe fyght wereꝺ ytake well thre score meꝺ & teꝺ, 16

that ham yoldeꝺ, & wereꝺ the heghest & the rychyst of al the sitè, such þat þay mẏght haue had for ham the sitè delyuered, or els as myche catel as thay wolden desyꝛ. Heruy of Mouꞑtmorthy, that to haꝺ was ẏcome, hẏm thrydsome of knẏghtes, & Reymond, 20 vp dyuers domes stroueꝺ what meꝺ sholdˀ do wyth har prysons[3]; ffor Reymond trauayllet about for to dylyuere haꝺ, as a maꝺ of reuthful mode, & þus seyd to hys feres: "lordynges, what ys vs

to done of ouꝛ wreched prisoners? I sey nat that man[4] shal on 24 any maner spaꝛ hys fomaꝺ; bot thay beth nat now fomen, both[5] beth meꝺ nat rebelle, bot yꝺ bataylle for to defend[6] har contrey ouercome. Me thynketh thay beth now yꝺ such state, that me oght bettyr haw mercy of haꝺ & yeve haꝺ lyfe, for to yeue otheꝛ 28 ensample to be boxoꝺ, thaꝺ cruely to do haꝺ to deth, whaꝛ-throgh þat otheꝛ, throgh ferdnesse of trust, þe lasse to yeldˀ haꝺ to vs." Whaꝺ Reymondˀ had such wordes I-seyde, yn al þe folke

was moste wi[lle][7] to graunt ham lyf, Arose vp Heruy amonge 32

---

[1] MS. lyfe.   [2] MS. sleue.   [3] pryson = prisoner.   [4] MS. maner.
[5] but: Sed hi non hostes jam, sed homines.—*Op.* v. 250.   [6] MS. defond.
[7] The ink has perisht: 'et murmure populi cum quodam quasi favore sub-secuto.' Gir. Camb., *Exp. Hib.* c. xv.—*Op.* v. 252, Rolls Series.

hoste was dys-comfite *and* toke ham to flyght / The othyr ham A.D. 1170.
folwid' into al the Playñ, and leyde on ham. So that in lytyl
space of tyme thay kyllyd' of ham **v. C.** *and* mo; and the most *ab altis in*
Parte of the othyr fellyn adoviñ into the see, of the hey Rokys, *mare rupi- bus prae-*
and dreynt ham-selfe // In this fyght was a knyght that was *cipitati sunt*
callid' William ferrand, that did ful wel *and* abowe al othyr; *infiniti.*
[1] he was a man that hade semblant as thegh he wer*e* on the
mych yuel; and therfor he Putte hym-Selfe at tymys ther the
moste Peryl was. For he roght not thegh dethe come betwen
hym and his Sekenys, or hit wer*e* mych grow on hym [1] /
Here the Pryde of Watyrforde felle; here al his myght went to *superbia*
noght; her-of come the Englysħ hope and conford'; and to the *cecidit.*
Irysñ, dred and wanhope. For hit was neue*r* ther-to-fore herde *horror . .*
that, of So few men, so grete a slaghte was done. But a lewid *desperatio.*
consayle thay diddyn, that ther-aftyr turned ham to myche
cruelte. For whan the Mastry was al har*e*, *and* al hare enemys
ouer*come*, In the fyght weryn take wel iije score men *and* teñ that *septua- ginta cives.*
ham yeldyn, *and* weryn the beste and the rycheste of the Cite,
Such that thay myght haue hade for them the Cite delyuerid', or
els as mych ryches as thay wolde desyre. Heruey of montmurthy, *pecuniam infinitam.*
that to ham was come, hym thyrdsome of knyghtis, *and* Reymond',
vp-on dyuers consaylis thoghten what thay sholde do wyth har
Prysoneris. For Reymond laborid' for thar delyverance, as man
of pitefull herte / And thus sayd to his fellowis: " Lordynges, what
is vs to done wyth our*e* wrechid' presoners ? I Sey not that man *de captivis nostris.*
shal on any man*er* spare his enemys; but thay byth nat now
enemys; but byth men not rebell, but in bataill forto defende
har contrey ouer*come*. Me-thynkyth thay byth now in such state,
that we owyth bettyr haue mercy of ham *and* yeue ham lyfe, forto *potius . . pietas ad*
yeue othyr ensampill to be boxum*e*, than cruely to do ham to *exemplum,*
deth; wher-for otheris wil truste the lasse to yelde ham to vs." *quam cru- delitas ad*
*Whan Reymond' Hade Suche Wordys y-Seyde, and al the fello- *tormentum.*
shippe Was most about to graunt ham lyfe, Aros vp heruey ney [*Fol.7 a.]

[1-1] vir carne quidem infirmus, sed corde firmissimus : imminentem, ut vide-
batur, leprae malitiam morte nimirum praevenire desiderans tam praematura
quam praeclara.—*Op.* v. 249.

D

A.D. 1170. hame al, & thys haɱ seyd: "Inogħ Reymond openly to vs hath

'Enough of Mercy! spoke of mercy & almes-dedes, vnked landes I-wonne, & nat wyth

Did Alexander and Caesar win by it? slagħ & wyth brenny[n]ge. Wheder Alexander & Iulius Cesar, that weren lordes of al þe world, wonnen londes by such wey, 4 I wold Reymond wold me answer. Whan thay comen to vs vel arrayede to fyghten, If þay hadde I-won ouer-hand & vs ouercome, wolden thay, for almesse & for reuth, haw had mercye of vs? nay, I trow nat. þerfor out-chese oɱ of two: Other do manly thynge, 8

Either kill the rebels quietly, wher-fore we bene ycome; & the folke þat ys rebbell ayeyn vs, wyth-outten any noyse, wyth wepne hertely brynge out of dawes;

or go home!' Other, yf we shollen do almes dede on heɱ, & haɱ saren, as Reymond hath seyd, out we wend to our shyppes, & turne ayeyn, 12 & let we the wreched men hold har lond, & brouken wythouten

As no gallows are handy, the rebels are drownd. any chalange." Heruyes dome lyket bettre than Reymondes; & weren the Cyteȝeyns to deth Idemed. Thay ne hadden no wone of warytres; & þerfor þey ladden haɱ to þe clyf of þe see, & put 16 haɱ adoun, & drent ham.

[CHAPTER XIV.]

Earl Richard Struguil The men-tyme, the Erl Rychard, wyth the power that he had arayed, was y-come to south wales; & whaɱ he hadde

[*Fol.7b.] wyth * gret reuerence y-done hys pylrimage at sent dauyes, he put 20 hym to saylle, & hade good wynd, came ẏnto Irland with two

lands at Waterford, Aug. 23, hundret knythtes & other, mor than a thousand. He arryued at weyseford on seynt Bertylmewes euen: Than was fulfẏlled a

fulfilling prophecies of Merlin and the Irish Saint Moling. prophecye that Merlyn seyd of hys comynge; 'þe brond shal 24 come to-fore þe borned fyr; And rygħ as the spark maked the brond come, Also þe brond shal make the fyr come after.' Anoþer prophecye, seẏnt Molynge seyd of that same: 'A mych man shall erne to-fore; & þe most heeddes of desmond & ek of leynestre 28 he shal defouly; & wyth streynth he shall noblych the wey opne to the wepned.' Amorow, whan the tẏthẏnge of haɱ was

Reimund joins him. They assault Waterford, Tuesday, Aug. 25. I-spronge, Reymond went hẏm to the Erle with furtẏ knẏghtes with mych gladnes; & amorow, after þe holy-daye, Thay went 32 comynly al to þe syte of Waterford, & assaylled the toun ful fersly; & twyes thay weren rebuked, & ful stalwarhlẏ, of þe Cyteȝeyns. Reymond, that by purueaunce & graunt of ham al was ymade

amonge ham al, *and* thus ham Sayde: "I-nowe Reymond opynly to A.D. 1170.
vs hath Spoke of mercy and almes-deddes, vn-kyd landis to wynñe
and nat wyth Slaght *and* wyth brennynge. whedyr Alexandyr *and*
Iulyus Cesar, that weryn lordys of al the worlde, wonnen londis
by such wey, I wold Reymond wolde me answere. whan thay *Cum ad*
com*m*yn to vs wel arrayed' to fyghten, If thay had the bettyr, *and* *nos expug-*
nandos
vs had ou*e*rcome, woldyn thay, for almesse and for Pite, haue had *instructis*
aciebus
mercy of vs? Nay, y trow not. ther-for chese oñe of two: Othyr *adve-*
to do manly thyng*e*, wher-for we ben come; and the Pepill that is *nerunt.*
rebel ayeynnes vs, wythouten eny noyse, wyth wepyn hertely berewys ham of lyfe / Othyr, yf we shall do almysdede on them,
and ham spare, as Reymond hath Sayd, go we to our*e* shippis, *and*
turnne ayeyn*e*, *and* lete we the wrechyd' pepil holde har lond', *and*
kepyn wi*th*out any chalange." Herueyes Iugement Plesid bettyr *membris*
confractis,
than Reymondes; *and* weryn the Citteseynnes to deth demyd'. *in maris*
Thay had no galosis; and therfor thay laddyn ham to the clyfe *praecipi-*
tium dati
of the See, and put ham adouñ, *and* drovnde ham al. *sunt.*

[CHAPTER XIV.]

T he men-tyme, the Erle Ry*ch*ard, wyth the Power that he *Capitulum*
had' arraied, was come to Suth Walis; *and* When he had *xiiij^m.*
wi*th* grete reuerence done his Pylgrymag*e* at Scynt Dauycs, he
Put hym to sayle, *and* had good wynd', come into Irland wy[th]
two hundryd' knyghtis *and* othyr, more than a thousand'. he
londid' at Weysford on Seynt Bartolomewes evyn. Then was
fulfillid' a pprophesy that Merlynge Sayde of his comyng*e*: "The *prophetia*
Merlini.
brond shal come to-for the brennynge fyr*e*, And ryght as the
Sparke makid the brond come, Also the brond shall make the
fyre come aftyr." Anothyr p*r*ophesy, Molynge Sayd of that same: *prophetia*
Molyng.
"A mych man shal erne to-for; *and* the moste hedis of desmond
and also of leynystre he shal defeuly; and wyth streynth he shal *capita con-*
culcans.
nobelych the wey opyn to the wepenyd'." A-morrow, when the
thythyngis spronge, Reymond went to the Erle wi*th* fourty
knyghtis wi*th* mych gladnys; and amorrow, aftyr the holy day
thay went holy to the Cite of Watyrford, and assaylid' the toun *bis viri-*
liter
ful fresly ; *and* twyes they weryn rebukyd', *and* ful boldely, of the *repulsi*
Citteseyn*es*. Reymond, that by Purueyaunce and graunt of ham *fuissent.*

D 2

A.D. 1170. prince, & formaꝺ of al the host, sawe & awayted a place good for
to assaylle: he cryed & cleped the wepned men to the assaut,

They take Waterford. & þay egrely assaylledeꝺ, & brakeꝺ yn-to þe sytè, & folke-mele
slowe the menꝺ yꝺ weyes & yꝺ houses, & waꝺ þe Cẏtè.   In ₄
rathnyldes touꝛ wereꝺ twey rẏche men ytake, bot þrogh prayeꝛ
of Macmorgh, that thedeꝛ was thaꝺ I-come, he was y-hold alyue.

Mac-murgh's daughter Eve is married to Earl Struguil. Macmorgh broght hys doghtyꝛ with hẏm, Eue by name, & spoused
hyꝛ to the Erle, & madeꝺ fast sekernesse betweꝺ ham.   Waꝺ thys ₈
was ydo al, þe Erle left menꝺ for to kepe the cytè, & turned hym
with the hoste to deuylyꝺ.

[CHAPTER XV.]

Macmorgh wyst that myche of the poweꝛ of haꝛ lond
was I-come to helpeꝺ ham of dyuelyꝺ, & haddeꝺ beset ₁₂

They march, thro' Glenda-lough hills, to Dublin. all þe wodde weyes & þe narow weys thetherward: he left tho
weyes, & lad the hoste throght the montaẏnes of Glyndelagh, al
harmeles, rẏght to the sytè. These cyteȝeyns, oueꝛ al otheꝛ, hated
wereꝺ of hym, & that was no wondeꝛ; ffor ẏn some tẏme thay ₁₆
sloweꝺ hys fadyꝛ yꝺ the cytè; & after the harme, thay dydde hyꝺ
mych shaꝺ, foꝛ thay burryd an hounde with hym yn the pute
that he was yn I-leyde. Thay sent messagers to þe Erle, &
namely the Erchebysshop laurence, & besoghteꝺ pees; & as thay ₂₀

Reimund and Miles of Cogan assail and take Dublin. wereꝺ spekyng of pees, on oon half was Reymond, & on the otheꝛ
halue a ful hardy knẏght, Myles of Cogan, with ẏonglẏnges well
coueytouse of battaylle & of gettyng. Thay assaylled the Cytè,
& breken In, & wan þe Cytè, wyth gret slaght of þe sẏtȝeyns. ₂₄

[*Fol.8 a.] *Natheles, the best parte of ham, wyth þe rychest & the derwarthest
thyngys þat thay haddeꝺ, yn botes escapeden, & wenten yn-to þe

Hasculf and the richest folk escape. north ylondes, wyth hastoyl, that was maẏstre yn the cyte, &
haꝛ lodesmaꝺ. That day byfel two Muracles yn the cyte: that ₂₈
on of the Croice, yn the modeꝛ chẏrche of þe trẏnẏte, whyche the
Cytȝeyns woldeꝺ haue I-ladde with ham yn-to the ylandes yn
the see; & for nothynḡ, thay ne myghth yt weccheꝺ out of þe
place. That otheꝛ, of a sergeant that hadde I-robbet the erche- ₃₂
bysshoppes paleys, & þer-after come to-for þe rcde, & offred a peny:
fyrst, & efte-sone, & at euery tym, the peny stert ayeẏne to hym.
he bethoght hẏm that god was nat wel I-quenyted of the robbery

al was made Prynce and forman of al the hoste, Saw and a-waytyď A.D. 1170.
a place goode forto assayle.   he cried *and* callid the wepenyd men
to the assaute anď thay egyrly assayliď, and brakyn Into the Cite,
and kyllid the men in weyes and in houses, and wan the Cite.   in
rathnyldys tour*e* weryn two ryche men take, *and* thay both wer*e*
be-hedyď. M*a*csaghlyn of olan was also take, but throgh Prayer Melaghlin
of M*a*cmur*gh*, that ther was than y-come, he was holde alyue. O'Phelan
                                                                is taken,
M*a*cmur*gh* broght his doghtyr wyth hym, Eue by name, and but kept
Spousiď hyr to the Erle and madyn fast syckyrnys betwen*e* *Ham// alive.
Whan this was done al / the Erle Lefte men forto Kepe the Cite [*Fol.7 b.]
and turnyde hym wi*th* the hoste to deuelyn //

[CHAPTER XV.]

M acmur*gh* vndyrstode that myche of the pepill of the Capi*tulum*
       contrey was come to helpe ham of the Cite of deuelyn, XVᵐ.
and hadde be-sette al the wodd-weyes and the Narrow-weyes *rias nemo-*
thedyrward. He lefte thay weyes, and lad the hoste throw the *rosas et
arctas*
montanys of Glyndelagh, al holde and sound, tyl thay come to the
Cite. The Citteseynes ou*er* al othyr hatid M*a*cmur*gh*; *and* they
wer hatyd of hym: and that was no wondyr. For in some tyme
thay slowyn his fadyr in the Cite; and aftyr the harme, thay dyd
hy*m* moche shame, for t*h*ay buryed an hounde wi*th* hym in the *cum cane
cires tumu-*
buryles that he was In-leyde. Thay send messangeris to the Erle, *larerunt.*
and namely the archebyschope Laurance, and besoghten Pees; and
as thay weryn Spekyn of pees, on oon*e* halue was Reymond and on
the othyr syde a ful hardy knyght, Miles de Cogan, wi*th* yonglynges
wel couetos of batail and of getynge: They assaylid the Cite, and
brokyn In, *and* toke the Cite wi*th* grete slaghte of the Citesen*es*.
Natheles, the beste parte of ham, wi*th* the rychest and the wourdyest
thynge*s* that thay haddyn, in botis escapedyn, and wentyn into the *naves et
scaphas . .*
north ylond*es* wyth hastoyl, that was Captayn in the Cite, and har *intrantes*
gouernour*e* / That day befel two Miraclis in the Cite: that one, of
the cros in the Cee churche of the trynyte, wych the Citteseyn*es*
wold haue take wyth ham into the Ilandys in the see / And for
no thyng t*h*ay myght not take hit out of the place. That othyr, *sicut in
'Topo-*
of a Sergeant that had yrobyď the archebysshope-is Place; and *ther-aftyr come to-for the rode, *and* offerid a peny: fryst, and har *graphia'
decla-*
aftyr, and in cuery tyme, the peny styrte ayeyñ to hym̃. he *ratur.*
bethoght hym that god was not aplesid of the robery that he had *Op. v. 129.*

A.D. 1170.

that he had y-do: he turned hẏm than, & let take al that he had y-nom[1], & bar̄ hyt ayeyn, & went to þe rode & offred; & hy[s] offrynge the[r] abode. Whan þe Erl hade a few dayes I-ordyned for the stat of þe Cytè, he left ther̄ Myles de Cogan, keper of þe Cytè & of þe contre, & a *par*tye of þe meyne wẏth hẏm. And by entycement of M*ac*m*orgh*, that bethoght hym of þe old enmyte that he hade to the kynge of Mithe, he went hym to þe contrey, branten, slowen, & robeden, & broghten the contre to noght, for none ne durst hym wythe-stond. Oconghur̄ of Conaght saw that he was the next—as man that seethe hys neghbors hous berne, he may drede of þe sparkes—he sent Messagers to M*ac*m*orgh* yn thys wordes: "Ayeyne þe four̄me of our̄ pees, thou hast imad come yn-to thys lond mẏch outcomen̄ folke. þe whẏlle that thou held the ẏn thẏ leynystre, we hyt tholleth euynly; Now thou, as man that naght ne the thynkest on thyn oth, ne no reuth ne hast of thyn ostage, the merres I-sete of thyn eldren lond, vnryghtfullyo u*er*goste. Make thẏn out-comen men wẏth-draw, & turne aẏeẏne, or els sothly we shul the send thy sones heede." M*ac*m*orgh* thys herd, & yaf hym̄ a prout answar̄, & sent hym to sey, that he ham̄ wold hold, & send aft*er* more & eke more; that he nold neu*er* reste tẏl he hadde I-wonne Connaght, wyth the kẏnge-dome of al þe lond, as hys eldren̄ su*m*tẏm hyt hadden̄ to-for̄ hẏm. Oconnoghur̄ had her̄ of grete dyspyte, & sore was atened, & let smyth of sonnes heed, þ*at* he had hym Itake fore ostage.

Earl Struguil leaves a force in Dublin, and ravages Meath. O'Conor of Connaught reproaches Mac-murgh, and cuts off his son's head.

[CHAPTER XVI.]

Aftyr this, worth gret spech ẏn-to all þe lond, & mych ferdnesse of the out-comen̄ men̄. Than gaddered ham al to-gedderes, al the clerkes & the wysmen̄ of þe lond at ardmagh̄; & of thys folkes comyng̃, was mych I-spoke, & longe dalyaunce. At þe laste, comẏnlẏ thaẏ accordeden̄ al her̄-to, that, for the syn̄ of þe folk, thys mesaduentur̄ ham ys bẏfal; namely, that whan thay fonden̄ englysshe-men̄ chyldren to syllen̄, that chepmen & robbers woldene brynge to the lond, thay * were wonet to by ham, & do ham yn̄ thraldome; & that throgh goddẏs owne

A Council of the Irish clerics is held at Armagh. The country's ill has come from enslaving English children. [*Fol.8b.]

[1] MS. ymon.

done. he turned̄ hym than, *and* toke al that he toke wyth hym, A.D. 1170.
and bare hit ayeyñ, *and* went to the rode, and offerid; *and* his
offerynge ther abode. / When the Erle had a few dayes y-ordaynyd
for the state of the Cite, he lefte there myles de Cogan, kepere of
the Cite and of the contrey, and a partey of the meynne wyth
hym.   And by entycement¹ of *Macmurgh*, that be-thoght hym̄ of ¹ *instinctu.*
the olde enemyte that he had to the kynge of Myth, he went hym As Mac-
to the contrey, brantyn, Slouedyñ and robedyñ, *and* broghten the hated
contrey to noght, for non ne durst hym wythstond.   Oconghoure O'Rourke
of connaght Saw that he was the nexte, (as a man that seth his (p. 2–4),
evyncrystyñ his house brenne, he may dred the sparkys ;) he send wasted.
messangeres to *Macmurgh* in these wordis : "Ayeyne the forume of *in insulam*
oure pees, thow haste made come into this londe mych strange *aequa-*
pepill. the whyle that thow helde the in thy leynystre we hit *nimiter*
tollid̄ euynly.   Now thow,—as man that noght rekyth of his *mus.*
trouth, ne no pite hauest of thyn hostage,—the meris y-sette² of- *positas ..*
thyn eldryñ lond, vnryghtfully ouer-goste³.   Make thy strangeres * [* Fol.8a.]
Wyth-draw, and turne ayeyne; othyr ellys Sothly we shall the ³ *insolenter*
sende thy Sonnys hede." *Macmurgh* this herde, and to hym yaue *excessisti*
a prowte answere, *and* Sende hym to Say, that 'he ham wold holde,
and send aftyr more, and eke more, / ande that he wold neuer
reste, til he had take *and* conquerid al connaght, with al the
kyngdome of al the lond, as his predessessouris had to-for hym.'
Oconghoure here-of had grete indignacioñ, and gretly ther-of was *indignans*
grewid̄; And he comandid to Smyte of his Sones hede, that he yafe *Rothericus*
hym for an hostage.

[CHAPTER XVI.]

Aftyr this, Spronge grete Spech in-to al the lond, *and* Capitulum
mych dreded̄ the strange comen men.   Than gadderid xvjᵐ.
ham to-gederes al the clerkys and the wysmen of the land̄ at
Ardmagh; and of this pepil-is comynge, was mych Speche and
longe delyaunce. At the last, comynly thay acordid̄ al herto,
that, for the synne of the Pepill, this mys-aduenture ham ys *tam a*
by-fall, specialy that whan thay foundyn Englysh-men childryn *mercatori-*
to sill, that Marchandis and roberes wold bryng to the lond, *praedoni-*
thay were woned to by ham, and pute ham in thraldome; And *piratis*

A.D. 1170. wreth hyt was, that as syllers wereñ to-fore y-broght yn thraldome,

also the byggers sholden after : ffoꝛ hyt was somtyñ that the

The English, folke of englond—The maner of har kyngdome was al I-hole—

whan thay had noñ otheꝛ thynge that þay myghten take to, rathaꝛ 4

ratherthan than thay wold any myssayse tholy, Thay weꝛ I-wont to syïleñ
suffer,
would sell haꝛ chyldren & haꝛ otheꝛ kynnesmeñ, botlñ ynto Irlond & ynto
their
children. otheꝛ londes. Theꝛ-foꝛ hyt may well be soth, that as the byggers,

also þe syllers, oft serued wel, throgh so loly gyltes to be y-broght yn 8

The Irish thraldome. Theꝛ hyt was yn þat consaylle be-heght, & by assent of al
resolve to
free all comynly I-set, that al the englysshe-meñ yn þe lond that yn thral-
English
slaves. dome wereñ, shold beñ delyuered, & frely let goo whodyꝛso they wold.

[CHAPTER XVII.]

Reports **H**er-aftyr spronge tythyngges of the Erle & of þe 12
are spread
in England englysshe-meñ ynto englond ; &, as maner ys, myche me
of Fitz-
Gerald's made more ; & that the Erl hade apropred to hym, nat only leynestre,
keeping
Irish land. bot otheꝛ londes also, that, by no ryght ne by law, to hyñ ne

Henry II to hys wyf longeñ. The kynge sent anoon, & forebeed that, 'out 16
forbids
ships to go no lond that were yn hys poweꝛ, ne shold no shyppen passe yn-to
to and
from Irland, ne no maner thynge for to brynge ; & al meñ that yn-to
Ireland;
and orders Irland waꝛ comen, shold ayeyn come yn-to englande, wyth-yn þe
all English-
men home. next estre, oꝛ they sholden be dysheryted & ex[y]led out of lond 20

for euer.' The Erl saw that he & hys wereñ narow belad, both

of hys men that hym wold leue, & eke that nothynge ne most

hym come out of otheꝛ landes, of þynge that hym nede was : by

Fitz- comune rede of hys men, he sent Reymond ouer to the kynge 24
Gerald
sends to that was feꝛ yn gascoyne, & thus hym sent to say : " By thy leue,
Henry II
in Gascony, lord, yf y am welle vndyrstond, y went ynto Irland foꝛ to help

thy trew man, Dermot Macmorgh ; þerfor, that al that of hys

and yields herytage, otheꝛ of oþers yn þe lond, almyghty god me hath I-sent, 28
his Irish
conquests as hyt come of thy graunt & of thy good wylle, also, I wyll that
to him.
hyt to the turne, to do theꝛ-wyth what the lyketh."

[CHAPTER XVIII.]

Reymond went to the kynge with such mandement ; & the
Thomas a
Beket is whyle that he folwed the kynges court, abydynge hys 32
martyrd.
answeꝛ, Thomas, the erchebysshoppe of Cantrebery [1], was martyred

---

[1] (*In margin, in a later hand :* The archebushop of canterbury called Tho.
Beckett. 1171.)

that, throw godis his owyn wreth hit was, that as the sylleris A.D. 1170.
weryn to-for broght in thraldome, also the byeris sholdyn be
brogh[t] in thraldome aftyr / For hit was somtyme that the
pepil of Englandˀ the maner of har kyngdome was al y-holde:
Whan thay had none othyr thynge that thay myght take to,
Radyr than thay wolde suffyr any dyssese, thay wold syll har *priusquam*
childyr and har othyr kynnes-men, both into Irland *and* into *inopiam ullam aut*
othyr landis.   Therfor hit may wel be trouth that, as the byeris, *inediam*
also the Silleris, ofte Seruydˀ well, throgh So wicked doynge, to be *sustinerent.*
broght in thraldome.   There hit was in that consayll promysydˀ,
and by assent of al comynly y-Set, that al the Englysñ-men
in the lond that in thraldome weryn, shold ben delyuerid, and
frely lette goo whedyr So thay wolde.

[CHAPTER XVII.]

HEre-aftyr spronge tythyngis of the Erle and of the *Capitulum*
Englysñ-men into Englond; *and* as the maner is, of mych *xvijm.*
thay mad more; and that the Erle had approperidˀ to hym, not only *fama de magnis*
leynystere, but othyr londis also, that, by no ryght ne lawe, to hym *semper*
ne to his wyfe partenydˀ// The kynge sende anone, and comandidˀ *majore, vulgante.*
that 'no shippe, out of no lond that Partenyth to hym, sholde Passe
into Irlandˀ, Ne no maner thynge forto brynge; and al men that
Into Irlandˀ war comyn, sholde ayeyñ goo into Englandˀ wythin the
nexte Estyr, Othyr they sholde be disherytid *and* exilidˀ out of
lond for euer.' The Erle saw that he and his weryn narrow bylad, *in arcto*
both of his men that hym wold leue, and also that nothynge sholdˀ *jam positos.*
come out of othyr landis of thynge that he had ned to / he toke
consayle of his men, and Sente Reymond ouer to the kynge, that was
fere in gascoyñ, and thus hym Sende to say: " By youre lycence *si bene*
lord, yf y be wel vndyrstond, y wente into Irlandˀ forto helpe yowr *recordor,*
trew man, Dermot M*acmurgh*.   Therfor, that al that of his *[*Fol.8 b.] i sic ad*
heritage, othyr of otheres, that y haue in the Land, that almyghty *eandem*
god to me * Hath sende, as hit come of youre graunt *and* of youre *pro libito vestro*
good wyle, [1] also y wille that Hit be turne to yow, to do ther-wyth *nutuque redibit.*
whate Plese yow."

[CHAPTER XVIII.]

REymond went to the kynge wit*h* such mandement; *and Capitulum*
the whyle that he folwid the kynges courte, abydynge his *xviijm.*
answere, Thomas, the archebisshope of Cantreberry. was martiridˀ

A.D. 1170.
yn englond, nat wyth-out mych blame to al þe lond-folk, both
lered & lewed. That erchebysshopp, after many-fold martyrdome
that he þolled, negh seuen yeȓ that he was banshed out of englond
for the ryghtes of holy chyurche, In sore & many wepynges, yn 4
double heeȓ about hys body—þat oñ, yn styd of shyrth ; that oþer,
yn stydde of breche—nyght & day yn holy prayeȓ & redynge
yn holy wrytte ; & o thynge that meste sorow broght to hys
hert, that al hys kyñ, men & wommen, yonge & old, wommen 8
lyggyne yn chyld-bed, & old men that fore eld yroked weren yn
heȓ cradelys, & all otheȓ, clerkes & lewed, that me myght wytt
that sybrede or otheȓ frendshypp haddeñ to hym, al thay wereñ
I-dryue out of englond ; & al they that wereñ of eld that þay 12
myghty othes swerȓ, swaren vpon the masse-boke that, as sone
as thay come ouer the see, thay shold go to þe erchebysshoppe,
& shew hym the * wrechednesse that þay suffred for hys sake ;
ffor he sholdˉ, for reuth of ham, turnen hys hert, & graunt þe 16
kynges wylle of þynge that he desyred. After such martyrdomes,
and many otheȓ þat he tholled yn hys lyue, whyche no manly
hert may bethynke to ful end, the hey martyrdome, that broght
hys soule to þe blysse of heuyn, & hys body to wyrshyppe yn hert, 20
otheȓ many þynges be-týdden that men Aght well vnderstond ;
þat ayeyns hys fomen yede, opyn heed, & opened þe chyrch durȓ
whyche the monkes hadden I-loke, & seyd þat 'meñ ne shold
no castell make of holy chyrche' ; & hys holy croune bade ayeyn 24
the naked swerdes for to smyte, & that yn the modyr chyrche,
heghest of al þe lond, & to-foȓ the weued, that he of fouȓ knyghtes,
wodeȓ than wood houndes, tholled fouȓ woundes yn the holy crouñ,
& [n]on without,—so as þe crouñ ogĥt betokne of proteccion to 28
clergy,—that he deth tholled yn the north syde of þe chyrche,
whyche betokneth Ihesu crystes passyoñ. & thus goddys owne
knyghte, wythouten any ferdnesse, tholled deth ; yn hys lyf of thys
world, chaunged wel selyly for þe lyf that euer shal lest without 32
end.   And as seynt Tomas-ys day, Apostle, ys þe fyft day afor
yold, so ys thys Thomas day þe fyft day afteȓ. That Thomas
was candel I-set yn þe este of þe world ; Thys Thomas yn þe west.
[That] was lyght to aly chyrche yn hyȓ yough, as [Thys] yn hyȓ eld ; 36

Arch-
bishop
Beket
sufferd
seven years
in exile,
personally,

and also
thro' his
persecuted
kinsfolk,

[*Fol.9 a.]
who
sufferd
for him.

Then came
his chief
Martyr-
dom.

He was
slain in
Canter-
bury
Cathedral
by four
knights,
before the
Altar.

The
Apostle
Thomas
died on
Dec. 21 ;
Beket on
Dec. 29.

iu England, not wyth-out grete reprefe to al the land-pepill, both *A.D. 1170.*
lerid and lewid. That archebisshope, aftyr manyfolde martyrdome
that he Sufferid, / ney vij⁰. yere that he was banneschid' out of *septennalis*
Englond for the ryght of holy church, In sore and many wepyngis, *fere exilii.*
In doubill here about his body,—that on in styd of shyrt, that *tam femo-*
othyr in styd of breche,—Nyght and day, in holy prayeris and *rali quam* *corporali.*
redynge in holy writte. And o thyng that meste Sorrow wroght *nec aetati* *parcente,*
to his hert, that al his kynnes-men, yonge and old, women lyggynge *nec sexui*
in chyldbed, and olde men that for elde yrokyd weryn in her *tam misera-* *bili san-*
cradelis, and al othyr, clerkys othyr lewid, that thay mygh[t] know, *guinis*
that weryn of his kyn͂, Othyr frendshipe haddyn to hym, al thay *universi* *proscrip-*
weryn dryw out of Englond'. And al thay that weryn of elde, *tione.*
that thay myght othys swere, Swaryn on the masboke, that 'as Sone
as thay come ouer the See, thay shold go to the archebyschope, and
Shew hym the mesury that thay Sufferid for his Sake ;' For he
shold, for Pite of ham, turnen his hert, and graunt the Kynge his
wyll of that, that he desyrid. Aftyr Such martirdom*es*, *and* many
othyr that he sufferid in his lyfe,—the whych in no mann*es* hert
may be thoght to ful end͂,—The hey martirdome, that broght his
Soule to the blysse of hewyn͂, and his body to vyrchip in Erth,
Othyr many thyngis be-fel that men aght wel vndyrstond ; that *quod ipse* *furibundis*
ayenes His enemys yede, opyn hede, *and* oppenyd the church-durre, *hostibus*
whych the Monkes haddyn y-loke, and sayd that 'men shold not no *templi* *fores*
castel make of holy church.' And his holy crovne bare ayeyn the *aperuit, et*
nakyd Swerdes forto smyte, and that in the modyr chyrch, heghist *aperto* *vertice*
of al the lond, and to-for the auter / that he of foure knyghtes, *gladiis* *occurrens.*
wodyr than wode houndis, *th*olled Foure wound*es* in the holy croun,
and [n]on wyth-out,—So as the crovn͂ oght to be know tokyn of *et nullum* *extra.*
*pro*texcion to clergy,—that he deth Sufferid in the north syde of the
church, whych be-tokenyth Ih*e*su cryst*es* Passion. and thus godis owyn knyght, wyth-out eny ferd, sufferyd' deth ; and his lyfe of
this world, chaunged' for the lyfe that eu*er* shal leste wythout end'.
And as seynte thomas-is day the apostyl, is the V. day afor yolde, ¹ *ille* *nascenti*
So is this Thomas-is day, the V. day aftyr. That thomas was candil *ecclesiae*
y-sette in the Este of the World; This thomas in the weste. ¹ [That] *lumen* *dedit, hic*
was lyght to holy churche in hyr youth, as [This] in hyr elde ; and *senescenti.*

A.D.
1170-1.
As the
Apostle
gave his
blood for
the early
Church, so
Beket gave
his for the
aged one.

Among all
saints, for

[¹ that
tofore]

Beket
alone were
all kinds of
miracles
performd.
He got a
man fresh
eyes and
genitals.

Merlin's
prophecy
of Beket.

[*Fol.9 b.]

Beket died
at 48 [that
is, 53-4],
on Dec. 29,
1170.
[T. MSS.
L. T. Ha.
Cl. n. Op.
v. 262 n.
4.]
Macmurgh
dies in
May, 1171.

& as he [the Apostle] commenced holy chyrche with hys blode whan
che was arerynge, Also thys, [Beket,] whan she had longe I-stond
& wox yn eld, & redy was to falle, wyth hys blode he ryght hyr vp,
& sette hyr yn ryght stydde. And as he t[oke hym] selue to 4
quellers ffor to arer þe seknes of holy chyrche, also thys ne douten
nat to taken hym-self to kene swerdes, & lydder men hondes, for
þe fredome of holy chyrche to sawe vnwemmed. The fourme of
hys martyrdome, twey verses a latyn shortly comprehendeth, that 8
thus mych ben to vnderstond : " ffor crystes spouse, vnder crystes
tyme, yn crystes chyrche, crystes owne leman deyed." Amonge
al the halwen that almyghty god wroght yn erth, of selcouth
myraclys for to showen har holynesse,—as the blynd to see, the 12
lame to gon, þe dombe to speke, the deue to hyr, lasers to clense,
paralys to festnen, y-dropesie & al other manere yueles to helen,
the dede to areren, yuel gostes to quethen, & al þe four elementes
to har commaundement hadden,—he alon was y-wyrshypped with 16
al these, & more þer-to, thar-to-for ¹ was nat herd ne sey ; ffor
a man that hade hys eghen I-draw out of hys heed, & hys manly
menbres y-kytte of & y-cast awey, come to hys tombe ; & þrogh
besechyng of hym, god hym sent newe. Of thys holy martyr, 20
Merlyn seyd thus yn hys prophecye : " A newe martyr shal aryse
with newe myracles, that yn the worldes endyng, yn the west
of þe world, by specyal vertue, mannys lymmes out I-draw & out
I-corue, ayeyn shald make come. Sorow shal turne ynto yoye, 24
whan þe sonnes shal sle þe fadyr yn hys modyr wombe ; prynces
& hey men * shal come out of þe este yn-to the weste, & lout ham
to þe newe martyres fot-stappes." Al þys was openly I-seyd of
þe holy martyr seynt Thomas ; he was þe whet corne þat fel yn 28
erth, & mych fruyt forth broght. In þe yer of burth-tyme .xlviij. ;
of hys sacryfiynge .viij. ; of hys exil .vij. ; yn the end of Decembre,
yn þe yere of our lordes yncarnacion .M.C.lxxj. ; & was poppe
of Rome, Alexandre the thyrd ; Emperour of Almayne, ffrytheryke ; 32
kynge of ffraunce, lowys. Whan the wentyr was I-passed, Dermot
Macmorgh deyed, þe begynenyng of may, & was bured at ffernes.
A man grett of body ; hardy yn fyght amonge hys folke ; of lange
& lome cryynge yn fyght, hys voys was somdel hors ; leuer hym 36

as he commencid holy church wyth his blod whan she was arerynge,   A.D.
1170–1.
Also this, whan she had long stond, and wox in elde, and redy was
to fall, wyth his blode he put hyr in good state, and therin
confermyd hyr.   And as he toke hym-selfe to them that hym
berewid the lyfe, forto arere the sekenys of holy church. Also this
doutyd not to take hym-Selfe to s[h]arpe Swerdes, & wickyd men   [*Fol.9 a.]
hondes, * For the fredome of Holy church to Saue Vn-Wemmede.   *ut eiusdem*
formam
The fourme of His Holy martirdome, two Versis of Lateyñ Sortely *conservaret*
comprehendyth, that thus mych ben to vndyrstond : " For crystis *illaesam.*
Spouse, vndyr crystis tyme, in crystis churche, crystes owyn leman *verus*
died." / Amongĕ al the holy Seyntes that almyghty god wroght for *amator*
obit.
in erth of voundyrfull miracles, for to Show har holynes,—as the
blynd to se, the lame to goñe, the dombe to Speke, the deue to *quod sepa-*
ratis
hyre, leperes to clense, Paralyse to festnen, ydropesye and al othyr *membris et*
maner sekenes to hele, the dede to arrere, the vickid Spyrytys to *proiectis,*
inaudito
ouercome, And al the iiije. elementes to har comaundement haddyn *more re-*
—he alon was y-wyrchippid with al thes.   For a man, that his *posuit.*
eghen was hym berewid, *and* his manly membris y-kute of and
cast away, come to his tombe; and throw besechynge of hym, god
hym sende newe // Of this holy martyr, Merlynge sayd thus in his Nota de
Sancto
prophesy : "A new martyr shall ryse, with new Miracles, that in Thoma.
the worldis endynge, in the weste of the world, by Special vertu,
manes lymes out y-draw and out y-corue, a-yeyn shal make come.
Sorrow shal make come Into Ioy, whan the Sonnes shal sle the *cum matris*
in utero
Fadyr in his modyr wombe.   Princes and hey men shal come out *patrem*
of the Este into the weste, *and* lout hame to the new martyr-is fote-*filii tru-*
cidabunt.
stappis."   Al this was opynly Sayd of the holy martyr Seynte
thomas.   He was the whet-corne that fel in Erth, *and* mych frute
forth broght.   In the yere of his berth-tyme, xlviij. ; of his Sacry-
fyynge, viij.; of his exil, vije.; in the Ende of Decembre, in the yere
of oure lord-is Incarnacion, Mł. Clxxj ; and was Pope of Rome,
Alexandre the iije. ; Emperoure of almane, Fryderik ; Kynge of
Fraunce, Lowys // Whan the wyntyr was ypassyd, Dermot Mac- Descripcio
Murcardi.
murgh dyed in the begynnynge of May, *and* was buried at Fernys. (*Op. v.*
A man grete of body; hardy in fyght amonge his Pepill; of lange *and* ²³⁷⁻⁸.)
ofte crȳinge in fyght. his voyce was Somdel hors; Leuer hym was

A.D. 1171.
Mac-
murgh's
character. was that man hym dredet than loued ; þe noble & þe ryche he
wold brynge to noght ; the mek [1] & the pouer he wold rere ; al men
ayeyns hym, & he ayeyns al.

[CHAPTER XIX.]

Hasculf, Aftyr that, about whyt-sontyde, hastoyl, that was some 4
tyme maystre of deuylyn,—as man that fayn was about for

with
Norsemen
in forty
ships, led
by John
the Mad,
lands to awreke hys old tene,—come wyt men of northwey & of þe north
ylondes, with ful grett folk, yn furty grett shyppes, & arryued
yn þe hauen of amlyffy, with haᷓ lodes-maᷠ, that hete Ioȟn the 8
Wood.   Thay wenten out of haᷓ shyppes, men well I-wepned,
sum with longe swerdes, some with Iren pletes & round sheldes
well I-bound about with Iren, swerdes & speres & axys ynowe,

& marches
to attack
Dublin.
Miles of
Cogan and
the English
meet him, & comeᷠ well ordeynly foᷓ to assaylle the toun on the eest half. 12
Miles de Cogan, kepeᷓ of þe Cyte, kyndly stalwardly, & hardy,
wyth wel choseᷠ folke, went out ayeyns ham, and yaf ham fyght ;
bot strong hyt was, to hold fyght ayayn so many with so fewe :
thaᷠ had he I-lost some of hys meᷠ ; & O knyghtes theygȟ was 16
I-cut with þe kappe of hys haubergeoᷠ wytht a dynt of a dennysȟ
ax.   nede he most turne yᷠ ayeyne at þe yate, tyll that Rẏchard
de Cogan, Myles brotheᷓ, wythe few men, that whylle stylly went
out at the south yate, & sharply becryed ham behynd, & smote 20
vpon ham.   throgh that, þat he come so fersly vpon ham, thay weᷓ
so afrygh, that thay wyst nat oᷠ whych syde thay shold kepe the

rout the
Norse, and
drive them
to their
ships.
John the
Mad is
slain. fyght : yn a lytell whyl thay waᷓ dyssconfyte, & toke ham to flyght
toward haᷓ shyppes.   these otheᷓ come ham betwene, & slowe ful 24
many : theᷓ was John the Wood I-slayn, & ful mych folk wyth
hym, throght Walter de Redlesford, that ful stalwarth was yn the
fyght.   Hascoyl was I-take fro the shyppe theᷓ he was to I-flow,
& I-broght alyues yn-to the Cyte, & hys lyf I-graunted for 28
raunceoᷠ ; bot as he stode yn court to-foᷓ Myles, he put forth

Hasculf
threatens
his con-
querors, lyddyrly a prout word & seyd, " wyt lytell poweᷓ we comen now,
& thys nas bot assaye of our myght ; bo[t] yf I lyue, aᷓ hyt be lange
to, shal come otheᷓ so mych as þese."   Whan thys was I-hard—for 32
yᷠ the mannys tonge hys oft lyf & deth, & me seyth eke, ' Tong
breketh boᷠ, thegh hym-self ne hawe none '—Myles bad that

_____
[1] MS. mok.   Lat. ' humilium erector.'

tha[t] a man hym dreddyd’ than lowyd; the nobil and the ryche A.D. 1171.
he wold brynge to noght; the meke and the Pouer he wold awaunce;
al men ayeynes hym, and’ he ayeynes al men //

[CHAPTER XIX.]

Aftyr that, about whitsontyd, Hastoyl, that was Somtyme Capi*t*ulum
Maystyr of Deuelyn,—as man that fayne was about forto be xix^m.
awengid of his old wreth,—come wyth men of North-Wey and of
the North ylondys, wyth many pepil, in fourty grete shippys, and *sexaginta*
londyd in the hauyn of Amlyffy, wit*h* har captayne that was callid *navibus.*
Ihoñ the Woode[1]. Thay wentyn out of har shippis, men wel *vel Vehe-*
wepenyd, Some wit*h* longe Swerdys, Some wit*h* Iryñ Platys and *alii*
roune sheldys, wel bound aboute wit*h* Iryñ, Swerdys and Speres *laminis*
and axes ynow, *and* comyn wel ordeynly forto assayle the tou*n* on *ferreis arte*
the Eeste halue. * Myles de cogan, Kepere of the Citey, Kynly [*Fol.9 b.]
Bolde and Hardy, Wyth Welle schosyn pepill, went out ayeynnes *innatae*
ham and yafe ham fyght; but stronge hit was to holde fyght ayeyn *tis au-*
so many wit*h* so few; than had he lost Some of his men; and o *dacia.*
knyghtes thegh was kut wit*h* the lappe of his haubergeoñ, wit*h* *cum panno*
a stroke of a dennysh axe. nedes he moste turne aye at the yate, *praecisa.*
tyl that Richard’ de cogan, Miles-Is brodyr, wit*h* few men, that
whyle went out at the south yate, and sharpely becryed ham *ipsos a*
behynde, and Smote vpon ham. throgh that, that he come so Fresly *acriter*
vpon ham, thay were so aferde, that thay wyst not on what Syde *excla-*
thay sholde kepe the fyght / In a lytyll whyle thay wer dyscom- *percussit.*
fyte, and toke ham to flyght toward har shippis. thes oþer come
ham be-twen, and kyllid ful many. ther was Ihoñ de woode *Johanne*
y-slayn, And ful mych pepil wit*h* hym, throw Water de Redeles- *Vehementi.*
ford, that ful bolde was in that fyght. Hastoil was take fro the
shipe ther he was to flede, and brogh[t] alyues into the Cite, *and*
his lyfe gravntid for Raunceou*n*; but as he stode in courte to-for
Miles, he sayd lewidly a prowte worde: "Wyth lytil pepil we come
now, And this was not but assay of oure myght; but yf y lyue,
ar hit be lange to, shal come othir so mych as thes." Whan this
was herde,—For in the manes tonge is ofte lyfe and deth; And as *linguae,*
hit is Sayd, Tonge brekyth bone, thegh hym-Selfe ne haue non,— *mors et*
Miles commandid that he shold anone out be-ladde, and to Smyte *rita.* Prov.
xviii. 21.

A.D. 1171. me*n* shold hym anooñ out lede, & smyte of þe heed.   & thus, foȓ
and is
beheaded.   hys hauteyn & prout spech, he lost þe lyf that thaȓ-by-foȓ mekely
hym was g*r*aunted.

[CHAPTER XX.]

[Fol.10 a.] Sone aftyr thys, many of thay that weren y-come 4
As Henry   yn-to Irland wyth the Erl, & eke to-fore,—for the kynges
II's edict
leaves   byddynge that come to ham, as hyt ys to[l]d a-fooȓ,—leften the
Struguil   Erl, & wenteñ yn-to england. The peple of yrland saw the erl
bare of
men and   narow beladde, both of hys meñ That hym left, & of vytalle that 8
food,   trukked, wheȓ-of he hade grete plente theȓ-by-fore out of eng-
the Irish   land. Thay gaddered ham to-gedders myche folk, al þe prynce
muster a
big army,   of the lond, wi*th* al haȓ poeȓ, & besegeden deuelyñ oñ eue*r*y
and besiege halue ; & that was throgh p*r*ocuryng̃ of laurence, Erchebysshoppe 12
Dublin.   of dyuelyñ, as men seyd, for loue of hys folk. he sent also hys
Gothred,   *lett*res, wi*th* Oconghours *lett*res, kynge of Connaght, to Gothred,
King of   kyng̃ of Manne, & to otheȓ prynces of þe norṫh ylondes, for to
Man, and
others,   be-sete the hauyñ of dyuelyñ ; & large yiftes & p*r*esentes ham 16
            yaue, & myche more hem behete, for to help*e* ham. &, for thay
            drede ham of al such man*e*re of aventu*r*es, Throgh that, that the
            englysshe-men hadden so wel I-conquered vpoñ þe yrysshe, Thay
with thirty comeñ the rather ham to help ; & yn lytell whyle came .xxxti. 20
ships, beset
Dublin   shyppys ful of stalwarth men wel arayed to fyght, & besetteñ the
Harbour.   haueñ of amlyffy. Whan the Erl & hys men wereñ well twey
After two   monthes beleyñ yn the syte of dyuelyn, & to ham come non help*e*,
months'
siege, and netheȓ of þe lond ne on watyȓ, & vytaylle fast ham slaked ; & (as hyt 24
when food   ys oft I-found, selde be-falleth ooñ harme that more [ne come]) come
is scarce,
            Donald, Macmorghes sone, of okenseley, to The Erl, & told hym
news   for that Robe*r*t steuenes-son was beseget yn hys castell that he had
comes that
Robert   rered at þe carryke, of þe Cyteȝeyns of weysford & the men of ken- 28
Stevenson   sely, well þre thousand men ; & few men had wyth hyɱ ; [&, but
is besieged
in Carrick hym] come socours by the þryd day, that of hym, ne thay that
Fort.   wi*th* hym wereñ, neue*r* no more to thynke. In the syte of dyuelyn,
Maurice   weȓ that tyme be-left wi*th* the erl, Moryche fytz-Geraud & Reymond, 32
and Rei-
mund Fitz- that from the kynge was comeñ newly ; sory for ham-self & for
Gerald
are in   hars : & thegh þey weren yn grett angwysshe foȓ ham-seleue, thay
Dublin.   wareñ yñ wel more foȓ haȓ good brotheȓ & for hys, that among*e*

of his hede. And this had he for his proude Spech loste the lyfe A.D. 1171.
that thar-by-for mekely hym was graundid.

[CHAPTER XX.]

S one aftyr this, many of them that weryn come into Irland Capit*ul*um
   with the Erle, and also tofor,—by the kyng*es* comandement xx^m.
that come to ham as hit is to-for told,—leften the Erle, and wentyn
into england. The pepil of Irland Saue the Erle narrow by-lad, *videntes*
both of his men that hym lefte, and of vytayle that trukked, *Hibernici*
                                                                comitem
wher-of he had grette plente ther-before out of Englond. Thay *et suos,*
                                                                 tam suo-
gaderid ham to-gederis mych pepill, al the p*rinces* of the londe *rum jac-*
                                                                   tura, quam
with al har Power, and be-segedyn Deuelyn on eu*ery* syd. and *victualium*
that was by procvrynge of laurance, Archebishope of Deuelyn, as *defectu ..*
                                                                 jam defici-
men sayd, for loue of his Pepil / Also he sende his le*ttres*, with *entes.*
o-conghoure-is le*ttres*, kynge of connaght, to Gothrede, kynge of
Man, and to othyr P*rinces* of the northe ylond*es*, for to be-Sette
the hauyn of Deuelyn ; and large yeftys and presentis ham yaue,
and mych mor ham promysid, forto helpe ham. and, for thay dred
ham of al Suche aventures, Throgh that, that the Englysh-men
haddyn So wel conqueryd vpon the Irysh, Thay comyn the radyr
ham to helpe. and in lytyll whyle came xxx^ti. shippis, ful of bold
men wel arrayid to fyght, and be-setten the hauyn of amlyffy.
whan the Erle and his men weryn wel two monthys besegid in the
Cite of Deuelyn, and to ham come no Soccovr on lond ne on watyr, [* Fol. 10
* And Vytayle ham falid, (and as Hit ys oft founde, Selde befallyth *sed cumu-*
one Harme that more ne comyth aftyr, and eu*er* gaderyth to helpe *lante*
                                                                    semper in-
more and more,) Come Donald, M*a*cmurghes sone of Okensely, to the *commoda*
                                                                     fortuna
Erle, and tolde hym, for that Robert Steuenes-Sone was besegid in *sinistra.*
his castel that he had rerid at the Karrike, of. the Citteseyn*es* of
weysford, and the men of Okenseley, wel iij^e. M^t. men; And few *quasi*
                                                                  tribus
men had w*ith* hym ; and, but hym come Socoure by the thyrd day, *virorum*
that of hym, ne thay that w*ith* hym weryn, neu*er* no more to *milibus*
thynke. In the Cite of Deuelyn, wer that tyme lefte w*ith* the Erle,
Morice fiz Geraud, *and* Reymond, that from the kynge was come
newely, Sory for ham-Selfe and for haris. and thegh they wer in *tam suo-*
                                                                  rum quam
grete angwysche for ham-Selfe, they weryn in wel more for har *sui non*
good brodyr, and for his, that among*e* his enemys was besegyd, in *mediocriter*
                                                                     anxietate
                                                                     turbati.

E

A.D. 1171.

Maurice
Fitz-
Gerald
harangs
his men :

" We were
the
highest :
we are
now the
lowest.

[* Fol. 10
b.]

" No help
can come
to us.

" Let us
fight !
Tho' few,
we've
heart, and
can beat
our naked
foes."

The
English
sally out,
in three
small
divisions
against
30,000
Irish.

Reimund
Fitz-
Gerald
fights best.

hys fomen was beseyget, yn place febly I-garnset, but a dych & a
hegge of thornes vpoñ, & lytell ost ston-wal. Moryce arose vp
to-fore the erl & the knyghtes, & seyde : " Nat to delytes, ne
ydelnes set to drawen, come we nat yn-to thys lande ; both[1] for to 4
sechen aduentures, & prouen ouȓ streynth vpon peryl of ouȓ
heedes. We haue I-stond awhyle & heghest, & now we bene
y-turned to the lowest, for so goth þe sykenesse of thys world ;
euery gladnesse ys endet wyth sorowe, & euery selth hath wnselth 8
at þe end. After þe bryght day, cometh the durke[2] nyght ; &
after, the durknesse of * þe nyght ys awey I-dryuen with þe lyght
of þe sone. Ar thys, the ouer-hand was yn all styddes ouȓ, &
plente of alle good ; nowe beth so belokeñ, that non help vs ne 12
may come, noþer by lond ne by watyȓ. On oþer halue, Robert
steuenes-sone, whos herdy herth opened vs þe wey yn-to þys land,
ys beseged feȓ wyt hys fomeñ yñ folk place. What ybyde we ?
haue we any hope that ouȓ lond-folk vs come to helpe ? thaȓ-to ne 16
tryst we nat ; foȓ we beth now yn such law I-sette, þat as þe
Iresshe weȓ, aȓ thys, to the englyshe, also þe englysshe beth now
to þe Iresshe. thaȓ-foȓ gow owt stalwartly, assayllen ouȓ fomen !
thegh we few be, we beñ meñ of herth, & wel I-wepned ! ne shal 20
neuer naked rascayll, thegh þey many be, haue myght ne poweȓ vs
to wyt-stond." Whan moryce hadde thys I-seyd, Reymond, þat
was I-smyte wyth the same sorow of herth, seyd to ham þe same
wordes, & mych moȓ, ' that thay wolldeñ allerformest smyth vpon 24
þe kynġ of konnaght, & hym that was heed, & formest & heghest
of ham alle.' Al that theȓ wereñ, heldeñ herto, & ren astryf to
wepne ham, & leppeñ to hors, & deled ham a thre, thegh thay
fewe wereñ. In þe formest, was Reymond with twonty knyghtes ; 28
In þe otheȓ, myles wyth .xxx[ti]. ; In þe þryd, the Erl & morice, with
fourty knyghtes & Squyerys ; & men an-hors & a-foot, to euery of
these I-sete, as hyt wold by-falle : thay went ham out of þe syte
stylly, about noon-dayes, & with so few meñ assayllydeñ añ 32
hostes of .xxx[ti]. thousand. Reymond, amonge the fyrst, smote vpon
ham ; & feyȓ to-foȓ al otheȓ : he smote tweyne throgh-out wyth a
speeȓ. Reymond & Moryce twey sonnes, Geraud & Alexandeȓ,

---

[1] but.   [2] MS. druke.

place febilly garnesyd, but a dyche and a hegge of thornys vpon, a.d. 1171.
and a lytil stone wal.   Moryce aros vp to-for the Erle and the
knyghtes, and sayd⁂: " Not to delytes, ne ydylnes, come we nat into *Non ad*
this land; but forto sechyn adventures, and proven oure Streynth *delicias,*
viri, non
vpon peril of oure hedys.   we haue stond awhyle, and hygh ; and *ad otia*
now we ben turnyd to the louyst ; for So is the schavnge of this *vocati.*
world.   the end of euery gladnes is Sorrow.   And euery Surnesse
hath vnsurnes at the ende.   Aftyr the bryght day, comyth the
nyght ; and aftyr, the durkenes of the nyght is a-way dryven with
the lyght of the Sone.   Afor this, the ouerhand was in al places
our, and plente of al goode.   Now ben we So belokken, that none *Auxilium*
helpe vs ne may come, nothyr by lond ne by watyr.   On the *nobis, nec*
mare
othyr Syde, Robert Steuenes-Sone, whos bolde hert openyd vs the *mittit, nec*
classis
way into this lond, is besegid fer with his fomen in febyll place. *inimica*
Whate abyde we ? haue we any hoppe that oure lond-pepil wil vs *permittit.*
come to helpe ? tharto ne trust we not / for we byth now in Such
lawe y-Sette, that ¹ as the Iryssh wer, or this, to the Englysh, Also *ut sicut*
the Englysh byth now to the Iryssh.   Wherfor go we out boldely *Hibernicis*
Angli, sic
assaylyn oure enemys ! thegh we fewe be, we ben men of herte and *et Anglis*
Hibernici
wel wepenyd ! ne shall neuer nakyd raskayl, thegh they many be, *simus.*
haue myght ne powere vs to wythstond."   Whan Morice had this
sayd, Reymonde, that was Smyte wyth the Same Sorrow of herte,
sayde to ham the same wordis, and mych mor, ' that thay woldyn
alther-formyst Smyte vpon the kynge of connaght / and he that was
hede and formyst of ham al.'   Al that ther weryn, heldyn herto, and
went to wepyn ham, and leppyn to hors, and delyd ham on thre,
thegh thay few were.   In the formyst, was Reymond, with twonty
knyghtes ; In the othyr, Milis, with xxxti.   In the thyrd, the Erle
and Morice wy[th] fowrty knyghtes, and Morice with fourty
knyghtis and Squyeris ; and men an-hors an[d] a-fote, to euery of
thys y-sette, as hit wolde befall.   thay went ham out of the Cite *hora quasi*
Softely, about noon dayes, and wyth So few men assayledyn an *post*
nonam.
hoste * of xxxti Mt. Reymonde, amonge the fyght, fryst Smote vpon [* Fol. 10
ham, and ferre to-for al othyr.   he Smote two throgh-out with b.]
a Spere. Reymond and Morices two Sonnes, Geraud and alex-

---

¹ In the margin, ' as we byth ynglys on to the yryssh, so we byth yryssh on
to the ynglys.'

A.D. 1171. thegh thay weṝ fyrst y-sete yn þe latest of þe host, throgh kynd

The little English host rout the 30,000 Irish, stalwardnesse hertly smytteꝺ out to the formest, & many dydden to deth. Alle þe otheṝ fresshely foloweden afteṝ; & yn lytell whylle dysconfited al þe hoste, & sloweꝺ so many, that no tonge 4 ne myght tell. Oconnoghouṝ, þat that tym satte yn bathe, vnnethe escaped: thay folwed the dyscomfytuṝ oꝺ euery halue

and return to Dublin with great spoil. They march (too late) to aid Fitz-Stephen. tyll þe nyght ham leth. Than thay turned ayeyne, & name haṝ pelfre, gold & syluyṝ, clothes & wepne & hors, & wenteꝺ wyth 8 mychel gladnesse yn-to þe syte. Amorow þay lefte good kypynge yn the syte, & turneden toward weysford by Odroon, wyth baners-y-lacet, foṝ to socouṝ Robert steuenes-sone.

[CHAPTER XXI.]

[Fol. 11a.] **T**he mene time, the folke of Weysford, wythe þe poweṝ 12

Fitz-Stephen's scanty garrison defend themselves bravely. of Okensely, wel thre þousand men, ayeyn haṝ othes I-sweṝ & haṝ trowth, Robert steuenessoꝺ al vnwardly, with fyue knyghtes & a few bow-men I-found withyn hys feble castel, thay stynt nat to assaylle. thay defendet ham full stalwarthly, thegh they fewe weṝ; 16 & namely a knyght that hete Wyllyam Not, aftyṝ Robert, ouer al otheṝ best dydde. Whan thay myght nat wyth streynth spede, thay bethoght ham that wyth falshed & wyth treyson they wold

The Irish deceive them; come wyth-yn ham. Thay sent to þe dyche twey bysshoppes, 20 that on of Weysford, that otheṝ of kyldaṝ, & otheṝ mo wyth ham yn habyt of relygyoꝺ; thay broght with ham massebokes, & Corpus domini, & relykes many, & sworne vp-on ham al, & vpoꝺ

swear Dublin is taken, and its Chiefs slain. haṝ owne soules, that 'dyuelyn was Itak; & þe Erl & morice & 24 Remond, & the englisshe-men, euerychon I-slawe; the host of leynestre & of Connaght comyng to ham-ward; & for good of

They offer the garrison a safe transport to Wales. hym, thay weṝ to hym y-come; that he shold yeld vp his castel, & me shold saue hym lyf & lym, & al his & al har good; for he 28 was ham so fre & so meke lord, me shold trewly brynge hym & his ouer in-to Wales ar the grete hoste of his fomen to hym

Their false words are believd, and the garrison are slain or imprisond. comen, that nothyng nold spaṝ hym.' Robert leued haṝ speche & haṝ fals othes; he came out & yeldet hym & his, to ham & to haṝ 32 trowth. Thay weṝ no raþer out I-comen, that me ne name ham euerychone; & some thay slowen yn þe place; some þay vndide & betten lidderly & bonden; & wyth ham selfe I-bounden, kesten

andyr, thegh they were fryst Sette in the laste of the hoste, throgh *A.D. 1171.*
kynly bolul [1] hertely Smyten out to the formyst, *and* many dyddyn *innatae*
to deth.   Al the othyr freschely folwedyn aftyr; And in lytyll *tamen*
strenuitatis
Space of tyme dyscomfyted al the hoste, and slowyn so many, that *indicio* ..
no tonge myght tell.   Oconghoure, that that tyme Satte in bathe, [1 ? *for* 'bolnys,'
vnneth Escapid.   thay folwid the dyscomfiture on euery halue tyll 59/14.]
the nyght ham lette.   Than thay turned ayeyñe, and toke har *victualibus*
et vecturis,
pilfre, gold and Syluyr, clothis, and wepyn and hors, *and* wentyn *spoliis*
with myche gladnes into the Cite.   A-morrow thay lefte good *quoque*
et armis
kepynge in the cite, and turned toward Weysford by Odrooñ, wyth *onerati.*
baneres ylacyd, forto Socoure Robert Steuenes-Sonne.

[CHAPTER XXI.]

The men-tyme, the pepil of weysford, with the Power of *Capitulum*
okenseley, wel iije. M[t]. men, ayeyñ har othis Sworne and har *xxjm.*
trouth, Robert Steuenes-Sonne al vn-wittynge, with v. knyghtes *Stephani-*
dem im-
and a few bowmeñ, fownde within his febil castel, thay stynte not *provisum.*
to assayle.   thay defendyd ham ful boldely, thegh they fewe were ;
and Specialy a knyght that was callid William Not, aftyr Robert,
ouer al othyr best dyd.   Whan thay myght not with streynth
Spede, thay bethoght ham that with falshede and with treysone *ad con-*
sueta
thay wolde come within ham.   Thay Sende to the dyche two *fallaciae*
bysshopis, that one of weysford, that othyr of kyldare, and othyr *tela fig-*
mentaque
mo with ham in habit of religioñ.   thay broght with ham masbokes *dolosa con-*
and Corpus domini, *and* relykis many, and Sworñ vp-on ham al, *currunt.*
and vpon har owyn Soulys, that ' Deuelyn was take ; and the Erle,
and Morice *and* Reymond, and the Englysh-men, euerychoñe were
Slayñ ; and the hoste of leynystre and of connaght comynge to ham-
ward ; and for good of hym, thay were to hym come ; that he sholde *Stephani-*
dae ipsius
yelde vp his castel, and thay wold Sawe his lyfe, and al his, and al *commodi*
har good ; for he was to ham so fre and So meke lorde, they wold *causa.*
trewely brynge hym and his ouer into walis, or the grete oste of
his enemys to hym were come, that nothynge wolde hym Spare.'
Robert belewid har Spech and har fals othys.   He came out, and [2] *alii ver-*
beribus,
yeldyd hym *and* his, to ham and to har trouth.   Thay were no *alii vero*
radyr out-come, than thay toke ham euerychone ; and Some thay *vulneribus*
graviter
Slowyn in the Place; Some thay vndide and bettyn vickydly [2]; *and* *afflicti.*

A.D. 1171.

willych In preson. Nat long ther-after, come soth tythyngges of

The Irish
traitors
burn Wex-
ford, and
go to the
Island of
Begeri,
with Fitz-
Stephen.
In the pass
of Odroon,
Striguil
defeats a
Leinster
force.

the dysconfytur of dyuelyn, & the Erles comyng toward ham.
the thraytours, whan thay hyt wysten, thay setten har own toun
of weysford afyr, & barnen hyte ; & wenten ham-self, with wyf & 4
chyld, & al har oþer good & har presons, ynto þe Iland of begger-
yng, þat hys I-sete yn the entre of the hauen of Weysford. þe
host of leynester come ayeyns hym yn Odrone, & yaf hym fyght
yn a paas of o thykke wood, strange yn hym selue, & comerous. 8
Ther wer many of the Irysshe y-slaw yn that fyght ; & þe Erl &
al hys camen hole & sound yn-to þe pleyne, sawe o man that he
þer forlese ; & meyler, our al other, as hys wone was, stalwardly

The Wex-
ford men
threaten to
kill Fitz-
Stephen
&c. The
English
hear of the
loss of the
Carrick
garrison,
and weep
for it.

hym thar byladde. ❡ After that, as thay comyn toward Weys- 12
ford, comen men ayeyns ham, & tolden ham the aduentur of
Robert, & of the tounes bernyng, & seyden ham sykerly, that 'yf
þay to ham wold vend anoon, þay wold sle har presons, & send
ham the heeddes.' Whan thus was y-hard among the oste, who-so 16
had I-hard þe wepynge, & the wenynge, & the sorow that thay
mad, he myght wel sygge that 'neuer-more sych reuth was amonge
men I-sey.' he was man that noon other was hys eunynge In all
goodnesse [1], & ensampell to all knyghtes that any stalwarthnesse 20

[* Fol. 11
b.]

wold begynnyge ; * ffor yn Wales & eke yn Irland many aduentures
both god & yuel had I-fond, that ofter weren hys aduentures hard,

Robert
Fitz-
Stephen
described.

thegh thay som tyme welcomen wyth hym. He was man mych
of body, [2]fayr vysage, soft & rody, nat ful becumliche ; grete 24
meet-yeuer, large & fre throgh al thynge, & of grett solace yn
Iappynge & pleynge ; bot to mych, & vnmesurable, he yaf hymself

Richard,
Earl of
Striguil
described.

lecherye [2]. The Erl was man of suche manere ; [3]he was samroed,
with grey eghen, wommanes vysage, & sproty, smal spech, 28
short nek [3] ; on al other manere he was of fayr body, & alonge
fre & meke ; ham that he hade nat to yeue to, he quemed ham
with fayr spech : out of wepne, he was as redy to otheres byddynge

---

[1] O virum, virtutis unicum, verique laboris exemplum.—*Op.* v. 271.

[2-2] vultuque decenti ; et statura paulo mediocritatem excedente : vir
dapsilis et largus, liberalis et jocundus, sed vino Venerique trans modestiam
datus.—*Op.* v. 271-2.

[3-3] Vir subrufus, lentiginosus, oculis glaucis, facie feminea, voce exili, colls
contracto.—Gir. Camb. *Op.* v. 272. Rolls Series.

andyr, thegh they were fryst Sette in the laste of the hoste, throgh *A.D. 1171.*

kynly bolul [1] hertely Smyten out to the formyst, *and* many dyddyn *innatae*

to deth.   Al the othyr freschely folwedyn aftyr; And in lytyll *tamen strenuitatis*

Space of tyme dyscomfyted al the hoste, and slowyn so many, that *indicio . .*

no tonge myght tell.   Oconghoure, that that tyme Satte in bathe, [1 ? *for* ‘bolnys,’

vnneth Escapid.   thay folwid the dyscomfiture on euery halue tyll 59/14.]

the nyght ham lette.   Than thay turned ayeyñe, and toke har *victualibus*

pilfre, gold and Syluyr, clothis, and wepyn and hors, *and* wentyn *et vecturis, spoliis*

with myche gladnes into the Cite.   A-morrow thay lefte good *quoque et armis*

kepynge in the cite, and turned toward Weysford by Odrooñ, wyth *onerati.*

baneres ylacyd, forto Socoure Robert Steuenes-Sonne.

[CHAPTER XXI.]

The men-tyme, the pepil of weysford, with the Power of *Capitulum xxjm.*
okenseley, wel iijᶜ. Mᵗ. men, ayeȳn har othis Sworne and har

trouth, Robert Steuenes-Sonne al vn-wittynge, with v. knyghtes *Stephani-*

and a few bowmeñ, fownde withīn his febil castel, thay stynte not *dem im-provisum.*

to assayle.   thay defendyd ham ful boldely, thegh they fewe were;

and Specialy a knyght that was callid William Not, aftyr Robert,

ouer al othyr best dyd.   Whan thay myght not with streynth

Spede, thay bethoght ham that with falshede and with treysone *ad con-sueta*

thay wolde come within ham.   Thay Sende to the dyche two *fallaciae*

bysshopis, that one of weysford, that othyr of kyldare, and othyr *tela fig-mentuque*

mo with ham in habit of religioñ.   thay broght with ham masbokes *dolosa con-currunt.*

and Corpus *domini, and* relykis many, and Sworñ vp-on ham al,

and vpon har owyn Soulys, that ‘ Deuelyn was take; and the Erle,

and Morice *and* Reymond, and the Englysh-men, euerychoñe were

Slayñ; and the hoste of leynystre and of connaght comynge to ham-

ward; and for good of hym, thay were to hym come; that he sholde *Stephani-*

yelde vp his castel, and thay wold Sawe his lyfe, and al his, and al *dae ipsius commodi*

har good; for he was to ham so fre and So meke lorde, they wold *causa.*

trewely brynge hym and his ouer into walis, or the grete oste of

his enemys to hym were come, that nothynge wolde hym Spare.’

Robert belewid har Spech and har fals othys.   He came out, and [2] *alii ver-*

yeldyd hym *and* his, to ham and to har trouth.   Thay were no *beribus, alii vero*

radyr out-come, than thay toke ham euerychone; and Some thay *vulneribus*

Slowyn in the Place; Some thay vndide and bettyn vickydly[2]; *and* *graviter afflicti.*

A.D. 1171.
willych In preson. Nat long ther-after, come soth tythyngges of

The Irish traitors burn Wex- ford, and go to the Island of Begeri, with Fitz- Stephen.
the dysconfytuȓ of dyuelyn, & the Erles comyng toward ham. the thraytours, whan thay hyt wysteᴺ, thay setten haȓ own touɴ of weysford afyȓ, & barnen hyte; & wenteᴺ ham-self, with wyf & 4 chyld, & al haȓ oþer good & haȓ presons, ynto þe Iland of begger- yng, þat hys I-sete yn the entre of the hauen of Weysford. Þe

In the pass of Odroon, Striguil defeats a Leinster force.
host of leynester come ayeyns hym yn Odrone, & yaf hym fyght yn a paas of o thykke wood, strange yn hym selue, & comerous. 8 Theȓ weȓ many of the Irysshe y-slaw yn that fyght; & þe Erl & al hys cameᴺ hole & sound yn-to þe pleyne, sawe o man that he þer forlese; & meyleȓ, ouȓ al otheȓ, as hys wone was, stalwardly

The Wex- ford men threaten to kill Fitz- Stephen &c. The English hear of the loss of the Carrick garrison, and weep for it.
hym thaȓ byladde.   ⁜ After that, as thay comyᴺ toward Weys- 12 ford, comeᴺ meᴺ ayeyns ham, & tolden ham the aduentuȓ of Robert, & of the toū̄es bernyng, & seydeᴺ ham sykerly, that 'yf þay to ham wold vend anoon, þay wold sle haȓ presons, & send ham the heeddes.' Whaᴺ thus was y-hard among the oste, who-so 16 had I-hard þe wepynge, & the wenynge, & the sorow that thay mad, he myght wel sygge that 'neuer-more sych reuth was amonge meᴺ I-sey.' he was maᴺ that noon otheȓ was hys eunynge In all goodnesse [1], & ensampell to all knyghtes that any stalwarthnesse 20

[* Fol. 11 b.]
wold begynnyge; * ffor yn Wales & eke yn Irland many aduentures both god & yuel had I-fond, that ofteȓ weren hys aduentures hard,

Robert Fitz- Stephen described.
thegh thay som tyme welcomeᴺ wyth hym. He was man mych of body, [2]fayr vysage, soft & rody, nat ful becumliche; grete 24 meet-yeuer, large & fre throgh al thynge, & of grett solace yn Iappynge & pleynge; bot to mych, & vnmesurable, he yaf hymself

Richard, Earl of Striguil described.
lecherye [2]. The Erl was man of suche manere; [3]he was samroed, with grey eghen, wommanes vysage, & sproty, smal spech, 28 short nek [3]; on al otheȓ manere he was of fayȓ body, & alonge fre & meke; ham that he hade nat to yeue to, he quemed ham with fayȓ spech: out of wepne, he was as redy to otheres byddynge

---

[1] O virum, virtutis unicum, verique laboris exemplum.—Op. v. 271.

[2-2] vultuque decenti; et statura paulo mediocritatem excedente: vir dapsilis et largus, liberalis et jocundus, sed vino Venerique trans modestiam datus.—Op. v. 271-2.

[3-3] Vir subrufus, lentiginosus, oculis glaucis, facie feminea, voce exili, colls contracto.—Gir. Camb. Op. v. 272. Rolls Series.

boundy[n] ; *and* w*ith* hym-Selfe y-bound, kesten vnmercyably in A.D. 1171.
pryson [1]. Not lang*e* ther-aftyr, come trew thythyng*es* of the dyscom-
fytur*e* of Deuelyn, and the Erlis comyng*e* toward ham.   the
traytour*es*, whan thay hit Vndyrstode, thay Setten har owyn toun*e*
of weysford afyre, and brentyn hit / And wenten hame-Selfe, w*ith*
wyfe and chylde, and al har*e* othyr good and har prisoner*es*, into the *ad insulam*
Iland of begeryn, that is at the Entrest of the hawyn of weysford. *Begeri . . .*
quae et
the Hoste of Leynystre come ayeynys hame in odroon, and yafe *sancta*
vocatur.
ham fyght in a paace of thyke wodde, strange in hym-* Selfe, and [*Fol. 11
a.]
comeros [2]. Ther wer many of the Iryssh Slayn in that fyght ; ande
the Erle and al his came hole and Sounde into the Playn, Saue
o man that he ther*e* forlese.   And Meyler*e*, ou*er* al othyr, as he
was woned, boldely hym ther*e* bore / Aftyr that, as thay comen †*ex parte*
toward weysford, came men toward hame, and toldyn ham the *quoque*
proditorum
aduentur*e* of Rob*er*t and of the toun*es* brennyng*e*, and † Sayd ham *firmiter*
asserentes,
Surly, that ' yf thay wolde to ham wende anoone, thay wolde sle har *quod si*
prisoner*es*, and Send ham the hedys.'   Whan this was herde amonge *ad illos*
accedere
þe hoste, who-so hadd herd the wepynge, and the lementacion and *forte prae-*
sumant,
the Sorrow that thay made, he myght wel say that 'Such Sorrow *praecisa*
was neu*er* amonge men Sey ' // He was man, that none othyr was *sibi suorum*
capita
his eunyng*e* in al goodnesse, and Ensampil of al knyghtys that any *statim*
cuncta
boldnys wolde begynne.   for in Walis, and also in Irland, many *remittent.*
aduentures both good and euyl had fovnde, that ofter weryn his Descripcio
aduentures hard, thegh thay Sometyme wel comyn w*ith* hym.   he *Roberti*
fiz Steuen.
was man myche of body, fayr vysage, Softe and rody, not ful be- A big man,
comlych ; good mette-yeu*er*, large and fre throgh al thyng*e*, and of liberal, but
lecherous.
grete Solace in Iaypynge ; but to mych, and vnmesurably, he yafe
hym-Selfe to Lechery //

   The Erle was man of Such man*ere* : he was wyth-out doute of Descripcio
grey eighen, womanes visage, *and* Sproty, smale Speche, Short *Ricardi*
Comitis.
neke : on al othyr man*er*, he was a fayr*e* body, and alonge fre and
meke.   thay that he hadd not to yew, he plesyd w*ith* fayr*e* Spech [3].
Out of wepyn, he was as redy to other*es* byddyng*e*, as thay to hym.

---

[1] in carceres, et vincula contruduntur.—*Op.* v. 271.

[2] quamquam in sui natura arcto nimis et invio, concidibus tamen plurimum
arte munito.—*Op.* v. 272.

[3] Quod re non poterat, verborum suavitate componebat.—*Ibid.*

as otheꝛ to hys: alle thynge he dydde by rede of hys meñ, &
nothynge wyth-out. Out of bataylle, he had more of knyght
thañ of host-ledeꝛ; yn bataylle, more ledeꝛ than knyght; & yn
al aduenturs of bataylle, he was stydfast, ful connynge, & tokne of 4
recet to al hys host; & for noñ vnhap he ne amayed hymself, ne
yn wanhope ne fel; ne for ne good chaunce, he ne made hym
the prutter ne þe more hautayñ; bot euer-more, yn al aduen[tu]rs,
of stydfast herth & trewe.   8

[CHAPTER XXII.]

Whan the erl hadde I-hard the trayson þat was I-done
to Robert, wytht myche sorow of hert he went hym
with the host to Watyrford; & þer he fond heruy of mountmorthy,
that thañ wase neweñ I-comeñ out of englond froṁ þe kynge, 12
& broght wryttes, & eke by mych amonested the erl that he
sails to
England,
and finds
Henry II
at Newn-
ham,
Gloster-
shire,
ready to
cross to
Ireland.
The Earl
yields
Dublin and
all haven-
towns to
Henry,
shold wend to the kynge. he hade shyppe redy, & good wynd;
he name heruy with hym, & went ouer; come to the contre
of clandechestre, to Newenham, ther he fond the kynge with mychel 16
host, redy to pass yñ-to Irland. & after myche speche betwene ham
ymade, & myche dalyaunce, throgh heruyes modelyng & comynge
about þe erle, & eke hys besechynge, the kynge name of hym
manred foꝛ to hold leynestre of hym; & the Erl graunted þe kynge, 20
dyuelyñ, & all the hauen tounes vpoñ þe see, with haꝛ Candredes
& castelles þer-vpoñ y-set; & that otheꝛ parte of hys conquestre,
he & hys heyres sholdeñ holdeñ of þe kynge & hys heyrs. Whan
thys was al on thys manere I-done, the kynge toke the wey yn-to 24
who goes
to Pem-
broke, and
waits
there for a
favourable
wind.
south Wales, & cam to pembroke; & theꝛ yn þe contre abode with
hys host longe whyle, aꝛ he had wynd foꝛ to passe. The whyle
that he was thaꝛ, he hadde houndes & haukes, as man that mych
delyted yn suche game. .O. day he went by the strond of þe see, 28
& baꝛ a mych goshawke of northwey vpoñ hys hand. Than sat
vp-oñ an hegh clyff ouer the strond, a faucoñ gentel, negh hys nest,
theꝛ he was woned to brede. The *goshake sawe the facoñ, &
a-bated to hym. the kynge that saw; & kest hym of hys hand; & 32
he nam hys flyght toward the facoñ, hym fore to henten: the
facoñ sawe hym comynge, & nam hys flyght an heghe, & escaped
of hym; þe goshawke turned ayeyne to þe kynges hand; & aꝛ

Al thynge he did by consayle of his men, and nothynge without / A.D. 1171.
Out of battayl, he had more of knyght than of hoste-leder; in
battayle / more ledder than knyght / and in al aduentures of *In praelio*
battayle, he was stydfaste, ful conynge, and tokyn of recette to al his *positus,*
fixum suis
hoste; and for no vnhape he was not aferde hym-Selfe, ne in van- *recupera-*
tionis et
hope ne felle; ne for no good chaunce, he was not the Pruttyr, ne *refugii*
signum
the heyer; but euer-more, in al aduentures, of stydfaste herte and *manebat.*
trewe.

[CHAPTER XXII.]

WHan the Erle had herde the trayson that was done to Ca*pitu*lum
Robert, with myche Sorrow of herte he went with al the xxij^m.
hoste to watyrford; and ther he founde heruey of montmurthy,
that that tyme was come out of England frome the kynge, and
broght writtes, and Eke mych amonneschyd the Erle that he sholde
wend to the kynge. he had ship redy, and good wynd; he toke
heruey with hym, *and* went ouer; come to the contrey of clandecestre,
to New-Enham, ther he found the Kynge with grette hoste, redy to
Passe Into Irland. and aftyr mych Speche betwen ham made, and
myche delyaunce, throgh herueyes medlynge and comynge about the *circum-*
ventu
Erle, and also his besechynge, the kynge toke of hym concayle forto *pariter et*
holde leynystre of hym; and the Erle graunted the kynge, deuelyn, *interventu*
and al the hawyn tounes vpon the see, with hare candredes and
castelis there-vpon sette; and that othyr Parte of his conqueste, * He [* Fol. 11
and Hys heyres sholde Holde of the Kynge and [his] Heyrys. Whan b.]
this Was on this manere done, the kynge toke the way into South
walis, and came to Pembroke[1]; and ther in the contrey abode with
his hoste longe tyme, ar thay had wynd to Passe. The whyle that
he was there, he hadd houndes and haukys, as man that mych
delytyth in Such game. O day, he went by þe see stronde, and bar
a mych goshauke of Norwey on his hande. Than Sate vpon an hey
clyfe ouer the stronde, a faucon gentyll, ney his neste, ther he was
wonyd to brede. the goshauke Saw the faucon, and abated to hym *laeva*
hym forto smyte. the faucon saw hym comynge, and toke his flyght *projecit*
an hey, and Escapid of hym. the goshauke turnyd ayeyn to the

---

[1] Et Penbrochiam veniens, pulcherrimam in brevi Milverdico portu [Milford
Haven] classem conjunxit.—Gir. Camb. *Op.* v. 273.

A.D. 1171.
is kild by
a Welsh
falcon.

he myght fully take to hym, the facoꝺ smote to hym from an heyght, & forcleue hym the rygge, & kest hym adoune dede at the kynges foote. Al thay that hyt saw, hadden ther-of myche wondyr. Than bade the kynge, that fro that tyme, the bryddes of that facons 4 neste shold euer-moꝛ be I-kepte to hys owne be-houe; & so thay weꝛ, euery yeyr; & yn al hys kynge-dome wer noꝺ so good facons I-found, ne so bold.

[CHAPTER XXIII.]

O'Rourke,
king of
Meath,

assaults
Dublin,
early in
September,
but is
beaten off
by Miles
of Cogan;
and his
son is slain.

The while that thys was, Roueryke, the kynge of Myth,— 8 awayted that the erl was out of lond; & Reymond & lytel folk was beleft ar dyuelyn, the syte & þe contrey for to kepe,— with mych folke come to dyuelyꝺ about myd-heruest, & assaylled the walles of þe syte with gret streynth & loly crye, & wend 12 wel to haue I-take þe syte, & al þat þer-In was. bote ther streynthys & stalwarthnesse, hyt mote nedes shewe hymself: Myles de Cogaꝺ & hys meꝺ preuely wenten out, & smote grymly vpon ham, so þat yn lytell whyl thay wereꝺ al dyscomfyted. Bot 16 roury hymself vnnethe escaped; & hys sone, a welle stalwarth man amonge hys folk, was thaꝛ I-slawe, wyth many other.

[CHAPTER XXIV.]

Nota: de [1]
primo
aduentu
Regis An-
gliae in
hiberniam
Henry II
lands at
Waterford
on Oct. 18,
1171,
fulfilling
prophecies
of Merlin
and St.
Moling.

Aftiꝛ this, whan the kynge had I-dyght al that nede was to so noble comynge ynto Irlond, he went to seynth 20 dauyes; & besoght the holy maꝺ, seynt dauy, with grett deuocion & mych wurshyppe. And tho wedeꝛ hym come, & wynd at wylle. He put hym to saylle; passed the see, hool & sound; & arryued at Waterford on seynt lukes day, with fywe houndred knyghtes, 24 & men, an hors an a foot, fulle many. Than was fulfylled a pro- phycye that Merlyn seyd: "out of þe Este shal come a fyꝛ bernynge, & shal Irlond al about for-swely." And seynt Molynge seyd þus: "Out of þe eeste shal come a stronge thondred, & shal 28 smyte yn-to þe weste, & al the streynth of Ormond adoun brynge." He arryued, the yeꝛ of hys kyngedome, senthe; of hys elde .xl.;

[1] Later note in right margin: 'For in Martilogis the king brought 400 great shippes into Irelande, and in short time subdued the whole lande, beinge governed by 5 kinges, all which submitted to the king, except the king of Connaght, who kept himself in woods and marishes.'

kyngys hand'; and, Ar he myght fully take to hym, the faucon smote A.D. 1171.

to hym from an hey, and for-clew hym the bake, and kest hym doune [1] *singulis*

rex annis,

ded at the kynges fote. Al thay that hit Saw, ther-of had grete *circa nidi-*

ficationis

wondyr. [1]Than comandid' the kyng*e*, that fro that tyme, birdis of *tempora,*

that faucon-is nesie shold eu*er*-more be kepe to his owyn behow; *propter*

falcones

and So thay were, euery yere. And in al his kyngdome wer *terrae*

none So good faucones y-found, ne so bolde. *illius, qui*

marinis

[CHAPTER XXIII.] *in rupi-*

bus exclu-

THe mene-tyme that this was / Roueryke, the kynge of *duntur,* *mittere*

mythe[1],—be-helde his tyme, and that the Erle out of lond was, *consuevit.*

and Reymond' *and* lytil peple was lefte at Deuelyn, the Cite and the *Capitulum*

xxiij^m.

contrey to kepe,—wyth mych pepyl come to deuelyn about myd

hervyst, and assaylid the wallis of the Cite w*ith* gret Streynth and

grymly cry, *and* wend wel to haue take the Cite, and al that therin

was. But ther streynthis *and* bolnys, hit mote nede Schow hym- *Sed quo-*

Selfe : Miles de Cogan and his men p*ri*uely wentyn out, and smote *niam* *virtus*

grymly vpon ham, so that in lytyll whyle thay weryn al dys- *claudi*

nescit; et

comfyted'. But Roury hym-Selfe vnneth Escapyd'; and his Son*n*e, *ignis op-*

a wel bolde man amonge his pepil, was ther Slayn, w*ith* many *pressus, in*

flammam

op*er*. *erumpit.*

[CHAPTER XXIV.]

Aftyr this, wh*a*n the kynge had dygh al that nede was to So *Capitulum*

nobyl comyng*e* into Irland', he went to Seynt Dauyes, and *xxiiij^m.*

besoght the holy man, seynt Dauy, w*ith* gret deuocion *and* myche

wyrchippe. and then wynde and weddyr hym come at wille. he *Nota* de

putte hym to sayle, and passyd the see, holde and Sounde ; and *primo* *aduentu*

londyd at Watyrford' on Seynte Luke-is day, w*ith* fyue hundred *Regis*

Anglie in

knyghtes, and men an hors and a foote, ful many. Than was fulfillid *hiberniam.*

a prophesy that Merlyn Sayd thus / " Out of the Este shal come

a fyre brennynge, and shal Irland al aboute forswely." And seynt

Molynge sayd thus, " Out of the Este shal come a stronge thondyr, *Veniet ab*

and shal smyte into the weste, and al the streynth of Ormond *aurora* *turbo*

adoune brynge." he londyt, the yer*e* of the kynge-dome, the Senfte ; *validus.*

of his age, the xl ; of our lordys incarnacion, M^t. Clxxij ; *and* was

---

[1] rex monoculus Medensis Ororicius . . . cum multitudine magna, circa
kalendas Septembris, Dubliniam venit.—*Op.* v. 274.

A.D. 1171. of our lordes Incarnacion .M.C.lxxij ; & was poppe, Alexander the
thryd ; Emperour, ffryderyke ; kynge of ffraunce, lowyse.

[CHAPTER XXV.]

Henry II
has Fitz-
Stephen

The kynge abode at Waterford a fewe dayes.   Theder
come the sytʒeyns of weysford, & broght to hym Robert 4
steuenesse-sone, as for gret seruyce, & yn hope of good reward ;
ffor as myche as he come yn-to Irlond, lond to conquer, wythout
auctoryte of hegher prynce, & yaue other, ensample for to comen
ynto the lond.   The kynge, at the byggynnyge, told of hym grete 8

[* Fol. 12
b.]

* vnworthynesse ; & edwyte hym, with grete thretynge, of that grete
boldnesse ; & lete take hym, y-bound as he was, & gyued hym to

put in
prison.

another, & put hym yn Rathnyldestour for to kepen.   Soine

The King
of Cork
does
homage to
Henry II ;

þer-after come the kynge of Corke, Dermot Maccarthy, & yeld 12
hym to the kynge, & dydde hym homage, & swar hym hold
othes, & delyuered hym ostages for to be to hym hold & trew,
& ber hym truage euery yer of hys land. ffrom thus, the kynge
went wythe the hoste to lysmore, & ther was twey dayes ; & fro 16
thus, went to Casshle.   Theder came donald Obreen, kynge of

so do the
King of
Limerick,

lymeryke, to hym vpon the watyr of ssur ; & for to hawe pees,
yeld hym to þe kynge yn al manere as Maccathy hadde done.
The kynge set kepers both at Corke & at lymeryke ; & to hym 20
comen the hoste of both contrees aftyr Maccathy & Obreen, & yeld

and all
the best
folk of
Munster.

ham to þe kynge, & becomen hys meyn by othes & ostages ; so that
ther was none that war of any name yn al Monestre, that by hys
good wylle ne yeld hym to the kynge.   Whan thys was al I-done, 24
the kynge, with mych wyrsshyppe & wyth ryche yiftes, lete euery

Henry II
returns to
Waterford,

man wend yn-to hys owne lond, & went hym-self by Tybrach
ayeyne to Waterford. þer was ayeyne Robert y-broght to-for hym.
The kynge saw hym, & bethoght hym of þe gret goodnesse þat 28
was yn hym, & of hys stalwarthnesse & hys hardy hert ; of many
good seruices that he & hys hadden I-done, wyth mych trauaylle
& grette perille of lyue : he had grett reuth of hym yn hys hert ;

pardons
Fitz-
Stephen,
and re-
stores him
his lands.

&, throgh besechynge of hegh men, al hys wreth, wyth good hert 32
he hym foryaf, & delyueret hym out of pryson, & lete delyuer
hym hys londes þat hym weren be-nomen, of Weysford & of þe

pope, Alexandyr the thyrd; Emperoure, Frederike; kynge of Fraunce, Lowys.   A.D. 1171.

[CHAPTER XXV.]

THe Kyng abod at Watyrforde a few Dayes. Thedyr come the Cytteseynys of Weysford, and broght to hym Robert Steuenes-Sonne, as for grete Seruyse, and in hope of good reward, for-as-mych as he came into Irland, lond to conquere, wythout auctorite of heghyr Prince, and yaue othyr ensampil forto come into londe. The kynge, at the begynnynge, tolde of hym gret Vnuorthynys; and reprewid hym, with grete tretynge, of that grete boldnes; and lette take hym, bound as he was, and gywid hym to anothyr, and Put hym in Rathnyldys toure forto kepyn. Sone ther-aftyr come the kynge of Corke, Dermot Maccharthy, and yelde hym to the kynge, and dyd hym homage, and Sware hym olde othis, and delyuerid hym hostagis forto be to hym holde and trew, and ber hym truage euery yere of his land. From thens the kynge went with the hoste to Lysmor, and ther was two dayes; and fro thens went to Cassell. Thedyr came Donal Obreyne, kynge of Lymerik, and to hym on the watyr of Sure; and for-to haue pees, yelde hym to the kynge in al maner as Macchardy hadd' done. The kynge Sette keperes both at Corke and at Lymerike; and to hym come the Best of both contreis aftyr maccharthy and Obreñ, and yelde ham to the kynge, and be-comyn his men by othis and hostagys, so that ther nas none that was holde of any reputacioñ in al Monester, that by his good wyll ne yelde hym to the kynge. Whan this was al done, the kynge, with mych vyrchip and wyth ryche yeftys, lette euery man wend into his owyn lond, And wente hym-Selfe by Tybraght ayeyne to watyrford. ther was ayeyn Robert broght to-for hym. The kynge Saw hym, and bethoght hym of the grete goodnesse that was in hym, and of his boldnys and his hardy herte, of many good seruyces that he and his haddyn doñe with mych trauayl and grete Perel of lyfe. He had of hym grete Pite in his herte; and, throw besechynge of good men, al his wreth with good herte he hym for-yaue, and delyuerid hym out of prisone, and delyuerid hym his londys that of hym wer take fro, of Weysford

[Fol. 12 a.]
Capitulum xxvᵐ.
quasi sub praetextu obsequii, eo quod Hiberniam citra ipsius assensum primus intraverit, aliisque malignandi occasionem praestiterit, vinctum et captivum adducunt.

rex videns virum tantis for-tunae peri-culis, et toties, ex-positum.

contrey about. Some syggen that the kynge lete to-draw the
traytours that hym betrayed ; Bot Maystre Geroud ne telleth
nothynge þer-of; & ther-fore I ne tel hyt nat to sothe, bot hyt
oght well be so.   4

[CHAPTER XXVI.]

Whan þe kynge had thus I-do, he left at Waterford, Robert
beranardesson, wyth mych meyne ; &, by Ossery, name the
wey toward dyuelyn. In that wyage, the kynge of Ossery came
to hym, & yeld hym to the kynge ; & whan he hade I-bydde 8
awhylle at dyuelyn, theder come Al þe heghest Iresshe-men of

leynestre, & besoghten pees, & yolden ham to the kyng. Roryke
O'conghour, the kynge of Connaght, ayeyns the kynges messagers
at the watyr shynnen,—that ys to wytten, hugh þe lacy & wyllyam 12
Al-delines sone,—ther he yeld hym to þe kynge ; & the kynge of
Myth Also ; So that ther nas none heght man yn Irland, that ne
come to the kynges owne body, or sent messagers for to be-comen
hys man, & yeld hym to hym, sawe only thay of vlnestre. Than 16

was fulfylled a prophecye that seynth Molynge seyd : "To-for hym
shall foot-*falle þe prynces, & trogh[1] boxom-fastines[2] the lyme of
pees shul vnderfonge." Merlyn seyd an-other : "Tho is lyght, the
foules of the Iland shollen togedder fle ; & the most of ham, with 20
har wenges I-brant, shollen ouerthrowen yn thraldome ; the fyf deles
shollen be broght yn-to on, & the syxt shal ouercome the strengest

places of Irland." Whan the mydwyntter came, many of the heghest
comen to þe kynges court to feste ; & myche wonder ham thoght 24
of the noble seruice that þey þer saw, & of the myche plente of
mete & of drynke, of bordes I-sette, & fayr clothes vpon ; the hegh
seruice of panetrye & buttellerie, & ryche vessels of gold & syluer ;
the many manere metes of kechen, on the manere of Englond, 28
whych thay had neuer þer-to-fore I-sey. After that þe fest was
heghly & fayr I-hold, euery man went wyth gladnesse yn-to hys
owne. In that tyme, weren bowemen at ffynglas I-horberowed,

& wenten ynto chyrche haye, & hewen adoun trees, that seyntes 32
by old tyme hadden þer I-sete : þer came sodeyn deth vpon ham,
euerychon. [See Giraldus's Topogr. Hibern. Opera, v. 135.]

----

[1] A later overline h is above the tr of 'trogh.'   [2] or 'fastmes.'

and of the contrey aboute. Some sayne that the kynge lette to- A.D. 1171.
draw the traytoures that hym betrayed. But Maystyr Geraud ne
tellyth nothynge ther-of ; and therfor y ne tell hit not for throuth,
but hit oght wel be so.

[CHAPTER XXVI.]

Whan the kynge had thus done, he lefte at watyrford, Robert Capitulum
Barnardessonne, with mych pepill ; and, by Ossory, toke his xxvj^m.
way to Deuelyn. In that vyage, the kynge of Ossory came to hym,
and yolde hym to the kynge. and whan he had bydd awhyle at
deuelyn, thedyr came all the heghyst Irysh-men of leynystre, and
be-soghten pees, and yeldyn ham to the kynge. Roryke Oconghoure,
the kynge of connaght, ayeynes the kynges messaungeris at the watyr *nunciis*
of shynnyn,—that is [to] Say, hugh de Lacy and Willam aldelines *regiis . .*
occurrit.
Sone,—ther he yelde hym to the kynge ; And the kynge of Myth also ;
So that ther was no man of any reputacioun that he ne come to the
* Kyngys owyn Body, or Sent messangeres forto Becomyn Hys man, [*Fol. 12
Saue only thay of vllyster // Than was fulfillid a prophesy that b.]
Seynt Molyng sayd : " To-for hym shal foote-fall the pryncys, and, *procident*
throgh buxumfastnys, the lyme of pees shal vndyrfonge" // Merlynge *principes,*
et fucato
sayd anothyr prophesy : " To his lyght, the foulys of the yland *sub foedere*
pacis
shullyn to-geddyr fle ; and the mest of ham, with har wynges *amorem*
y-brante, shullyn ouer-throwyn in thraldome [1]. the fywe delys *conse-*
quentur.
shal be broght into one, and the Syxte shal ouercome the Strongyst *sextus*
placis of Irland" / Whan the Mydwyntyr came, many of the heghest *Hiberniae*
moenia
men comyn to the kynges courte to feste ; and mych wondyr thay *subvertet.*
had of the nobil seruyce that they ther Sawe, and of the mych plente
of mete and of drynke, of bordys sette, and fayre clothis vpoñ ; the
hey Service of panetrye and buttellerye, and rych wesselis of golde
and Syluyr ; the many maner metys of kechen, on the maner of Englond, whych they had neuer ther-to-for Seyn [2]. Aftyr that the feste
was ryaly holde, euery man went wyth gladnys into his owyn. In
that tyme weryn bow-men at Fynglas y-herberowid, and wentyn
Into church-hay, and hewyn adoñ trees that Seyntys by olde
tym had ther Sette : there came Sodayn deth vpon ham eueryoñ.

---

[1] corruent in capturam.   [2] Why wasn't this crane bit englisht ? ' carne
gruina, quam hactenus abhorruerant, regia voluntate passim per aulam vesci
coeperunt.'—Op. v. 280.

A.D. 1172.

Henry II,
wishing to
purify
Irish life,
assembles
the Clergy
at Cashel.

The lond was than yn good pees by-for þe kynge, &
þe pees wel I-hold : the kynge had wel y-hard that þe
folk of the lond was of vnclene lyf, & ayeyne god & holy chyrche ;
he thoght that he wold brynge the folk ynto better lyf, & myche 4
desyr hadde ther-to ; he leth assembly al þe clergye of þe londe
at Casshell, & that me enquered & herd openly the fylthede of
the lond-folk yn whych thay ladde har lyf; & setten hyt yn wrytte,
vnder the bysshoppes sele of lysmore, that was eke legat of þe 8
court of Rome, & heghest of dygnyte ouer al thay that ther wer ;
& þe statutes of holy chyrche Whych yit men halte, yn þe manere
þat holy chyrche ham holte yn Englond, he lete thar sette : whych
statutȝ, yn the wordes that thay weren ther I-swewed, ys non 12
harme thegh me expresse ham here :—

NARACIO. [CHAPTER XXVIII.]

NARACIO.

The Synod
at Cashel,
under the
Romish
Legate,
the Bishop
of Lismore.

In the yer of our lordes Incarnacion M.C.lxxij, the
forme yer that þe kynge of england, henry, Irland wan ;
Crystyen, bysshoppe of lysmore, & legat of þe court of Rome[1]; 16
Dougher, Erchebysshoppe of Casshell ; laurenȝ, Erchebysshoppe
of dyuelyn ; Cathel, erchebysshoppe of Connaght ; wyth leed
bysshoppes, Abbotes, priours, & many other prelates of holy
chyrche yn Irland, throgh the same kynges commaundement 20
comen to-gedder yn þe See of Casshel ; &, for þe state of holy
chyrch to brynge yn-to better fourme, helden ther har conssaylle.

Statutes or
Constitu-
tions made
at it :—
1. Irish-
men shall
put away

[† Fol 13.
b.]
their
concubine
kins-
women,

and marry
legally.
2. Children
shall be
baptized in
church
fonts.

To thys conseyl, comen these from the kynge I-sent : a noble man
Rolf, abbot of byldewdys ; Ralf, Erchedekene of landaf ; Nychol 24
the prest, & other many, the kynges clerkes & hys messagers.
The statutes or constytucions of that consaylle ben these here
I-wrytten, & by the kynges auctoryte' I-stablet. ⓒ The fyrst ys,
that crysten men In Irland shvllen leuen har kynnes-wommen 28
† & her sybbes, whyche þay have ar thys I-hold to har wylle out of
spoushode, & lawfully spouse other wommen, & spousehede lawfully
hold[2]. That other ys, that the chyldren, at þe chyrche dorre
shullen ben I-primseined[3] of the prestes hond, & yn þe holy 32
fantstones yn har moder chyrches to be I-fulled[4]. The thrydde,

[1] Late sidenote in MS. : ' Establishment of orders for the Clergy, and
matters of Religion.'

[2] repudiato cognatarum et affinium contubernio, legitima contrahant matri-
monia, et observent.—Op. v. 282.   [3] catezizentur.   [4] baptizentur.

The lond was than in good pees by-for the kynge, and the pees *Capitulum* ^xxvij^m.
wel holde. the kynge herde that the pepil of the londe was
of vnclen̄ lyfe, and̄ ayeȳn godd and holy churche. he thogh[t] that
he wolde bryng the pepil Into bettyr lyfe; and mych desyr had
therto. he Sende for al the clergy of the lond at Casshel; and that
he Enquerid and herde opynly the fylthed of the lond-pepill in *tam enor-*
mitatibus
whych thay lad har lyfe; and Setten hit in writ, vndyr the Bi- *quam*
schopis sele of lysmore, that was also legat of the courte of rome, and *spurcitiis.*
heyghest of dygnyte ouer al thay that there were. and the Statutes *Statuta*
Cassellen-
of holy church, whyche yit men halte [1] in the maner that holy church *sia.*
ham holte in England, he lette thare Sette: Whych Statutes, in the [1] *quae ad-*
huc extant.
Wordis that thay weryn ther Shewyd, is none harme thegh y
expresse ham here:—

[CHAPTER XXVIII.]

IN the yere of oure lord-is incarnacyon M꜀. Clxxij, the fryste *Capitulum*
^xxvij^m.
yere that the kynge of En[g]land, henry, Irland conquerid [2],
Crystyn, Byschope of Lysmore, and Legate of the Courte of Rome;
Dougher, Archebyschope of Cassel; Laurance, Arcebishope of
Deuelyn; Cathel, Arcebyschope of connaght; with othyr Byschopis, *Catholicus*
Tuotue-
abbotis, pryorys, and many othyr prelatys of holy church in Irland̄, *nensis (Co-*
nactensis,
by the same kyngys comaundement comyn to-geddre in the Cee of *Harl. 177).*
Casshel; and, for the State of holy church to bryng into bettyr state,
heldyn ther har consayle. to this Consayle comȳn thes frome the
kynge, that is to say: a nobyl-man Rolfe, Abbote of byldewais; Ralfe,
Archedekyn of landafᶦ; Nycol the Preste, and othyr many of the *Nicolaus*
capellanus.
kyngys clerkys and his messagers // The Statutes or constytuciones
of that consayle ben this her writtyn, And by the kynges auctorite
Stabelid̄ // The fryst is, that crystyn men In Irland̄ sholde lewe jᵐ.
har kynnys-women, whych thay haue ar this holde to har will out *cognata-*
rum et
of Spoushode, and lawfully spouce othyr women, * and Spoushode *affinium.*
Lawfully Holde // The Seconde is, that the chyldryn at the church ijᵃ.
[*Fol. 13
dore sholde be y-primseined of the prestes honde, and in the holy b.]
fantstonys in hare modyr chyrchis to be yfullid̄. The thyrde, that iijᵃ.

² conquesid, MS.

F

A. D.
1171-2.
3. Tithes
to be paid.
that eue*ry* crysten man lawfullych pay hys tethynges to hys
pa*r*oche chyrche, of corne & of al othe͞r thynge that a ye͞r hym
aneweth [1]. ❡ The ferthe, that al þe londes of holy chyrche & ha͞r

4. Church
lands to be
left in
peace.
possessiou*n*s, of al herthly askynge be quyte; & namely, that no 4
kynges ne other heye men, ne he͞r sonnes, ne he͞r meygnees, mette
ne herbrowe yn chyrche londes, ne ask, ne wyth streynth ne be so
hardy to take; & that Cursed me[te] that four syth a ye͞r was wonet
to be asked y͞n chyrche tounes, & of the next neghbors, neue*r* eft 8

5. Clergy
not to pay
any of
kinsmens
fines for
Man-
slaughter.
be asked. ❡ The fyft, that of manslaghttre that lewed men doth,
whan man maketh fy͞n w*ith* hys foma͞n, the clerkes that ben hys
kynnes-me͞n, no þynge ne yeue ne yeld ther-to; bot, as thay be͞n
gyltles of the dede, also be thay harmles of þe payement. ❡ The 12
syxth, that wha͞n a man ys seke, he shal make testament openly

6. Wills to
be made
openly.

Property to
go to family
in thirds,

or halves.
to-fo͞r hys prestes of the pa*r*orch, & to-fore hys neghbors; & aft*er*
hys dettes & se*r*ua*u*ntes hyre out take. dele hys catel a thre; yf
he hath wyf & chyldre͞n, that on to hys spoused wyf, that other 16
to hys shyldre͞n, The thryde to hys testament. And yf he hath
non chyldren by spouse, the good be y-deled bytwene hym & hys
wyf, eue*ry* Ilyche; & yf the wyf deyeth, the goodes be I-deleth
a thre bytwene the housbond, & the chyldren, & the wyf. ❡ The 20

7. As to
funeral
services.
.vij. that wha͞n a man othe͞r a woman deyeth, ha͞r wathe [2], & the
se*r*uyce of holy chyrche, & the buryeng, be man-shyply I-done.

8. All folk
to go oft to
Church.

All Ser-
vices to be
in the
English
way.
❡ The .viij. that al me͞n & wo*m*men wyrshyppe holy chyrche, & oft
go to chyrche; & holy chyrche y͞n al se*r*uyce be goue*r*ned on the 24
ma*n*e*r* that hyt ys yn England. In al these thynges, the kynge
ynto the lond come, many defautes we͞r yn the land I-found,
& mych horynesse or oryble synnes that me ne aght nat to speke
of, that—throgh g*r*ace of god, & by the kynges pu*r*ueyaunce & hys 28
myght—weren amendet, & yn bette͞r wonne I-broȝth. ❡ The
prymat of Ardmagh was nat at thys conssaylle, ne thede͞r myght
come, for he wase old Man & feble; Bot he come the͞r-after to

In winter,
no ships
can get to
Ireland.
dyuely͞n, & g*r*aunted yn al thyn͞g the kynges pu*r*ueyaunce. In 32
thys tyme was the wede͞r so stronge, & the wynd so aweyward,
that yn al the wyntyr ne myght no shyppe com oue*r* yn-to Irland.

---

[1] 16th century side-note : ' the privileges and frydom gyve*n* to the church, and
londs ther of.'   [2] ? mistake for ' wache,' or *th* used for *k*, as on p. 67, l. 4.

euery crystyn man lawfully pay his thethis to his Parashe church,   A. D.
of corñe, and of al othyr thynges that a yere hym aneweth // The   1171-2.
iiije. that al the landis of holy church and har Possessiones of al $animalium,$
Erthly askynge be quyte ; and namely, that no kyngest, ne othyr hey $frugum,$
men, ne her Sones, ne her menyes, mete ne herbrow in church $ceterarum-$
londys, ne aske / ne with streynth ne be So hardy to take ; and that $tionum.$
Cursed met that foure tymes a yere was wonyd to be askyd in   nothynge.]
church tounes, and of the nexte neghbores, neuer aftyr to be axed [1].
The Ve, that of manslaghtre that lewid men doth, whan men makyth   ve.
fyne with his enemy, the clerkys that ben his kynnys-men, nothynge $quolies$
ne yeue therto ; but, as thay ben gyltlest of the dede, also thay be $inimicis$
harmeles of the pament. The vje. that whan a man is seke, he $suis com-$
shal make testament opynly, to-for his preste of the parash and   vjª.
to-for his evyncrystynnes and aftyr his dettis and his seruauntes   [‡ MS.
vagis out-take, dele his catel athre. yf he haue wyfe and chyldryn,
that on to the Spousyd wyf, that othyr to his chyldryn, the thyrd
to his testament. And yf he haue no childe [by] Spouse, the good be   [2] $inter$
y-delid betwen hym and his wyfe, euery y-lyke. and yf the wyfe $liberos$
deyeth, the good be y-delid at thre [2], betwene the hosbonde, and the $bipartiri$
chyldryn, and the wyfe / The vije, that whan a man oper woman   vjª.
deyeth, har wache, and the seruyce of holy church [3], and the burienge,
be wyrchiply done // The viije. that al men and women wyrchip   viijª.
holy church, and ofte go to church ; and holy church in al seruyce be   [3] $et missa-$
gouerned on al maner that hit is in England. In al thes thynges, $liarum ex-$
the kynge Into the lond come [4], many defautes were in the land found, $multimoda$
and mych felth or orribil synnys that y ne oght not to Speke of, $malorum$
that,--by the grace of god and by the kynges purueyaunce and his $genera.$
myght—weryn amendid, and in bettyr state broght // The Primat
of Ardmagh was not at this consail, ne thedyr myght come, for he   [5 Harl.
was olde man and febill. But he come ther-aftyr to deuelyn, and   chapter
graunted in al thynge the kynges Purueyaunce [5]. In this tyme was   and leaues
the weddyr so stronge, and the wynd so aweyward, that in al the   out the
wyntyr ne myght no shipp come ouer Into Irland. the kynge   white cow |

---

[1] et quod de villis ecclesiarum cibus ille detestabilis, qui quater in anno
a vicinis comitibus exigitur, de cetero nullatenus exigatur.—*Op.* v. 282

[4] ? abl. abs.—Nam ante ipsius adventum in Hiberniam —*Op.* v. 283

A.D.
1171-2.
The kynge went to Watyrford, & abode ther a whyle, & ful mych
desyre adde for to hyr tythynges from beyont see. & of the

[* Fol. 14
a.]

Henry II
gets the
best Irish-
men on his
side.

knyghtes that he fond *yn Irland, he drogh to hym sleghly for
o coste the beste : as Reymond, Myles de Cogan, wyllyam Masturel, 4
& other, for to make hys part þe strenger, & the Erles parte the
fobler[so]. ⁋ After the myd-lente, come shyppes yn-to Irland, that

A.D. 1172.
He hears
bad news :

hard tythynges hym broght, & lydder, bothe out of engeland & out
of fraunce, And normande, & other londes ; ffor ynto Normandy 8
weren ycome twey cardinalles, from the poppe Alexander y-sent
(that oon heght Albertus, & that other Theodynus), for to serchen
& enqueren of the holy martyres deth, seynt Thomas : ryghtful
men, as me vnderstond, & to that lawfully y-chosen / natheles thay 12
weren Romayns ; & such folweth oft coueytyse ; &, bot the kynge

the proba-
ble Inter-
dict on his
land, and

come the rather to ham, the kyngedome of england, & al the londes
that he was lord of, sholden be entredyted. & (as me fynd oft ¹,
good aduentures comen oft slowly & aloon, bot mesaduentures 16
ne cometh neuer-more aloon ;) wyth thay tythynges comen other
mychel wers, & of more perylle ; ffor the kynges sone, henry, the

the
treasonous
conspiracy
of his sons.

eldest, whyche he so fayne was obout to crowne kynge of England,
& other tweyn of hys bretheren, (that throgh yought & foolrede 20
hym folwed, & many drogh to ham, both of england & of beyend
þe see,) waren I-swore to-gredder to entre vp-on the kynge, & bynyn
hys londes, The whyle that he was yn Irland : & wel may be
that hyt was I-purueyed bytwen ham, ar he ynto Irland wente.   24

He is
grievd,

⁋ Whan the kynge thys herd, he was ² yn grete anguysshe.
sory he was at the begynnyge, þat he, gyltles, was I-retted of the
holy mannes deth ; sore he was afred that hys londes shold bene
I-shent throght that lydder dede of hys sonne ; sore hym for- 28

as he
wanted to
fortify Ire-
land,

thoght, that he the lond of Irland so sone most fore-lete, whyche
he hade y-cast for to streynth with castell, & stable yn pees, the
next somer that was to comen. Of al thys, he was yn many
thoghtes ; & spake ther-of fyrst to hymself, þer-after to hys men. 32

and keep
it.

Aftyr many redes, he sent some of hys ynto England by-fore hym ;
& ther-after he puruyed how he myght sykyrlychest kepe Irland.

¹ MS. est.   ² MS. way.

wente to watyrford, and abode ther awhile, and grettely desyr hadd A.D.
forto hyr thythyngis from be-yont see. And of the knyghtes that 1171-2.
he found in Irland, he drew to hym wylely for o Purpos, the beste,
as Reymond, Miles de cogan, Willam Masturel and othyr, forto A.D. 1172.
make his parte the strongyr, *and* the Erlis parte the febelier / Aftyr
the myd-leynte, come shippis into Irland that [1] screwid thythyng*es naves ad-*
hym broght / out of England, and out of Fraunce, And Normandye, *reniunt,*
tam gravi-
and othyr lond*es.* For into Normandy weryn come two cardynalis, *tatis nun-*
from the pope Alexandre Sende,—that one was callid Albert, *and ciae, quam*
pravitatis.
that othyr Theodoin,—forto serche and e[n]quere of the holy martires
deth, Seynt Thomas. (ryghtful men, as y-vndyrstode, and to that
lawfully chose.) [2] Natheles, they were Romanys ; *and* such * folwyth [* Fol. 13
ofte covetys [2] ; and, But the Kyng*e* come the Sondyr to Hame [3], the b.]
[3] *nisi citius*
Kyngdome of England, *and* al the londys that he was loid of, *eis rex*
Sholdyn be Entredytyd, and (as y fynd ofte, good aduentures comyn *occurrerit.*
ofte Slowely and aloon, but mysaduentures ne comyth neu*er* more
al-oon.) Wyth thay thythyngys, comyn moche wors, and of moche
more Pere*y*l.   For the kyng*es* sone henry, the eldyst, whych he So
fayn was to crovne kyng*e* of England, *and* othyr two of his
bretheryn (that throw youuth and fooly hym folwid, *and* many drew *fratrum*
puerili
to hame both of England *and* of beyonde See,) war*e* Swern to-giddre/ *levitate*
to Entyr vpon the kyng*e* and take his landis, The whyle that he *secuti,*
pravissimo
was in Irland : And hit may wel be, that hit was Purveyed be-twen *consilio.*
ham, ar he into Irland went // Whan the kyng*e* this herde, he was in
grete a[n]gwysche : Sory he was at the begynnyng*e*, that he, gyltles,
was yretted of the holy manys deth [4].   Sore he was aferd, that his
londes sholde ben shente throw that vngoodly dede of his Sonnes.
Sore hym forthoght, that he the londe of Irland so sone moste leue, *tam incar-*
tellare
the nexte Som*er* that was to come. Of al this, he was in many *quam*
thoghtys, and spake therof fryst to hym-Selfe, theraftyr to his men. *firma stabi-*
lire pace.
And aftyr many consalys, he Send Some of his men into England
to-for hym ; And there-aftyr he Pvrueyed how he myght Svrly kepe
Irlande /

[1] thad, MS.   [2-2] sed tamen Romani.—*Op.* v. 285.
[4] se tanta tam immerito suspicione notari.—*Ibid.*

A.D. 1172.

Henry II
leaves
Leaders
at Dublin
to keep
Ireland,

and sails
from Wex-
ford on
Easter
Monday.
At St.
Davids, in
Wales,

a Welsh-
woman
complains
to him,

[Fol.14 b.]

he goes on,

and she
appeals
for ven-
geance on
him, to the
stone of
Lechlavar,
the
'speaking
stone'
(prophesied
of by
Merlin

which lies
over a
stream N.
of the
church
yard.

As a corpse
was carried
over it, the
stone
spoke.

He left at dyuelyn, the cyte & the contray to kepe,
hught de lassy, wyth .xx.^{ti} knyghtes ; Robert steuenes-sone,
& Moryce fytz Geraud, wytht other .xx.^{ti} at Waterford ; hunfrey
de boun, Robert Bernardesson, & hugh de Gundeuyl wyth .xl.^{ti} 4
knyghtes ; At weysford, wyllyam Al-delines-sone[1] & phylppe de
Breuse wyth .xx.^{ti} knyghtes. And a morow after Estre .day
herly, he dydde hym to saylle at Weysford, & arryued at
seynth dauyes, sone after none. Whan he come a lond, he went 8
wyth grete deuoccion to the modyr chyrche, as a pylgrymage,
a-foot, with a burdon yn hys hond. Come the chanons of the
chyrche ayeyne hym at the whyte yate, & with fayr processioun,
with mych reuerence, & with mych manshype, hym receyued. As 12
þe processyoun yede a rewe to-for hym, come a walche womman,
& fel hym to þe feet, & made a myche mone, yn hyre langage,
of the bysshope of that place. The [kynge] stode, & herd hyr
mone ‖ of an ynterpretour-es mouth that hyt hym told ; & for he 16
went forth, & dydde hyr no ryght anoon as tho wolde, she smote
hyr handes to-gyddre, & bytterly began to crye tofore ham Al,
a walshe langage, “ A-wreke vs to-daye, lahlauar ! A-wreke our
kynred & our folke of thys man ! ” Thay that vnderstode hyr 20
speche, put hyr away, & fore-bade hyre cryynge ; & sho so myche
the more cryed yn the same manere, & hoped to an old prophecye
that Merlyn seyd : “ The kynge of england that shal wyn Irland
shal be I-woundet yn Irland of a man with a rede hond ; & as 24
he cometh ayeyne by south wales, he shal deye vpon lehlauar : ”
Þat was þe name of a stone, that lay ouer a streme by north the
chyrche heye of seynt dauyes, yn stydde of a brygge. The stone
was of Marbel wel fayr, & smothe of mannes geynge, & hadde 28
.x. feet yn leynth, & .vi. yn brede, & a foot thykke. And ys ‘lehlauar,’
a walshe, as mych to sygge as ‘ a spekynge stone.’ And hyt was
ytold, that som tyme as me bar a dede body ouer that stone,
he began to speke ; & wyth the spech he claue throghout ; & yit 32
the clyft ys I-sene, & yit yn-to thys day me be-bereth no dydde
body ouer that stone. The kynge come to that stone, & bethoght

---

[1] Weisefordiae, vero Guillelmo Aldelini filio, Philippo de Hastinges, et
Philippo de Breusa.—*Op.* v. 286. [William Fitz-Audeline.]

HE lefte at Deuelyn the Cite and the contray to kepe *Capitulum*
Hugh de Lacy with xx^{ti}. knyghtes, Robert Steuenes-Sone *xxix^m.*
and Morice fiz-geraud, wyth othyr xx^{ti}.; at Waterford Humfrey de *A.D. 1172.*
bonn, Robert Barnardes-Sone and Hugh de Gondeuyl, with xl. *Hugone de*
knyghtes / At Weysford, Willam Aldelines sone *and* Philip de *Gunde-*
Bruse, with xx^{ti}. knyghtes. And amorrow, aftyr estyr-day, Erly *villa.*
he did hym to Sayle at Weysford *and* londid at Seynt dauyes
sone aftyr noone. Whan he come alond he went wyth grete
deuocion to the modyr church as a Pylgrymage afoote with a *devoto*
stafe in hande. Come the chanones of the church ayeynes hym *peregri-*
at the white yate; and wyth fayre processioun[1], wyth mych *more,*
reuerence *and* wyth mych wirchip, hym resceiwid. And as the *baculoque*
Procession yede arew to-for hym, come a Walch woman, *and* fel *suffultus.*
to-for his feete, and made mych mone in hyr Speche of the Bischop
of that Place. He stod, and herde hyr complaynte of an inter-
pretoure-es mouth that hit hym tolde; and, for he wente forth, and *quoniam*
did hyr no ryght anoone as sho wolde, She smote hyr handis to- *jus suum*
giddyr and bittyrly began to cry to-for ham al in walch Speche: *tinenti non*
"A-wreke vs to-day, lathlauar! wreke our kynred and our pepil *est assecut i.*
of this man!" Thay that vndyrstode hyr Speche, Put hyr away,
and forbade hyr cryynge. She so mych the more cried in the *[3] ab homine*
Same maner, and hopid to an olde prophesy that Merlynge sayde[2]: *manu in*
"The kynge of England that shal conquere Irland [shal be wounded *vulnera-*
in Ireland of a man[3]] with a rede hand, and as he comyth ayeyn by *tum.*
South walis, he shal dye vpon lethlauar": that was the name of *flumen*
a stone, that lay ouer a streme[4] by north the churchey of Seynte *jacens.*
dauyes, instyd of a brige. The stone was of marbill, * Wel fayr *[* Fol. 14*
and smoth of men goynge, and was of x fote in Leynth, and vj in
Brede, and O foote thykke. And is 'lethlauar' in walch, as mych
to say as 'a spekynge stone': and hit was tolde, that Some tyme *Lapis*
that whan ther wase a dede body y-bore ouer that stone, he began *loquax*
to speke; *and* wyth the speche he clewe throgh[5]-out; and yit the *ipso conatu*
clyfte as Seyn. And sithyn on-to this day, thay berryth no ded *medius.*
body ouer that stone. The kynge come to that stone, and bethogh[t]

---

[1] canonicorum ecclesiae processionem . . . invenit.—*Op.* v. 286.
[2] alludens illi fictitio vulgari, nec vero Merlini proverbio, quo dici solebat.—
Op. v. 287.   [5] throght, MS.

A.D. 1172.
hym of that prophecye. & he stode at þe stones end & grymly hyt

Henry II walks over the stone, and asks 'Who'll now believe the liar Merlin?'
be-hold; & awhyle ther-after, boldely yede ouer a good paas. & whan he was ouer, he turned ayeyne to þe stone, & deynously þus seyd : " Who shal heten-forward beleue Merlyn the leyer ?" A man stode 4 þer besyde & herd, & wold, hys thankes, saue þe prophetes sawe, Answard the kynge & seyd, " Thou art nat that kynge that shal Irland conquer ; ne Merlyn ne speketh nat of the." Thus the kynge went yn-to the chyrch, yn seynt Andrees & seynt dauyes 8

He hears Mass, and goes to Haverford, and Normandy.
wyrshyppe I-sette, & herd hys masse of a preste that was I-found fastynge, as god wold. After masse, he eete hys mete ther, & after mete wente to hauerford, than ouer .xl. myle ; ffrom thens he wente hastyly yn-to englande ; out of enland yn-to Normandy, & come 12 to-for þe cardynalls with mych buxumnesse at Custance. Ther,

He swears that he didn't slay Beket, but he does penance,
after myche dalyaunce & many wordes I-spoke, he excused hym by othes of þe holye Martyres deth, that he was nat by hym I-slaw ; bot he ne for-sok nat that he nas for hym ; & þerfor he vndretoke 16 such penaunce as holy chyrche hym wold loke. Þe cardynals, he sent ayeyne wyth myche wyrshyppe ; & noon he went to þe marche, & ther he spake with the kynge of ffraunce. þer, (throgh besechynge of hegh men, & namely of phylepe þe erl of flaundres, that from 20

and makes peace with King Lewis of France.
seynt James was ryght than I-come,) the pees was made betwene the twey kynges, of the wreth that was betwene ham for the forseyd martyres deth ; ffor-thy that þe kynge of ffraunce, with other mychel & myghty men, name an hand to the erchebysshopp 24 whan he shold turne ayeyne yn-to England, [ayeyn] the pees betwen the kynge & hym. ffor þer was pees thus y-made betwene the kynges, al the harme þat the sones with har allyees hadden throght to do, was I-lost tyl þe next yere theraftyr.   28

[CHAPTER XXX.]

[Fol. 15 a.]
Wnder this, as the lond of Irland was yn good pees vnder ham that weren In lefte, the lond for to kepe, byfelle that a day of parlement, at a certeyne place, was betaken

Hugh de Laci and O'Rourke, King of Meath, meet.
by-twene hugh de lacy, whom the kynge had I-yeue dyuelyn to 32 kepe with trust, And þe kynge of Myth. a nythe, whan the parlement shold ben a morow, a knygh[t] that was Moryce fytz Geraudes neuew, & Robert Gryffyn by name, thoght yn hys

hym of that prophesy, and he stod at the stone his ende, and grymly A.D. 1172.
hit be-helde; and a whyle ther-aftyr, boldely yede ouer a good
pace. *and* whan he was ouer, he turnyd ayeyne to the stone, *and*
deynously thus sayde: "Who shal, fro this forth, beleue Merlynge *verbum hoc*
the lyer?" A man stode ther bysyd, and herde, *and* wolde, his *indig-*
nanter
thankes, Sawe the prophet-is Saynge, Answerid the kynge and *emisit.*
Sayde, "Ye ben not that kyng that shal Irland conquere, ne
Merlyng Spekyth not of yow" / Thus the kynge went into the
church of Seynt Androwis and seynte dauyes, and herde his
masse of a preste that was founde fastynge, as god wolde. Aftyr
masse he ette his mette and aftyr mette went to hauerford than *quasi per*
miliaria
othyr xv myle. Frome thens he went forth hastely Into England, *duodecim*
out of England into Normandy and come to-for the cardynals *abinde*
distans.
with mych buxumnesse at Custaunce. Ther, aftyr mych delyaunce
and many wordys spoke, he excusid hym by othys of the holy
martyris deth that he was not by hym Slayn, but he forsoke
not that he was for hym. And ther-for he vndyrtoke such
Penaunce as holy church wolde hym enyoyn. the Cardynalls,
he sende ayeyn with mych wirchip; and anoone he went to the *ad mar-*
chiam cum
marche, *and* there he spake wyth the kynge of Fraunce. There, *Francorum*
(throgh besechynge of good men, *and* namely of Phylippe the Erle *rege Lodo-*
vico . . .
of Flandris, that frome Seynt Iamys was than come,) the Pees was
made betwen the two kynges, of the wreth that was betwen ham
for the forsayd martires deth; [1] For-they that the kynge of Fraunce, [1] *puta*
with othyr mychel men *and* myghty / And vndyrtoke to the *quem*
Anglorum
archebischope, whan he shold turne Into Englan, afeyn the pees *rex archi-*
praesuli in
be-twen the kynge *and* hym. For ther was Pees thus made *Angliam*
betwen the kynges, al the harme that the Sonnes, with hare *reddituro*
allyences, haddyn thoght to do, was left til the nexte yere *. . . fide-*
jussorem
ther-Aftyr. *donaverat.*

[CHAPTER XXX.]

VNdyr this, as the lond of Irland was in good pees *Capitulum*
vndyr ham that weryn lefte, the londe for-to kepe, by-fel *xxxᵗʰ.*
on a day, that a certayn Place, to a parlement was sette, be-twen
Hugh de Lacy, to whom the kynge had yewe Deuelyn to
kepe wyth truste, and the kynge of myth. On a nyght, whan *et regem*
monoculum
the Parlement sholde ben amorrow, a knyght, that was Morice *Ororicium*
fiz-geraudes eme, *and* Robert Gryffyn by name, thoght in his *Medensem.*

A.D. 1172. slepe that he saw a mych flote of wylde swyne yernynge vp-on

Griffith
Fitz-
Gerald's
dream : he
saves
De Laci, &
Maurice
Fitz-
Gerald.
hugh & moryce ; & a boore amonge ham, myche & grysly ouer al
other, come toward ham, & with hys tuskes wold haue smytten
ham & I-slawe, yf he stalwarthly ne had y-come betwene, & 4
I-slawe the bore, & I-holpe ham bothe. A morow, thay went to þe
place ther þe parlement was I-sette, at a place that me hath seth

The inter-
view is at
Rorik's
Hill.
y-cleped 'rorykes hylle' : ffyrst thay helden har parlement from
ferr, by messagers goynge betwen ; ther-after thay name sekernesse 8
of othes I-sworne, & comen to-geddre by forward ; natheles few,
& ylych fale on ether halue, and thay vnwepened,—bot the one, her
swerdes ; & the other, her sparthes,—& ether of har folke somdel

Griffith
keeps seven
trusty
knights
near.
fer from ham.   Gryffyn, that with Moryce was to the parlement 12
I-come, was ful thought-ful of the vysyon that he sawe. he name
to hym seuyn knyghtes of hys owne kyn, than that ho moost
truste to har stalwardnesse, & drowen ham on the on halfe of
the hylle, as neyght as thay myght leppen vpon har stedes, with 16
sheldes about har nekkes, & speres an-hond ; & for a coste,
pleneden & prykkeden har hors ayeyn other, so that, yn whych
halue the parlement turned, throght encheson of such pley thay
myght be fonden Redy.   Roryk & hugh helden har parlement 20
of many thynge ; bot of nothynge thay myght nat accord, & begyn

O'Rourke
treacher-
ously at-
tacks De
Laci.
to departe a wrethe.   The traytour Roryk had yn hys thoght þe
trayson þat he hadde I-purueyed. he made semblant, & draw hym
by-halues as for to pyssen, & made tokens to hys men that thay 24
hastely shold come to hym.   Whan he thys hadde I-done, he
turned ayeyne wyth hys sparth an hegh, hys wysage al blak with

Maurice
Fitz-
Gerald
warns De
Laci,
ful snel goynge.   Moryce was Iwarned of hys neueu, of the
vysyon that he sawe ; stod, & beheld al thys. he hent out þe 28
swerd, & cryed vpon hugh, & mynyed hym, & dyd hym-self ayeyne
the traytour, for to defend hym.   The traytour ran to hugh, hym
for to smyte ; har latymer yed betwene hym & the dynt ; & he

who is
saved by
his inter-
preter, and
[∥ Fol. 15
b.]
escapes
alive.
smote hym of the oon arme, fast by the sholdre.   Moryce stode, & 32
campled wyth hys swerd ayeyne the sparthe, & lowd cryed to har
men. & ar hugh myght be yn any state, hym-self for to helpe,
throgh grete hastynge, he felle twys ∥ abak ; & vnnethe, throgh
helpe of Moryce, that hym defendet thus, Hugh escaped wyth hys 36

Slepe that he Saw a mych flote of wylde Swyn yernynge vpon
Hug*h* and Morice; *and* a bore amonge ham, mych *and* grymly *horribilem*
ouer al other, come to ham, *and* wyth his tuskys wolde haue *prae aliis.* *et grandem*
smytten ham Slayn, yf he boldely ne had come betwene, *and*
Slayne * the Boore, and Holpyd Hame Both. On the morrow, [*Fol. 14
thay Went to the Place ther the Parlement was sette, at a place b.]
that Sedyn is callid "Rorike-is hille." Fryste thay heldyn har
Parlement from fere, by messager*es* goynge betwen; ther-aftyr thay
toke Surtey, *and* othis Sware, *and* comyn to-giddyr aftyrward.
Natheles fewe, *and* ylyke many on euery syde, *and* thay vnwepeny*d*,—
but the on, her Swerdys; the othyr, her Sparthes,—and her felle- *praeter*
chip in euery syde fere fro ham. Gryffyn, that wyth Moryce come to *dios tun-* *hinc gla-*
the Parlement, was ful thoghtful of the vysion that he Saw; he *tum, inde* *secures.*
name to hym Sewyn knyghtis of his owyn kyn, tham that he
most truste to har bolthenys, and drowen ham on the one halfe
of the hille / as neye as thay myght, Leppen vpon har stedes,
with sheldis about har nekk*es*, *and* Sperr*es* in honde, and for oo *ex indus-*
Purpos pleydyn and prikkedyn in the felde ayeyne othyr, So that *mentis* *tria torna-*
in what syde the Parlement turnedyn, throgh encheyson of Suche *Gallicis*
Pley, thay myght be foundyn redy. Rourik and Hugh kepten har *faciebant* *praeludia*
Parlement of many thyngis; but in nothynge thay myght acorde,
and begon to de-Pert, as in wrethe. The traytoure Rourik had
in his thoght / the trayson that he hadd Purueyed: he made
semblaut, and drow hym be-sydis as forto Pissyn, *and* made tokyn *simulans*
to his men that thay hastely sholde come to hym. Whan he this *gendum.* *ad min-*
had done, he turned ayeyne wit*h* his sparth an hey, his face al *vultu*
blake wit*h* ful snel goynge. Morice was warnyd of his eme by the *pallido.*
vysyon that he sawe; stode, and be-helde al this. he toke out
his Swerde, and cried vpon Hugh, *and* mynyd hym, *and* did hym- *prae-*
Selfe agayn the traytoure, forto defende hym. The traytoure rane *suscitans.* *muniens et*
agayn hugh, hym forto smyte. har latymer yed betwen hym and *viri inter-*
the stroke; and he smote of hym the oone harme of, fast by the *letali* *pretis . . .*
shuldyr. Morice stode, and camplid wit*h* his Swerde ayene the *brachium* *vulnere*
Sparthe¹, *and* loude cried to har men. And ar hugh myght be *amputarit.*
in any state², hym-Selfe forto helpe. throgh grete hastynge. he fel *securim* *¹ contra*
twies a-bac; *and* vnneth. throgh helpe of Morice. that hym defendid *confligebat.* *gladio*

² staste, MS.

A.D. 1172. lyf. The whyll that thys was, Rorykes men ful many come to hys
clepynge, out of dales & wodes about, yernynge to ham wyth
speres & with sparthes, for to brynge hugh & Moryce out of
dawes. Than Gryffyn & hys felewes comen yernynge vp on har ₄

O'Rourke hors styffly to ham. þe traytour saw ham comynge, & lep to hors
that to hym was broght, & wold do hym to flyght; & as he lepe,

is slain by vp come Gryffyn, & wyth hys spere smote hym & hys hors throgh-
Maurice
Fitz- out, & slowe hem bothe. Wyth hym wer I-slayne þay that, yn so ₈
Gerald. mych perylle, the hors hym broght; & hy[s] heed I-smytten of, &
yn-to england þer-after to the kynge I-sent; & al hys men yn-to al
the feldes dyscomfyte, & I-slawe ful many. Rolf, Robertes sone fytz
Stephen, was the other stalwardthest that daye yn the felde ¹.   12

[CHAPTER XXXI.]

[Fol.16 a.] **M**orice was a mane ful wyrshypful & chamfaste; vysage
Maurice wel colowred; becomlyche; lytel of body, sumdele more
Fitz-
Gerald þan lytel, & lasse than metlych. of hert, & body, wel I-thewed;
described. nothynge hauteyne. of k[i]ndly goodnes, he was good; & leuer 16
hym was be good, than be sey good; hys maner was euer-more to

He spoke hold hym methelyche. man of short spech & lytel, bot of fayr
little, wordes, as he that more hadde yn hert than yn mouth, more of
wytte & reyson þan of spech. ²Nat forthy³, whan tyme was, & nede 20
to sp[e]ken, to good reyson forth brynge,—as lettred as he was, as

was very wytty he was ². In thynge that byfell to bataylle, swyth hardy,
bold, but
not fool- & vnnethes of stalwarthnesse any was hys bettre; natheles, of
hardy, perille to take, he was nat to hastyf ne to fool-hardy. bot as he was 24
thus, & of purueaunce thynge to begynne, Also he was stronge &

was strong stydfast yn thynge Whan he hyt hadde begune. he was sobre, wel
and sted-
fast. I-thewed & chaste, lawful, & stydfast, without blame.

A.D. 1173.   [CHAPTER XXXII.]

In April, **I**n the next auril ther-after, þe yonger kynge henry, þe 28
Henry II's
three sons, kynges sone, the lyddernysse that he hadde I-thoght to hys

¹ The twelve lines on the back of fol. 15, 'a bak (p. 74, at foot) . . . felde,'
were first written by mistake on fol. 16, but afterwards struck out.

²⁻² Et tamen, cum sermonem res exigebat, ad sententiam dicendam sicut
serus, sic scientissimus.—Op. v. 297.   ³ ? MS. Rat fortly.

thus, Escapid wyth his lyfe. the whyle that this was, Rourik his A.D. 1172.
men, ful many, come to his callynge, out of dalis and woddis about,
rynnynge to ham w*ith* Sper*es* and Sparthes, forto berew hugh *and* *cum jaculis*
Morice the lyfe. Than gryffyn and his fellouys come rynnynge *binis et securibus*
vpon har hors styfly to ham. the traytou*r*e Saw ham comynge, *amplis.*
and lep to hors that to hym was broght, *and* wolde do hym to
flyght / And as he lep, vp come gryffyn, *and* wyth his spere
smote hym *and* his hors throght-out, *and* slayne them both. wyth *cum ipso,*
hym were Slayn thay that, in so myche Peril, the hors hym broght / *tribus ejusdem fami-*
and his hed Smytten of / *and* into England theraftyr to the *liaribus.*
kynge hit sende; and al his men into al the feldis discomfite, and
Slayn ful many / Rolfe, Rob*er*t-is Sone, fiz-Steuyñ, was the othyr
boldyste that day in the felde.

[CHAPTER XXXI.]

MOrice was a man ful wyrchipphul *and* shamefaste; [1]vysage *Capitulum* xxxj^m.
 wel colorid; becomlych; lytil of body, sume-whate more *Descripcio*
than lytel *and* lasse than metlych. of herte and body, wel thewed ; *Maurici fiz-*
nothynge couetynge. of * Kyndely goodnes, He was good[1]; ande *geraud.* [*Fol. 15
Leu*er* hit Was to Hym to Be good, than to Be sayde good. his a.]
man*er* was eu*er*-mo*r*e to holde hym methelyche. man of Shorte
Speche *and* lytyll, but of Fayre wordis, as he that more had in *plus pectoris habens quam*
herte than in mouthe, more of witte and Reysen than of speche. *oris, plus rationis*
Nat forthy, whan tyme was, and nede to Spekyn, to good reyson *quam ora-*
forth brynge,—as letterid as he was, as witty he was. In thynge that *tionis, plus*
befel to battayl, Swyth hardy. But as he was thus, *and* of *sapientiae quam elo-*
Purueyance, thynge to begyn, Also he was stronge *and* stydfast *quentiae.*
in thynge whan he hit hadd begonne. [2]he was sobyr, wel
condicionyd *and* chaste, lawful and stidfaste, wyth-out blame[2] /

[CHAPTER XXXII.]

A.D. 1173.

IN the nexte Aurel ther-aftyr, the yongyr kynge henry, the *Capitulum*
 kyng*es* Son*n*e, the Wickidnys that he had thoght to his xxxij^m.
fadyr done / nolde no longyr helle, wyth his two bretheryn that

---

[1-1] vultu colorato, decentique ; mediocri quadam modicitate, tam mediocribus minor, quam modicis major ; vir tam animo quam corpore modificato, nec illo elato, nec hoc dilutato ; innata vir bonitate bonus.—*Op.* v. 297.

[2-2] Vir sobrius, modestus et castus ; stabilis, firmus atque fidelis.—*Ibid.*

A.D. 1173.

fadyr nold no lenger hellen ; with hys twey bretheren—that ys to

Henry,
Richard
and Geof-
frey, get
French
help, and
rebel.

wytte, the Erl of peytou & the erl of brytayn [1]—wenten to the
kynge of ffraunce, whose doghter he hadde I-spoused, & purchased
helpe of hym for to werr vpon hys fadyr. The enchesoñ wher-for 4
hyt was, Mayster Geraud ne telleth nat, ne I ne cañ nat sey ; bot
many hegh & Ryche men he hadde to consaylle & to helpe, both
of England & of beyend the see ; many openly & wel ; most, illy &

Henry II

dernely. The old kynge, the yonger kynges fadyr, for the fortune 8
that hym come to oñ euery halue so vnwarly, was ful sorowful.

draws most
of his men
from Ire-
land. They
come to
him at
Rouen.
[† Fol. 16
b.]
He com-
mits Ire-
land to
Earl
Striguil and
Reimund
Fitz-
Gerald.

℃ Nathales, throgh gret sleght & hegh herth, he made fayr semblant,
& heped to god ; & oñ euery syde that he myght, yn al maner he
besoght help.   He sent messagers ynto Irland, & mad come ouer 12
to hym the meste parte of the knyghtes & of the good meygne þat
he ther hadde I-lefte. Thay come to hym at the cyte of Ruem,
& he bethogh hym that † hyt was perylle to leue har lond vnkepet;
ther he betoke þe Erl Rychard al þe lond to kepe, & sette to hym 16
Reymond as hys other hand ; ffor the erl for-soke al out & out, þat
he that kepynge wold nat receyue, bot yf he hadde Reymond with
hym for to helpe.

[CHAPTER XXXIII.]

Most Irish,
hearing
of the
Princes' re-
bellion,
turn
against
Henry II.

The Erle [&] Reymond, with har power, wentten yn-to 20
Irland ; &, for the folk of yrland hade y-hard of the mych
stryff that was betwene the kynge & hys sonnys be-yent the see,—
as folk þat styddefast ys yn vnstedfastnesse, & lawfully ham holt
to vnlawfulnesse,—the most parte of the prynces of þe lond, ayeyn 24
har trouth I-found, þay turned ayeyn-to the kynge. The erl hadde
sone I-spend the traysour that he broght ouer wyth hym ; & whan
the meygne lacked spendynge, & nat spedden yn prayes takynge
vnder heruy, that was conestable ouer the meygne, & euer hadde 28

The Eng-
lish de-
mand to
be put
under Rei-
mund Fitz-
Gerald.
They in-
vade
Offaly, in
Leinster,

enuy to Reymond, Thay wenteñ ham to the erl comynly by one
accorde, & sey hym wel, that ' bot yf he wold sete Reymond ouer
ham, thay wold leue hym euerychone, & wend yn-to england; oþer,
that wel wors was, thay wold turnet to har enemyes ayeyns har 32
heed.' As the meygne wold, Reymond was I-sette ouer ham ; thay
name than hert to ham, & wenten vpon the Ofolanes yn the dees,

———
[1] Pictaviae scilicet et Britanniae comitibus.—Op. v. 297-8.

is to Say, the Erle of Peytou *and* the Erle of Brytayn, wentyn ^{A.D. 1173.}
to the kynge of Fraunce, whose doghtyr he had Spousid, *and* *ad Lodo-*
vicum,
Purchasid helpe of hym forto were vpon his fadyr. The encheyson *Francorum*
wherfore hit was, Maystyr Geraud ne tellyth not / ne I ne can *regem.*
not say ; but many hey men he hade to consayl and to helpe,
both of England *and* of beyonte see ; many opynly *and* wel ; *multo*
plures
[more] falthyr pryuely. The olde kynge, the yongyr kyng*es* fadyr, *occulte*
for the fortvne that to hym was fal on eu*er*y syde so vnwyttyngly, *habens, et*
fautores.
was ful Sorroful. Neu*er*-the-las, by grete Sotylte *and* hey herte,
he made fayre semblante, *and* trystid to god ; *and* on eu*er*y syde
that he myght, in al man*er* he besoght helpe. he sende messager*es*
into Irland, *and* made come ou*er* to hym the meste Parte of the
knyghtes and of the good mennye that he ther lefte. Thay come
to hym at the Cite of Ruem. *and* he be-thoght hym that hit was *ad urbem*
Rothoma-
Peril to leue har londe vnke*p*te : ther he be-toke the Erle Richard, *gensem.*
al the londe to kepe, and sette to hym Reymonde as his othyr *custodiam*
illam sus-
hande ; For the Erle forsoke out and out, that he that kepynge *cipere*
omniᴀo
wolde not rescewe, but yf he hadde Reymond wyth hym, hym *renuerat.*
forto helpe.

[CHAPTER XXXIII.]

The Erle and Reymond, wi*th* har men, wentyn Into Capi*tul*um
Irland ; and, for þe Pepil of Irland had herde of the grette ^{xxxiij^m.}
stryfe that was betwene the kyng and his Son*n*es be-yount the
See,—as Pepyl that stydfast is in vnstydfastnes, *and* lawfully ham *gens sola*
constans
holde to vnlawfulnes,—the most Part of the Pryncis of the londe, *incon-*
agayñ har trouth y-founde, thay turned agayn the kynge. The *stantia.*
Erle had spende the tresoure that he broght ou*er* wyth hym ; *and* *deficien-*
tibus
whan the fellochipe lackid spendynge, *and* not Speddyn in Prayes- *quoque*
takynge, Vndyr heruey, that was constabil ou*er* the men*n*y, and *stipendiis.*
eu*er* had envy to Reymond ; Thay wenten ham to the Erle
comynly by oone acorde, *and* sayde to hym wel, 'but that he
wolde sette Reymonde ou*er* ham, thay wolde lewe hym eu*er*ichone,
and wende Into Englande ; othyr, that wel wors was, thay wolde
turne to har enemys agayn*es* hame' / And as the men*n*y desyrid,
Reymonde was sette ou*er* hame. thay take then herte to ham, *in Offelᴀnos*
insur-
and wenten vp-on the Ofelanys in the deseses, and toke grette *gentes.*

A.D. 1173.   & name grett *prayes*, arrayed ham nobly wyth hors & wepne.

Lismore,   From thens thay wentteñ to lysmore, & the cyte, & al þe contre
&c., and
take much   about, robbeden & *prayeden*, & by the see wey senten many grete
prey.   *prayes* to Watyrford ; & of pylfre & thynge that thay namen, thay 4
fylled .xiij. far costes that wereñ I-come fro Wat*er*ford yn-to the

The   hauen of dongaruame. As thay weɼ wynd abydynge, theɼ come
English
fleet fight a   þe men of Cork from by west, by the see, yn xxxij shyppys, & many
Cork fleet,   men theɼ-In, for to take thay other. Theɼ was the fyght styffely 8
I-yeuen, of these twey fletes yn the see : That oon assaylled that
other grymlych w*it*h stones & w*it*h sparthes ; the otheɼ wereñ
welle I-wepned, & w*ith*-stode styffly w*it*h arblastes & w*it*h bowes.

rout it, and   At þe end, thay of Corke weren descomfyted & ou*er*-come ; heɼ 12
kill its men,
and take   shyppys I-take ; heɼ men I-slawe, & I-caste yn the see. Adam de
their prizes   herford & phylep de Wellsse, that weren I-sette ou*er* thay yong-
to Water-
ford.   lynges, w*it*h mo shyppes & grete beyetes of wepne & of pylfre, to

Reimund   Watyrford wenten w*it*h grete yoye. Reymond herd speke of thys 16
marches,   fyght, & tythynges to hym come ; he toke w*it*h hym xx*ti* knyghtes
& an hundreth bowmen, & went by the see wey thederward.
Than come to hym tythynges þat dermot, þe prynce of desmond,
was, w*it*h myche hostes, comeñ to lysmore, to helpe ham of Cork. 20

Dermot   Reymond went hym thederward. Þe prynce that herd, & turned
daren't
face him.   ayeyne, & durst hym nat abyde. And Reymond went fortheɼ yn-to
Reimund   the contrey, robbed & *prayed*, so that he hadde w*it*h hym at hys
has 4,000
cattle.   turny[*n*]ge aye toward Watyrford, four thousand kyne ; & as thay 24
[‖ Fol. 17   wer comynge ‖ by narow weyes wyth har *praye*, come the Ireshe-
a.]
The Irish   men of þe contray, & henten a party of har kyne, & wenten al
take some.   quytten w*it*h ham to wodde. þe crye arose, & Reymond [1] (as man
that eu*er* was forɼost redy) went aftyr, w*it*h oñ p*ri*uisant man an 28

He pur-   hors wyth hym ; come to the woddes ense [2], theɼ the theues
sues them
into a   weren an hydynge. Whan he hadde I-faylled of þe preye, &
wood.   wolde turne ayeyne, hys felewes folyly entyced hym for to wende
yn-to þe wodde, & he so dydde. Whan thay weren wel w*it*h-yn, 32

---

[1] The Latin text gives this exploit to Meiler : Gir. Cambr. *Op.* v. 309–10,
‘ et in primis Meilerius, ut erat praeceps semper et probus, satellite quodam
comitatus equestri, praedones usque ad silvae condensa est persecutus.’
[2] Ends.

Prayes arrayed ham nobely with hors and wepyñ. From thens A.D. 1173.
thay wentyn to lysmore; *and the Cite and the contrey about, [*Fol. 15
robbodyn and preedyn, and, By the See-wey, Sendyne many gret b.]
prayis to waterford; and of pilfre and of thynge that thay toke,
thay fillid' xiije. farcostes that weryn come from watyrford' into *naviculas
the havyn of doūn-garvan. As thay were wynde abydynge ther, *tredecim.*
come the men of Corke from be weste, by the See, in xxxijti. Shippis,
and many men therin, forto take the othyr. ther was the fyght *bellicosis*
fressely yewyn of this two flittes in the See. That oone assaylid *refertae viris.*
the othyr grymly with stones and with Sparthis; the othyr wer
wel wepenyd, and wythstod styfly with arblastes and with bowes[1].
At the Ende, thay of Corke weryn dyscomfyted and ouer-come;
Her shippis take, her men slayne, and caste Into the See. Adam
de herforde and Philippe[2] the wellsshe, that weryn sette ouer
thay yonglynges, with mo shippes and gret begetes of wepyn *cum armis*
and of Pylfre, to Watyrford wentyn with gret Ioy. Reymond' *et oneribus.*
herde speke of this fight, and tythynges to hym come : he toke
with hym xxti. knyghtes and an hundrid bowmen, and went by *per mari-*
the see-way thedyrwarde. Than com to hym tythyngis that *timam viam.*
Dermot, the prince of desmonde, was with r.yche hostys comyn
to lysmore, to helpe ham of Corke. Reymonde wentyn hym
thedyrward'. the prince that herde, and turned agayn, and durst
hym not abyde. And Reymonde wente Ferdyr Into the[3] contrey,
robbid and Prayed, So that he hadd with hym at his turnynge
agayn toward watyrford, iiije. Mt. kyne. and as thay were comynge
by naroweis wyth har Pray, come the Iryssh-men of the contray, *ad silvas*
and tokyn a party of har kyne, and wentyn al quyte with ham to *de plano.*
wodde. the cry aros, and Reymond, as man that euer was formyst
redye, went aftyr, with one pryuisant man an hors with hym, come
to the woddys syd ther the thewis were an-hydynge. Whan he had
falid of the pray, and wolde haue turne agayne, his fellowis folely *juvene in-*
Enticed hym forto wende into the wodd; and he so dide. Whan *stigante temerario*

---

[1] dum isti lapidibus et securis acriter impetunt, illi vero, tam sagittis quam
laminis ferreis quibus abundabant, promptissime resistunt.—*Op.* v. 309.

[2] Philpippe, MS.

the the, MS.

A.D.
1173-4.
Reimund is
attackt,
but cuts
his way
thro' his
foes.

the Irysshe-men rysse to ham on euery halue, & leyd ham oñ,
& anooñ-ryght the yonge mañ was al to-hakked to-for hym; he
yarne to snellych for to socuŕ hym, & was assaylled oñ euery
halue; & he, as man, hent out the swerd & leyd on about hym, 4
& smot of that mañ the hond, þat otheŕ the arme, þe þryd the
heede by þe sholdres; thus he opened hym the wey, & come out
to hys men, & brogĥt twey sparthes fast on hys sheld, & thre on
hys hors [1]; bot all hool & sound, & harmeles of body, he escaped. 8

A.D. 1174.

[CHAPTER XXXIV.]

Whan thys was y-done, & the meygne was noblych
      arrayed both byl ond & eke by watyŕ, come tythynges
to Reymond, that hys fadyŕ Wyllyam fytz Geraud was dede.

Reimund
goes to
Wales.
Hervey is
made Con-
stable.

Reymond went ouere yn-to Walys, to take seysyne yn hys fadyŕ 12
landys; & heruy was the whyle eft [2] y-made conestable of þe
meygne: he wold fayne entremette hym to do some thynge the
whyle that Reymond was out of londe, & made the Erl & the
meyne wend to Cassell for to weren yn Monestre; he sent eke 16
after the meyne of dyuelyn to come to ham. And as thay come
throgh Ossery, & laye a nyght yn a place thaŕ thay supposed to
be al sykeŕ, Obreen, the kynge of thomone, was sykeŕ, & awayted

Donnell
O'Brien
slaughters
the Dublin
men.

haŕ comynge by good spies. he aroos with mych folk vpon hem 20
erly a day yn the mcrowenynge, & smot vpon ham vnwyttyngly,
& slogh fouŕ knyghtes that wereñ ouer ham, & fouŕ hundret
ostmen. Whan the tythynges heŕ-of come to the Erl, he turned
ayeyne to Waterford with mych shame, & held hym thaŕ as man 24
that was beseget, that he cam nat fro thennes. And for thys

The Irish
massacre
the Eng-
lish.

aduentuŕ, the folk of Irland wyth oo hert al to-gyddre aresen vpon
the englysshe, & slow ham yn-to al theŕ thay myght ham fynd.
The kynge of Connaght come eke ouer the shynen yn-to Myd, 28
& fond al þe castels wast & voyde; he brant & keste ham adoun
to ground, tyl he come ryght to dyuelyñ. The Erl saw þat he
was narow by-ladde: by consaylle of hys men, as the last remedy
of lyue, he sent hys lettres to Reymond ouer yn-to Walys, yn these 32

[1] tres secures Hibernicas in equo confixas, duasque in clipeo portans.—Gir.
Camb. Op. v. 310.   [2] MS. est.

thay wer wit*h*-In the Irysh-men rysse to ham on euery halue *and*
leyde on ham, *and* anoone the yonge man was al to-hackid to-for
hym. He rane forto socoure hym, *and* was assaylid on eu*er*y syde.
And he, as man, toke out his Swerde, *and* leyde on aboute hym, *and*
Smote of, that man the honde, that othyr the harme, the thyrde the
hede by the sholdris; thus he oppenyd the wey, *and* come out to
his men, and broght two Spare*s* faste on his shelde, and thre on his
hors; but al holde and Sounde *and* harmeles of body he Escapid.

A.D.
1173-4.

exserto
gladio,
viam sibi
vir ani-
mosus viri-
bus ape-
ruit.

[CHAPTER XXXIV.]

A.D. 1174.

Whan this was done, *and* the meyne was nobely arrayed
both by londe *and* also by watyr / come thythyngis to
Reymonde, that his Fadyr willam fiz-geraude was dede. Reymond
wente ou*er* into Walis, to take seysyne in his Fadyr landis; And
heruey that tyme was made constabil of the meny. he wolde fayn
entremitte hym to done sumthynge, the whyle that Reymonde
was out of londe; *and* made the Erle *and* meny wende to cassell
forto werryn in monestre. He sende also aftyr the meny of
deuelyn to come to ham. And As thay come throgh Ossory,
and lay a-nyght in a place thar thay demyd to be al Sure,
Obreen, the kynge of Thomonde, was Sure, *and* awayted hare
*comynge By good Spies. He aroose, wit*h* mych Pepil, vppon
Hame, erly a day in the mornynge, *and* Smote vppon ham vn-
wittyngly, *and* killid iiij^e. knyghtis *and* weryn ou*er* hame, *and*
CCCC men. Whan the thythynges herof come to the Erle, he
turned agayne to Watyrford with mych shame, *and* helde hym
ther as man that was besegid, that he came not fro thennes.
And for this aduenture, the Pepil of Irland wit*h* oo herte al-
to-giddyr arysen vpon the Englysh, *and* Slowen ham in al places
that thay ham myght fynde // The kynge of Connaght come also
ou*er* the shynnyñ into Myth, *and* found al the Castelis waste *and*
woyde. he braunt and keste ham doune to grounde, til he come
ryght to Deuelyn. The Erle Saw that he was narrow bylad: by
consail of his men, as the laste remedy of lyue, he sende his
le*t*tres to Reymond, ou*er* into Walis, in thes wordis: "As rath as

Capitulum
xxxiiij^m.

aliquid
agere
videretur.

[*Fol. 16
a.]

qui aliis
praeerant.

unanimiter
insurgunt.

in arcto
jam posi-
tum.

G 2

A.D. 1174.　wordes: "As rathe as thou hast I-sey these *lettres*, ne leue nat to

Striguil asks Reimund's help, and promises him his sister Basile.

come to soco*ur* vs wyth good myght: & thy desyr of basyle, my
sustre, lawfully for to spouse, anone at þy comynge, wythout faylle
thou shalt haue." Whan Reymond hadde thys I-herd, both for the 4
maydnes loue þat he so longe hadde desyred, & for to proue hys
stalwardnesse, & soco*ur* hys lord yn hys mychele nede, wyth Meyler̄,
hys emes sone, he dyght hym al þat he myght yn such hast, so

[‖Fol. 17 b.]
Reimund sails, lands at Wexford,

that he hadde thretty ‖ knyghtes of hys owne kyn, & thre hundert 8
bowmen, the choyse of al Wales: he put hym to saylle, & arryued at
Weysford yn fyftene shyppes. That same tyme, the men of Weysford
hadden I-p*ur*ueyed ham to vndo al þe englysshe, wher̄-so me myght
ham fynde. Whan thay sawe the shyppes comynge yn þe hauyṅ, & 12
baner*es* that thay wel knowe; þroght þat comynge so fersly, that

and brings Striguil safe from Waterford.

trayson̄ was y-lefte; & anoon̄ Reymond went wyth hys men to
Waterford, & broght thens the Erl stalwarthly to Weysford.
ffresel, that was keper̄ of Wat*er*ford, went after̄ the Erl by þe 16
wat*er* of Sur, yn botys wit*h* hys men; &, as þay wer̄ yn the watyr̄,
the lydder gyddes that hym shold lode [1], slowe hy[m] & al hys men,
& turned ayeyne to the Cyte, & gadered ham to-gedder al þe

The Irish in Waterford slay the English there.

Irysshe-men, & smyt vpon̄ þe englesshe, & slowe al that thay 20
myght fynd yn hous & yn wey, men & wom*men*, yonge & old,
wit*h*out any sparynge, saue thay that escaped yn-to Rathe-
vyldestour̄; & throgh ham was the toun̄ I-saued, tyl the traytou*rs*
þer-after come to pees, & euer ther-after the lasse beleued & loued. 24
Reymond, whan he hadde thys I-se[u]yd the Erl, he miniyed the

Striguil's sister Basilia weds Reimund.

Erl of hys beheste. The Erl sent anoon̄ to dyuelyṅ aftyr hys
suster̄, and went neuer̄ from Weysford, fort sho was wit*h* mych
wyrshyp*p*e I-spoused to Reymond. Whan he was I-spoused, & 28
al þe day was Ihold yn yoy, gladnesse, & mych plente of mete
& drynke, & the nyght aftyr, yn delytes of chambre as ham beste

King O'Conor destroys all Meath.

lyked, came tythynges that Oconghour̄, kynge of Connaght,
hadde I-destrued al myght, & was I-come wyth myche power̄ 32
yn-to the contrey of dyuelyṅ. Reymond was nat slowe, nether̄

Reimund marches after him.

for loue of hys fayr̄ wyf ne for the moche feste, bot anoon̄
a morowe he toke hys men̄ wyth hym, & went toward dyuelyṅ.

[1] *for* lede.

ye haue sey thes *lettres*, ne lette not to come to socoure vs w*ith* A.D. 1174.
good myght : *and* you*r*e desyre of Basyle my Sustre, lawefully forto *et deside-rium tuum,*
Spouse, anone at youre comyng*e*, w*ith*-out fayl ye shall haue " // *in Basilia sorore mea*
Whan Reymond hadd this herde, both for the maydes lowe that he *tibi*
so longe had desiryd, *and* forto prow his myght, *and* socoure his *legitime copulanda.*
lorde in his mychel nede, w*ith* Meyler, his emys sone, he dight hym
al that he myght in such haste, so that he myght haue / *and*
hadde xxx*ti*. knyghtes of his owyn kyne,*and* CCC bowmen, the coyse *de electa*
of al Walis.   he putte hym to sayle, *and* arryued at Weysforde in *Kambriae juventute.*
xv. shippis.   that same tyme, þ*e* men of Weysforde hadd Purveyed
ham to vndo al the Englysh, wherso thay myght ham fynde.
Whan thay Saue the chippis comyng*e* Into hawyn, and baner*es*
that thay wel knew ; throw that comyng*e* So Fresly, that trayson *adventu tam subito.*
was lefte ; and anoone Reymonde went wyth his men to watyrforde,
and broght thens the erle boldely to Weysforde.   Fresell, that was *Fretellus,*
keper of watyrforde, wente by the watyr of Sure in botis w*ith* his *custos.*
men ; and, as they wer*e* in the watyr, the liddyr gides that hym *ab iniquis Ostmannis.*
Sholde lede, slayñe hym *and* al his men, *and* turned agayn to the
Cite, *and* gaddrid' ham to-geddyr al the Irysh-men, *and* smyte
vpon the Englysh-men, *and* slayne al thay that thay myght fynde
in hous, in wey, men *and* women, yonge *and* olde, w*ith*-out any *in plateis et domibus.*
sparynge, Saue thay that Escapid' into Rathevyldestour*e* ; *and*
throgh ham was the touñe Sawid, tyl the traytorys ther-aftyr
come to Pees, *and* euer ther-aftyr the lasse belewid *and* lowid. /
Reymond, when he hadd thus I-Sawid the Erle, he mvnyed the
Erle of his prom*es*.   the erle sende anoone to deuelyn aftyr his *revocatam a Dublinia Basiliam,*
suster ; *and* Wente neu*er* frome Weysforde till that she was, w*ith*
myche wyrchipp, Spousid to Reymonde.   Whan he was spousid,
and al the day was holde in Ioy *and* gladnys, *and* mych Plente
of mette and drynke, and the nyght aftyr in delytes of chambyr, *in thalami deliciis*
as ham beste plesyde / Came tythyngis that o-conghoure, kynge of *nocte con-*
Connaght, hadd destrued al Myth, *and* was come w*ith* grete hoste *sumpta.*
into the contrey of Deuelyn.   Reymond was not Slow, nethyr for *nec vino,*
lowe of his fayr*e* wyffe, ne * for the moche feste ; But amorrow He *nec venere, retardatur.*
toke His men W*ith* Hym, *and* Went towarde Deuelyn.   O-con- [*Fol. 16 b.]

A.D. 1174.
O'Conor
retires.

Reimund
rebuilds his
Castles and
restores
peace.

Oconghour hadde þer-to-forne assayed hys mayne, y-douted hym
the more; he ne abode nat wyth hym, bot was gladde to take
homward. Reymond let restore & arere that was destrued throgh
þe werr, & fale castels ryght vp, & broght yn-to rather state; 4
& for dred of hym, the lond wax yn good pees a good whyle, that
none Iresshe-man ne durst hym styrre, wer to begynne.

A.D.
1173-4.

Henry II
livd in
strife.

The worst
was, that
his trusted
Body-
guard
deserted to
his rebel
sons.

[CHAPTER XXXV.]

This while the kynge was yn mych stryf, wel two yer,
ayeyn hys thre sonnes & har allyes, both yn englande 8
& yn normandy & garioigne; & so was I-peyned with trauaylle
yn wepne & wakynge nyght & day, that no man ne myght more.
Bot, for ne wors fomanne may be, þan thay that man moste
trusteth to, o thynge was, that meste tene hym dydde: that þe 12
knyghtes that he hadde I-chose, hys body to kepe, yn whose
hondes hys lyf & hys deth he be-taght, for the moste dele euery
nyght wenten to hys sones pryuely; so that, whan the kynge
oft-tymes asked aftyr ham, thay war nat I-founde. Natheles, the 16
bataylle that was of so dotous begynnyge, hadde so good endynge
that, for the vnryght that hys sonnes hym dedde so vnk[i]ndely,

But he won
all fights,

hyt semete bettre tha[t] he soght by power of god, than by erthly
power; ffor yn al places, the ouerhand was hys. And as hyt semete 20
fyrste that hyt was for wreth of seynth Thomas-es deth that þat

[||Fol. 18
a.]

vnhape hym || betydde, Also hyt semed þer-aftyr, Whan he
hadde I-done asseth to holy chyrche, & pees made wyth the
holy martyr, wyth teres & repentaunce of herte, al hys tene, 24

by God's
help.

throght goodys helpe, hym turned to gladnesse: ffor aftyr the
mych tene & trayson þat he hadde Itholled al two yer, at þe
laste was þe bataylle I-smytten, at the whych, betwen the twey

His sons
were
routed, and

ostes, Ther war the kynges sonnes dyscomfyt, progh Rauf de 28
Glanuyl, that was mayster of þe kynges hoste. Ther was I-take
þe kynge of scotland, & þe erl of shestre, & þe erl of leycestre,
& so fele gret men, bothe of england & of beyent see, that vnnethe
me fond prisons to ham. Ther, aftyr al þe trauayl þat þe kynge 32

obliged to
make
peace (a
false one

hadde, & þe enuy, & þe costes al two yer, come þe sonnes to þe
fadyres pees, & maden asseth, falsly, as hyt was þer-aftyr wel
I-shewed yn deede. Of þus vntrowth, spake Merlyn yn hys

ghoure had thertofor assayed his meny, *and* douted hym the more. A.D. 1174.

he wolde not abyde hym, but was glade to take homwarde. *et castris*
Mediae...

Reymonde lette restore and arere that was destrued by the werre; *dirutis...*

And fale casteles ryght vpe, and broght into radyr state.   *and for* *jam repa-*
ratis et in

dred of hym, the londe wax in good pees a goode whyle, that none *statum*
redactis.

Irysh-man ne durst hym not styre, werre to begynne.

[CHAPTER XXXV.]   A D.
                                                   1173-4.

This whyle the kynge was in myche stryfe, wel two yere,
agayn his Sonnes *and* har allience, both in Englande and in *Capitulum*
*xxxv*ᵐ.

Normandy, *and* gascoygne ; *and* So was peyned *with* trawail in
wepyn, nyght and day, that no man ne myght more.   But, for no
wors enemy may none be, than thay that a man trusteth moste to,
O thynge was, that most angyr hym didd : that the knyghtes that he *illi quoque*
hadd chose his body to kepe, in Whos handis his lyfe and his deth *quos cu-*
bicularios
he betoke, for the mor Party, euery nyght wentyn to his Sones *sibi milites*
elegerat.
priuely ; So that, whan the kynge ofte-tymys askyd aftyr hame, thay
were not founde.   Natheles, the battayll that was of So doutos
begynnynge, hadd So good Endynge that, for the vnryght that his
Sones hym didde so vnkyndely, hit Semyd bettyr that he foght by
Powere of god, than by Erthely Powere.   For in al Placys, the ouer-
hande was his.   And as hit Semyd fryst, that hit was for wrethe of
Seynte Thomas-es deth that that vnhape hym befell, Also hit
semyd ther-aftyr, whan he hadd done asseth to holy churche, *and*
pees made *with* the hooly martyr, *with* terys and repentaunce of *propiti-*
ante nobili
herte, al his tene (by godys helpe) hym turned to gladnys.   For *martyre*
Thoma,
aftyr the mych tene and trayson that he hadd sufferid al two yere, *lacrimis et*
At the laste, was the battayl Smytten, at the whyche, be-twen the *devotione*
jam pla
two hostys, Ther were the kynges Sonnes dyscomfyte, by Ralfe de *cato.*
Glanvil, that was Maystyr of the kynges hoste.   Ther was take
the kynge of Scotlande, and the Erle of Chestre, and the Erle of
leycestre, and So many grete men, both of England *and* of beyonte
See, that vnneth thay found prisonys to ham.   Ther, aftyr al the
trauail that the kynge hadde, and the Envy, and the costys al two *umbratili-*
que magis
yere, come the Sonnes to the faderis Pees. *and* madyn asseth, falsly, *quam vera*
as hit was ther-aftyr wel Shewid in dede   Of this vntrouth, Spake *concordia*

Merlin of Celidon's prophecy of the Rebellion of Henry II's sons.

prophecyes, & seyde : " The sonnes shullen agylte aycyn þe fadyr̄ for hys gyltes, & the rather gylte shal be enchesoñ of þe gyltes þat after shullen comen. The sonnes shullen aryse vpon þe fadyr̄ ; & for to awreke hys felonye aycyne þe wombe, the tharmes shal 4 swer ham togydder̄. In the man of blode, the blode shall aryse, & wanhoply shal hys pynsynge be, tyl that scotland þe penaunce of hys pylgrymage bewepe."

[CHAPTER XXXVI.]

Henry II had grey eyes, a red face,

The kynge henry the other̄, was[1] a mañ saunrede, roune 8 heed, & round grey eghneñ ; roghly lokynge, & rede yn wreth ; vysage rede bernynge, grete speche, neke somdel logħ of þe sholdres, brest thyk, armes staluarthe, of flesshy body ; &, more

and a big belly, tho, to lessen it, he'd hardly rest his body. All day he was out hunting, and rode a high trotter ;

of kynde than of glotony, grete of wombe ; for he was, as to prynce 12 belongeth, [of] mete, & of drynke ful meen & for-berynge[2] ; &, for to a-quenche that gretnesse, he put hymself to ful mych trauaylle, that wnneth he lete hys body haue eny reste, ether̄ by day other̄ by nyght ; ffor, wynter, & somer, he arose euer more yn the dawn- 16 ynge, & herd fyrst hys seruyce of holy chyrch ; ther̄-aftyr, most what al þe day he wold ben out, other̄ wyth houndes other̄ wyth hawkes, for yn thay two thynges he delyted hym swyth mych wythal ; & vnnethe he wold ryde any amblynge hors, bot myche 20 trottynge hors, for to trauaylle hys body the more. Aftyr al hys trauaylle a-day, vnnethe he lete hys body haue a lytell reste for to syte to hys mete the whyle that he eete ; & anoon aftyr mete,

at night he stood.

& namely aftyr sopper̄, anoon he wold aryse & stonde, & so dryue 24 forth al þe meste parte of the nyght, so that al þe court was

When once he'd seen a man, he knew him again.

oft ennyede ther̄-of. þe man that he ones yn lych beheld, euer̄ eft he hadde knowleche of hym ; & dynge þat he hadde ones herd, euer̄ eft he hyt wold vnderstond ; þe man that he ones hated, 28 vnnethe he wold euer̄ eft[3] loue ; & man that he ones loued, vnneth

---

[1] vir subrufus, caesius (= lentiginosus), amplo capite et rotundo, oculis glaucis, ad iram torvis, et rubore suffusis, facie ignea, voce quassa, collo ab humeris aliquantulum demisso . . . corpore carnoso, et naturae magis quam gulae vitio, citra tumorem enormem et torporem omnem, moderata quadam immoderantia ventre praeamplo. Gir. Cambr. Op. v. 302.

[2] Erat enim cibo potuque modestus ac sobrius ; et parcimoniae, quoad principi licuit, per omnia datus. Gir. Cambr. Op. v. 302.   [3] MS. est.

merlynge in his prophesies, and Sayde : " The Sonnes shullyn agylte
agayn the Fadyr for his gyltes ; and the radyr gylte shall be encheyson of the gyltes that aftyr shullyn come.   The Sones shall aryse
vpon the fadyr; and forto aw[r]eke his felony agayñe the wombe, the *et ob scele-*
tharmes shal Swere ham to-giddyr. In the man of blode, the blode $\frac{\text{ris vindic-}}{\text{tum in}}$
shal aryse; *and* wanhoply shal his Pynsynge be ¹, til that Scotland *ventrem*
the Penaunce of his Pylgrimage bewepe. '   *viscera con-*
jurabunt.

[Chapter XXXVI.]

The kynge henry the othyr, was a man same rede, rounc Cap*itul*um
hede, *and* rounde grey eyyn ; row lokynge, *and* rede in wreth ; $\frac{\text{xxxvj}^{\text{m}}.}{\text{Descripcio}}$
Visage rede, brennynge ; * grete Speche ; neke somdel shorte of the Henrici
Soldrys, breste thyke, of fleschy Body ; ande, mor*e* of kynde, than of $\frac{\text{regis tercij.}}{[\text{*Fol. 17}}$
glotony, gret of wombe ; for he was, as to prynce belongyth, of a.]
mete *and* of drynke ful meen *and* for-berynge ; and forto aquenche
that gretnes, he put hym-Selfe to ful mych trauayl, ² that vnneth he *immo-*
lette his body haue enny reste, othyr by day othyr by nyght.   For $\frac{\text{derata}}{\text{corpus}}$
Wyntyr and Som*er*, he aros euer-more in the dawnynge, and herde *vexatione*
fryst his s*er*uyce of holy church ; theraftyr, most part al the day he *torquebat.*
wolde be out, othyr w*ith* houndys or w*ith* hauke*s* ; for in thay two
thyngys he delyted gretly w*ith*-al / *and* vnneth he wolde ryde any
hamlynge hors, but mych trottynge hors, for to trauail his body the
more. Aftyr al his trauayl a-daye, vnneth he lette his body haue
a lytil reste forto sitte to his mette. the whyle that he ette, *and*
anoone aftyr mette, *and* namely aftyr soper, anoone he wolde arysse
and stonde ², and So dryue forth al the moste Parte of the nyght, So *totam*
that al the courte was ofte wery of his wakynge.   the man that he $\frac{\text{statione}}{\text{continua}}$
onys in lyche be-helde, eu*er* he hadd knowlege of hym ; and thynge *curium*
that he hadd̃ ones herde, eu*er* aftyr he wolde hit vndyrstonde. $\frac{\text{lassare}}{\text{consue-}}$
the man that he onys hattyd, vnneth he wolde eu*er* aftyr loue ; *and* *rerat.*
man that he onys lowyd, vnneth he wolde eu*er* aftyr hate.   Whan

---

¹ ut desperabilis fiet afflictio.—*Op.* v. 301.

²⁻² sibi nec pacem ullam nec requiem indulgebat.   Venationi namque
trans modestiam deditus, summo diluculo equo cursore transvectus, nunc
saltus lustrans, nunc silvas penetrans, nunc montium juga transcendens, dies
ducebat inquietos : vespere vero domi receptum, vel ante coenam vel post,
rarissime sedentem conspexeris.—*Op.* v. 302.

Henry II
described.

he wold euer eft hate. Whan any vnhappos hym befelle, noman
meker ; efte whan he was yn sekernesse, no man sterner. Suert
ayeyn the bold, meke wyth ham that weren vnder y-broght, hard

He lovd
meekness,
and hated
pride.

amonge hys owne, & priuely large amonge vnkouth ; & openly 4
mekenesse & debonerte he louede ; pryde & hauteynesse he hated,
& wold brynge vnder fote.

A.D.
1174-5.

[CHAPTER XXXVII.]

Henry II
does not
forget his
Ireland.

Thegh þe kynge wer wel longe yn grete nuy & grete
anguyshe throght hys sonnes, as hyt ys to-fore I-told, 8
natheles, amonge other nedes, he ne foryet nat hys Irland. He
lete take the lettres that war Imade yn the consaylle of Casshele,
of the vnclene lyf & the horyble synnes that the folk of Irland

[*Fol. 18
b.]

lyueden In, || other-wyse than crysten men oght lyuen ; & the 12
lettres, al ensealed as thay wer, he sent by hys messagers to the

He gets a
grant from
the Pope,
of the Lord-
ship of Ire-
land, and a
charge to
reform the
folk to the
laws of the
Church,

Court of Rome, to the pope Alyxsander that than was ; & thar
he dydde the purchace, that by auctoryte of the pope, & by hys
concent, was to hym I-graunted the lordshype of the lond ; & þe 16
lond-folke, that crysten shold be, & al clene was out of ryght
reule of crystendome & ryght byleue, to bryngen yn-to ryght
lawe of holy chyrch, yn the manere of England. That pryuelege
forth, wyth another, that rather was purchaced of þe pope Adrian, 20
that was to-fore Alexander, was I-sent ouer yn-to Irlande by
Nychole, pryour of Walyngeford, & Wyllyam Aldelines sone ;
& was a consaylle of al the clergye of Irland I-gaddered to-gyddre

No[ta]
teno[rem]
bullee
[A]drian.

at Waterford : ther wer the pryueleges I-shewed & I-radde 24
solempnelych to-fore ham, & I-graunted heghlygh by consente-
ment of al the comynes. The forme of thay preuyleges, as thay
wer endyted yn the Court of Rome a latyne, ne myght I nat
comly setten yn Englyshe ; & þerfor I hyt leue ; bot the meste 28
streynth ys thys :—Whan the pope Adryan hadde herd opynly
the euyle lyf, & þe synfule, that þe folk of Irland ladden, wors than
wyld bestes, & out of constytucions of holy chyrch & ryght byleue,

to with-
stand sin,
and better
had doings.

he graunted the kynge that he shold ynto Irland wend, for to 32
adresse & sprede þe termes of holy chyrch, for to wythstond & lete
the ruyne of syn, for to Amend the lyther thewes, & sette þe good,

any vnhappis hym be-felle no mane mekyr. Whan he was in
sickyrnys, no man sternyr. Smyrte agayn the bolde, meke wyth ham *clemens in*
that weryn vndyr-broght ; harde amonge his owyn, ande Pryuely *subactos.*
large amonge strange men; *and* opynly meknys *and* debonerte he *diffusus in*
lowyd ; Pryde *and* hauteynesse he hatyd, *and* wolde brynge vndyr- *extraneos.*
fete.

[CHAPTER XXXVII.]

A.D.
1174-5.

Thegh the kynge were wel longe in gret angwysche throgh *Capitulum*
his sonnes, as hit is to-fore tolde, natheles, amonge othyr *xxxvij*ᵐ.
nedys, he foryate note his Irlande.   he take the letteres that ware *suae tamen*
made in the Consayl of Cassell, of the vnclene lyfe and the horribil *inter agendum*
Synnys that the Pepil of Irland lyuedyn In / In othyr wyse than *Hiberniae non im-*
crystyn men oght lyue ; and the *lettres*, al Ensealid' as thay were, *memor.*
He sende his messagers to the Courte of Rome, to the Pope *ab Alexan-*
Alysandyr that than was, *and* thar he did Purchase that, by *dro tertio, tunc prae-*
auctorite of the Pope and by his concent, was to hym grauntyd the *sidente, privi-*
lorchippe of the londe, *and* the londe-Pepill that crystyn shold be, *legium im-*
and al clene was out of Ryght rule of crystyndome and ryght *petravit.*
belewe, to brynge into ryght lawe of holy church, in the man*er* of ¹ *quod idem rex ab*
England.   That pryvylege forth, wi*th* an othyr ¹ that radyr was *Adriano... perquisi-*
Purchasid of the Pope Adriane, that was to-fore Alexandyr, was *erat.*
sende ou*er* Into Irlande by Nycole, pryoure of Walyngeforde, *and* *in publica audientia*
Willam Aldelines-sone ; and was a consayle of al the clergy of *ejusdem privilegii,*
Irland' y-gadderid to-giddyr at Watyrford.   ther wer the pryuy- *cum uni-*
legis y-shewyd, *and* y-radd Sollempnelych to-fore ham, *and* grauntyd *versitatis assensu*
hyghlych of al the comynys. The fourme of thay Pryuylegis, as *solemnis*
thay wer endyted' At Rome a-latyne, y may not comly sette in *recitatis facta fuit.*
Englys̄h, and therfor y * Hit Leue ; But the mest streynth is this : [*Fol. 17
Whan the Pope Adryan Hadd Herde opynly the evyl lyfe, and the b.]
synfull, that the Pepell of Irland laddyn, wors than wilde bestis, *Nota teno-*
and out of constitucion*es* of holy churche *and* ryght be-lewe, he *rem bulle Adriane.*
gra*un*ted' the kynge, that he sholde into Irland wende, forto
adresse and sprede the termys of holy church, forto wythstonde *and* ² *et vitio-*
lete the ruene of synne², forto a-mende the wickid dedis. *and* sette *rum plan- taria inde*
the good'; forto En[e]che religion of crystyndome, So that hit were *exstir- panda.*

A.D.
1174-5.

for to eneche relygyoun of crystendome, so that hyt war wyrshype
to god, & helte to the soules ; & the folke of þe londe, manshyply
hym shold vptake, & worthly as lorde ; saue ryghtes of holy chyrche

But every
house in
Ireland is
to pay the
Pope 1*d.* a
year.

vnwemmed ; & to seynt petyr & þe holy modyr chyrche of Rome, of 4
euery hous a pany to rent, a yer, yn Irland, as yn England.   Thys
pryuelege was I-purchased of þe pope Adryan ; & a clerk hyt
purchased, that hette [1] Ihoū of Salusbury ; & the pope, by the
same clerk, sent to the kynge a gulden rynge, yn name of Seysyne 8
of the lond.   the pope Alexandre next aftyr hym confermed that

All oppo-
nents are to
go to the
Devil.

same yift ; & euery eþer of ham amonested & parted from god
almyghty, & betheght þe deuyl al ham that yn any tyme þer-
ayeyne wold come.   12

A.D. 1174.

[CHAPTER XXXVIII.]

Now again
for our
Knights'
deeds in
Ireland.
Hervey of
Mont-
maurice,
jealous of
Reimund,

Off þe kynge And of hys sonnes, & of the purchace that
þe kynge dede, ys Inowe Itold shortlyche : now we
wyllen turne ayeyne to our knyghten gestes yn Irlande.   The
lond of Irland was yn good pees vnder Reymond-ys kepynge ; bot 16
heruy of Mountynorthy,—that euer hadde enuy to Reymond, & saw
that hys selth & hys wyrshype wex euer more & more,—fore he ne
durst nat openly showe the felony that was yn hys hert, he
bethoght that he wold dernely ; he made hym semblant of myche 20
loue ; besoght ful yorne þat he most allyaunce haue to har kynrede,
& namely, that he moste haue to wyue a gentyl-wommañ, Moryces

marries
Nesta
Fitz-
Gerald.

doghter, fytz Gereud, that hegh Neste.   Thys mayd was hym
Igraunted, & he hyr spoused ; & þat þe kynrede sholden the 24
faster be Ibound togydyr, by procurynge of Reymond & of hym
eke, þe Erl yaf helyn, hys sustre, to Wyllyam, Moryces eldest sone :
þe erl sent eke aftyr Moryce, that was than Iwent ynto Walys ;
& at hys comynge, he yaue hym þe haluendele of Ofelañ, & þe 28
castel of wykynlo ; & þat oþer haluendele he yaue Meyler.   In the

O'Brien,
King of
Limerick,
rebels.

tyme þat þe pees was, & þe lond yn good state, byfel that Obren,
the kynge of Thomon, ayeyne hys trouth & ayeyn the kynges pees,
began to withdrawen hym from the kynge, & noght nold be 32
bowynge to hym, ne to ham that wer vnder hym yn þe lond.

---

[1] MS. 'sette' for 'hight, hette, or hete,' p. 94, l. 22 below : ' per Johannem
Salesberiensem,' v. 316.

vyrchipp to god, *and* helth to the Sowlys ; *and* the Pepil of the

londe, manshiply hym sholde vp-take, *and* worthy as lorde ; Saue the

ryght of holy church vnwemyd ; and to seynt Petyr *and* the holy

modyr churche of Rome, of euery hous a peny to rent, a yere, in

Irland as in Englancl. This pryuylege was Purchasyd of the Pope

Adrian. / And a clerke hit Purchasid that was callid Ihon of

Salysbury ; *and* the Pope, by the Same clerke, Sende to the kynge

a golde rynge, in tokyn of Seysyn of the londe.   And the Pope

Alexandyr nexte aftyr hym confermyt that Same yfte ; And euery

othyr of ham amonessed *and* Partid from god almyghty, *and* betoke

the deuyl al ham that in any tyme ther-aycynnes wolde come.

A.D.
1174-5.

*salva beato
Petro, et
sacro-
sanctae
Romanae
ecclesiae,
sicut in
Anglia sic
et in Hiber-
nia, de
singulis
domibus
annua
unius
denarii
pensione.*

A.D. 1174.

[CHAPTER XXXVIII.]

O Ffi the kynge and of his sonnes, and of the Purchas that
the kynge did, is y-now tolde Sortelych.   Now we will

turne agayñe to oure knyghten gestis in Irlancī // The londe in

Irland was in good pees vndyr Reymonde-is kepynge ; but heruey of

montmorthy,—that euer hadd envy to Reymonde, and Saw that his

goodnes and his wyrchippe [wex] euer more and more,—for he ne

drust not opynly show the felony that was in his herte, he be-thoght

that he wolde Pryuely / he made to hym semblant of mych loue ;

be-sogh[t] gretly that he sholde alyaunce haue to har kynryde, and

namely, that he haue to wyue a gentyl woman, Morices doghtyr,

fitz-geraude, that was callid Neste.   This mayde was to hym

grauntecī, and he hyr Spousecī. and that the kynred sholde be fastyr

bounde to-giddyr, by procurynge of Reymonde *and* of hym also, the

Erle yaue Ellyn his sustyr, to Willam, Morices Eldyst Sone.   the

Erle sende also aftyr Moryce, that was than went into walis ; and at

his comynge, he yaue halfe to hym of Ofelan, and the castel of

wickylow ; *and* the othyr halfe he yaue to Meyler.   In the tyme

that the Pees was, and the londe in good state, befel that Obreen,

the kynge of Thomonde, agayn his trouth *and* the kynges Pees,

began to wyth-drawe hym frome the kynge, *and* wolde not be

bowynge to hym, nethyr to ham that wer vndyr hym in the londe.

*Capitulum
xxxviij^m.*

*Videns ..
ejusque
successus
de die in
diem am-
plius pros-
perari.*

*Nota
matrimo-
nium inter
Herucium
contrahi et
Nestam
filiam
Maurici
fitz-geraucī.*

*medium
Ophelaniae
cantare-
dum . . .
cum Wi-
kingelo-
nensi
castro.*

[Fol. 19 a.]
A.D. 1175.

Reimund marches to Limerick ; but is stopt by the Shannon.

Reymond told þer-of myche vnworthynes, & yn lytyl whyle gadered to-dedderes [so] hys hoste, so that he hadde an hundert knyghtes & .xx.[ti], thre hundret other an hois, & .cccc. bowmen afote, & about al-halwen-tyde went toward lymeryke. Whan thay wer theder 4 I-come, thay hadden grete lette of the grete watyr of þe shynen, that was betwen ham & þe sytè, so that thay myght nat ouer wende : the yonglynges—that wel coueytouse wer ham self to auaunce, her stalwarthnesse to showe, & also wynnynge to gete & to 8 hawe,—weren wel sore a-tened þat thay myght nat ouer to þe syte that was ham so neght, for þe watyr þat was so depe & so streit rennynge betwene, & eke so stony by the grourd. As the formest of ham waren houynge vpon þe waterys brynk, was a yonge 12

His nephew, Davy the Welshman

knyght amonge ham, newly I-dobbet, fayr & stalwa[r]th, Reymondes Neuowe, that hete Dauy the Welsse [1] : thregh grete couetyse that he hadde, ouer al other to wyn the formest pryce, ne dredet nat to do hym-self to so horyble perylle of deth ; he smote hys hors with 16 the spores, & ouer-threwe adoun ynto þe watyr, þat was so depe & so stony. the horse was myche & stronge, & come sone vp

swims the river aslant ;

aboue the watyr wyth hym. he wyssed the hors sydlynge ayeyns the watyr asquynt, & come ouer on the other syde, & cryed to hys 20 men, & seyd that he hadde a ford I-found. bot, for he fond no man

but as only one knight follows him, he swims back.

þat hym wold felowe, bot o knyght that hete Geffrey Iudas [2], he turned ayeyne by that same wey, & þe knyght with hym. he come ouer hole & sound ; bot þe knyght, þrogh þe streyntnesse of þe 24 watyr, was I-throw adoun, he & hys hors, & y-drent to-for ham al.

Meiler then

Whan Meyler, that theder was wyth Reymond I-comen, þys saw, he hadde grete enuy that such hardynesse shold be I-teld of any other, & nat to hym : vpon the hors þat hym bar, he put hymself 28

crosses the Shannon.

yn the watyr, & hardylyche, wyth-outen any ferdnesse, passed ouer þe other syde. The cytzeyns sawe hym comynge so al-oon ; thay comen ayeyn hym, some for to kepe hym vpward at hys comynge out of þe watyr, for to mak hym turne ayeyne ; other, to vndo hym 32 ryght yn the watyr. The knyght was stalwarth, & boldly putte hym vp bytwene twe perylle :—on on halue, þe wode-yernynge

---

[1] David agnomine Walensis. _Op._ v. 321.

[2] Galfridus Judas. _Ibid._

Reymonde tolde therof gret vnworthynys, *and* in lytyll whyle A.D. 1175.

gaddrid to-gidderis his hoste, So that he hadd an hundred knyghtes *circa*

and xx^{ti}, thre hundrid oþer an hors, and CCCC bowmen afoote ; and *kalendas*
Octobris.

aboute al-halwyn-tyde wentyn toward lymerike. whan thay wer

thedyr come, thay hadd gret lette of * the watyr of the Shynnyñ, [*Fol. 18
a.]

that Was Betwen Ham and the Cite, So that thay myght not ouer-

wende. the yonglynges—that wel couetos were ham-selfe to *juventus,*
tam lucri

auaunce, har myght to show, and also wynnynge to gette *and* to *quam*

haue,—wer sore greuyd that thay myght not ouer to the cite that *laudis*
cupida,

was ham so nyghe, for the watyr that was to depe, and so Streyte *tanquam*

rynnynge betwen, *and* also so stony by the grounde. As the *ad aquas*
Tantali

fryste of ham was abydynge vpon the watyres brynke, was *posita.*

a knyght amonge ham newely dobbid, fayre *and* stalwarth, Rey-

mondes Eme, that was callid Dauy the Welsse : throgh gret *horren-*
dumque

couetyse that he hadd, ouer al othyr to wyn the formyste price, he *mortis*

dreddit not to do hym-Selfe to so horribill Perel of deth. he *periculum*
laudis

smote his hors with the Sporis, *and* ouer-threw adoūne Into the *amore con-*
temnens.

watyr, that was depe *and* ful of stonys. the hors was mych *and*

stronge, *and* come Sone vp abow the watyr with hym. he wissed *Cursum*
itaque

the hors sydlynge ayeynes the watyr asquynt, *and* come ouer on the *fluminis*

othyr syde, and cried to his men, *and* seyde that he had a forde *lateraliter*
obliquans.

founde. but, for he found no man that hym wolde follow, but

O knyght that [was] callid Geffrey Iudas, he turned agayn by that

Same wey (*and* the knyght come with hym) holde and Sounde ; but *militem*
illum, in

the knyght, throgh the Strey[t]nys of the watyr, was caste doun, he *redeundo,*

and his hors, *and* drounde to-for ham all / whan Meyler, that *amnis im-*
petuosi

thedyr was with Reymonde come, this Sawe, he hadd gret envy *violentia*
raptum, ad

that Such boldnys sholde be tolde of any othyr, and noght of hym : *ima sub-*

vpon the hors that hym bare, he Put hym-Selfe in the watyr, *and* *mersumque*
non re-

boldely, wyth-out any ferde, Passid ouer the othyr syde. The *duxit.*

Citteseynys Saw hym comynge out of the watyr so al-oone : thay

came agayn hym, some forto kepe hym vpward at his comynge out

of the watyr, forto make hym turne agayn ; othyr, to vndo hym

ryght in the watyr. The knyght was stronge, and boldely Putte

hym vp be-twen two Perelis :—on oone halue, the wode rynnynge

A.D. 1175.

Meiler is
stoned and
shot at by
the Lim-
erick men.

Reimund

calls on his
troops to

save
Meiler.

He and all
his host
swim the
Shannon,
and take
Limerick.

[||Fol. 10
b.]

Which was
the boldest
of the
three?
Davy,
Meiler, or
Reimund?

watyr so grysly ; on other haluc, hys fomen, that with stonys & with
fawes hym leyden on, both at þe watyr, & vpon the wallys of the
toun, þat ryght vpon the watyr stode. He pute hys sheld & hys
heed wyth the helme ayeyns the dyntes, & hertely held hym amydde 4
al þat harme, alone, wythout any helpe, ful unseker on al syde : þe
crye was ful horyble on euery haluc. And Reymond, that was at þe
last of þe hoste, as hede & lodesman & prynce of al þe hoste, herde
the crye, & wyst nat yit what hyt was. He come anoon hastyly 8
thrughe al þe hoste, tyl he come to þe watyr; & when he sawe hys
neueu on that other syde, so narowe byladde, & on al syde besete
so narowe, he hadde grete angwysshe yn hys hert ; & sharpe &
byttyrly bygan to cry to hys felowes : " Men that so stalwarth 12
ben of ryght kynd, & yn so fele Anguysshes with vs hath your
streynth assayed, cometh forth, men ! the way ys open to-for vs,
& the ford that noon of vs ne couth, throgh hardynesse of our
y-found. folow we now the herty knyght, that so stronge ys 16
byladde, & let me hym neuer so neygh to-for our eghen be I-shent ! "
With that word, Reymond was þe fyrst that put hym yn þe watyr ;
& al þe hoste aftyr dyde ham yn aduentur, & yn goddys grace,
& wenten our al quyte, bot o knyght that hete Guy, & twey fote- 20
men. her fomen flowen [2] to-fore hem ynto the Cytè, & thay braken
yn aftyr, & wan the cytè, & slowen ful many of þe cytzeyns, &
dreyntten. Thay fonden ther so myche gold & syluer & other
rychesshe, that for that, & eke for the maystre || that god ham sent, 24
thay told lytel of the perylle & the lostes that thay hadde ther-to-
fore. Nowe arede ye, whyche was the hardyest of these thre
knyghtes? whether he, that wythout any man to-fore hym, put
hym yn-to the watyr for to techen al the other the weye ; Ather 28
he, that, aftyr ensample of hym, & the horyble death of ham that
weren I-dreynt to-fore har eyghen, passed the watyr, & al-one sette
so hardyly hys body to mark amonge so many fomen ; Other he,
that aftyr ham both, so hardyly & so boldly, with al the hoste, put 32
hym yn so gret perylle ? Thus was, as the [3] tyme, lymeryk I-wonne

---

[1] MS. fawes. Lat. creberrimis lapidum jaculorumque jactibus *Op.* v. 322.

[2] MS. slowen. Lat. fugatis in urbem hostibus, v 322.

[3] ? for 'at this.'

watyr so grymly; on the othyr syde, his enemys, that wyth stones *A. D. 1175.*
and with fawis hym leydyn on, both at the watyr, *and* vpon the *creberri-*
wallis of the toun, that ryght vpon the watyr stode.   he Put his *mis lapi-*
shelde and his hede wit*h* the sallet [1], agayn the strokys, *and* hertely *lorumque*
helde hym amyd al the Perelis al-one, wit*h*-out any helpe, ful [1] *galeam*
vnsur*e* on al sydis / the cry was ful horribill on euery syde.   And *clipeumque*
Reymond, that was at the laste of the hoste, as hede and ledder and *praeten-*
prynce of al the hoste, herde the cry, *and* wyst not what hit was. *dens.*
he come anoone hastely throw al the hoste, til he come to the watyr;
and whan he Saw his eme on that othyr syde, so narrow besette, *acriter ex-*
he hadd grete angwysche in his herte; and sharpe and bittyr began *clamavit:*
to cry to his fellouys, " Men, that So bolde ben, of ryght kynde, and *bus virtutis*
in so many angwyschis wit*h* vs hath your*e* streynth proued, come *insitum*
forth, men! they way is oppenyd̄ to-for vs; and the forde that noone *novimus a*
of vs knew, throgh boldnys of our*e* is founde.   followe now the herty *quorumque*
knyght that so stronge is by-ladde; *and* lette we neu*er* so ney to-for *gustiis ani-*
our*e* eyyne be shente!" wyth that worde, Reymonde was the fryste *mositatis*
that * Put Hym in the Watyr; and al the Hoste aftyr did Ham in *perti*
aduentur*e*, and in goddys grace, *and* wenten ou*er* al quyte, (but *Nota p̄a*
o knyght, that was callid Guy, *and* two footmen,) [2] her enemys *captionem*
kylledyn to-for hem, into the Cite [3], *and* Slowyn ful many of the *limeric.*
Citteseyn*es*, and dreyntyn [2].   Thay foundyn ther so mych golde and [*Fol. 18
Siluyr, and othyr riches, that for that, and also for the Maystry that b.]
god ham sende, thay tolde lytel of the Perel and the lostis that thay
hadd ther-to-fore.   Now ared þe, whyche was the boldyst of this
thre knyghtes: Whedyr he that, wit*h*-out any man to-for hym, put *Elige,*
hym in the watyr forto techyn al the othyr the wey; Othyr he that, *lector,*
aftyr Ensampill of hym, and the horribil deth of ham that weryn *rorum au-*
drovnde to-for har eyyn, Passid the watyr, *and* al-one sette so *mum.*
hardy his body, to marke, amonge so many ennemys; Othyr he that,
aftyr ham both, so hardy and so boldely, wit*h* al the hoste, Put hym
in so grette Peril.   Thus was as this tyme lymerike take on

[2–2] fugatis in urbem hostibus, non sine grandi civium strage, muros statim
irruperunt; et urbe potiti cum victoria, spoliis plurimum ditati et auro,
periculi damna lucri simul et laudis honore compensarunt.   v. 322–3.

[3] The English copier of this MS. has jumpt from the first ' Cite ' to the
second—see lines 21, 22 opposite,—and put ' killedyn ' = ' slowen ' l. 22 opp.
for ' flowen,' l. 21 opp.

A. D. 1175.
Three Victories on a Tuesday, the day dedicated by heathens to Mars.

one a tywesday [1]; Watyrford I-wonne one a tywesdaye, & dyuelyn also : noght for o coste was that day awayted þer-to, bot as hyt byfelle by cas & by adwentuꝛ; & nat wythout skyle, ffor the tywesday, by hethen men day yn the old world, was I-sette to a god 4 that day cleped Mars, & was I-hold god of bataylle; & on that day thay fonden, þat whoso bataylle besoght, he shold spede betteꝛ than yn oþer dayes.

[CHAPTER XXXIX.]

Reimund Fitz-Gerald

Now I wille yowe telle these twey stalwarth knyghtes, 8 Reymond & Meyler, whych thay weren. Reymond was a man brod of body, [2] somdel more than metlyche, yolowe heꝛ & sam-crysp, grey eyghen & depe, somdel heyghe nose, neb rody,

was a farseeing, self-restraind man,

wel I-hewed, glad semblant & cleeꝛ [2]; man of moche methe & of 12 grete purueyaunce; nothynge delycion, nothcr of mete ne of cloth; heet & cool, al I-lyche, wel he myght suffre; man of mych trauaylle; tholmode yn wreth; as redy he was to serue, to queme ham that he was ouer, as to be I-serued of ham. Whan he hoste 16 ladde, he was so besy about to kepe the host, that oft he left

watchful at night,

slepe al the nyght, & wandredde about, spyenge & crynge for to look þat noon harme ne shold betyde, & for he wold euer fyrst be redy, yf hyt nede wer. & shortlych to sygge hys thewes & hys 20

liberal,

maneres, he was man free & meke, queynt & purueynge; & thegh he wer swyth hardy & wel taght yn wepne, of quenyntyse & of

and most skilful in War.

sleyght yn syght, & of selth yn bataylle, he passed al otheꝛ [3]; & thegh he yn both weꝛ myche to preyse, he was betteꝛ leder of 24 hoste þan knyght.

[CHAPTER XL.]

Meiler lookt dark and stern.

Meyler was a man of durk semblant; blak eghen, & rogh lokynge; sterne semblant; of body, somdel more than methlych; ful stalwarth, wel I-brested, smal mydel [4], armes & other 28

---

[1] Later note in margin : 'Theꝛ-aftyre hyt was I-socoured one a tywsday.

[2-2] staturaeque paulo plus quam mediocris ; capillis flavis et subcrispis, oculis grossis, glaucis et rotundis, naso mediocriter elato, vultu colorato, hilari, ac sereno. Op. v. 323.

[3] et quanquam animosus plurimum, et armis instructus, prudentia tamen rebus in martiis et providentia praecellebat. v. 324.

[4] staturae paulo mediocri plus pusillae ; corpore tamen pro quantitatis captu pervalido ; pectore quadrato, ventreque substricto. v. 324.

a tyvysday, theraftyr hit was socourid on a tywysday, waterford A.D. 1175.
was take on a tyvysday, and deuelyn also. noght for oo Purpos *nec per in-*
was that day wayted therto, but as hit befell by case and by *dustriam*
aduenture, and not *with*-out skylle. For the tyvysday, by hethyn *casu solo*
men tyme in the olde worlde, was sette to a god that is callid Mars, *contigisse.*
and Was holde god of battayle; And on þat day thay fovndyn, that
who-so ba†tayl be-soght, he sholde spede bettyr that day than in
othyr dayes.

[CHAPTER XXXIX.]

NOwe y wille you telle thes two bolde knyghtes, Reymond *Capitulum*
and Meyler, whych they weryn // Reymond was a man *xxxix^m.*
brode of body, somdel more than metlych, yolowe here, and sam- Reymundi
crysp; grey eyyn and depe, Somdel hegh nose, face rody we[l] hewid, *Le gras.*
glad, semblante, *and* clere; man of mych mette *and* of grete Puruey- *Vir mo-*
aunce / nothynge delycious, nothyr of mete ne of cloth; [1] hette *and* *providus,*
colde, al y-lyke, wel he myght suffyr; man of mych trauail; *nec cibo*
tholmode in wreth; as redy he was to Serve, to queme ham that he *delicatus.*
was ou*er*, as to be s*er*uyd of ham [1]. Whan he hadd lost, he was so
byssy about to kepe the hoste, that ofte he lefte Slepe al the nyght,
and Walkid about, Spyeng*e* and crieng*e* forto loke that noone harme
ne sholde befall, and for he wolde eu*er* fryst be redy, yf hit nede
were. And Sortely to Say his condicionys and his maner*es*, he was
man fre and meke, queynt and Purueyyng*e*; *and* thegh he wer *providus*
Swyth hardy, *and* wel taght in wepyn, of queyntyse and of Sleght *et prudens.*
in fygh[t], *and* of Selth in battayl, he Passid al othyr; and thegh he *quidem*
in both wer*e* mych to Preyse [2], he was bettyr ledder of hoste than *militis*
knyght. *sed plus*
ducis.

[CHAPTER XL.]

MEyler was a man of durke semblant; [3] blake eyyne and rogh *Capitulum*
lokyng*e*; sterne Semblante; of body, somdel more than *xl^m.*
metlych, ful bolde, wel brestyde, smale myddyl, armys and othyr *nigris et*
torvis.

---

[1]—[1] caloris et algoris ei patientia par: vir patiens irae, patiensque laboris.
Quibus praesidebat prodesse magis quam praeesse, potiusque minister quam
magister videri volens.— *Op.* v. 324. (No Latin here for 'Whan ... nede were.')

H 2

lymmes ful bony, more synowy than fleysly. he was knyht ful

Meiler was never afraid of any enterprise.
hardy & enuyouse ; he was neuer aferde ne agryse to begynne thynge yn fyght that any man oght done hym on, Ather wyth otheꝛ y-meued[1]. In euery fyght, he was þe fyrst to begynne, & the 4

He 'd win or die. But he, and all the knights, robd the Church.
laste that hyt wold leue. Al þe stalwarthnese that any man myght do, he wold passe, or suffre deth; the maystrye & prys to wynne, otheꝛ deye,—nothynge he ne sette betwene. Of al thynge, bothe these knyghtes weꝛ to preyse myche wyth-al, neꝛ hyt that thay, 8 throgh couetyse, oft byname holy chyrch heꝛ ryghtes; bot more harme ys, & mychel to mourne, that defaute haddeꝰ meste al ouꝛ

Praises of the Fitz-Stephens, Fitz-Geralds, St. Davids, Fitz-Henrys, Fitzhughs, &c.
knyghtes from the forme begynnynge. What was Robert steuenessoꝰ & hys sonnes yn haꝛ tyme ? what, Moryce fytz 12 Geraud & hys sones ? what, Robert debarry, of whom ys to-fore I-told ? what, myles de seynt dauy ? both Robertes & Moryce neueuen, with þe formest boldly come ynto Irland ? what, Robert fyz henry, Meyleres brotheꝛ ? what, Reymond de Cante- 16 tone ? what, Robert de barry the yonge ? what, Reymond hues-

The memory of their pluck and grand deeds shall never die out.
sone ? what, otheꝛ of the selue gentrye, many & I-nowe, whych hyt waꝛ stronge to namen al by nam ? for no mane ne myght hyt bethynk, bot haꝛ stalwarthnesse ne heꝛ good deddes shold neuer 20 wend out of mynd. Thay weꝛ a folke & a kynrede, on two halue, kyndly, stalwarth, & hardy ; on other halue, of þe kynde of ffraunce,

[*Fol. 20 a.]
& theꝛ of wel I-taght yn wepne of myche * nenbre (?) of kynred & kynd stalwarthnesse euer more to heꝛ ende. Whan Reymonde 24

A. D. 1175.
hadde I-wonne the sytè of lymeryke, he ordeyned & puꝛueyed how the cytè myght be best I-kept; he lete brynge thedeꝛ

Reimund victuals Limerick, and leaves his cousin, Miles of St. David's, in charge of it.
vyttaylle on euery halue grete plente, & lefte þer Myles of seynt dauy, with fyfty knyghtes & squyers an-hors, & ccc bowmen, 28 & with þe other parte of the hoste wyth yoy & gladnesse al harmles turned ayeyne ynto leynestre.

[CHAPTER XLI.]

Hervey of Montmaurice euvies
The lond was þan yn good pees vnder Reymondes kep-ynge, so that non Iresshe-man ne durst hym stur to 32 mysdom. Heruy of Mommorthy, that euer hadde enuy to hym,

---

[1] Miles animosus et aemulus; nihil umquam abhorrens, quod aggredi quis vel solus debeat vel comitatus, v. 324.

lym*es* full bony, mor*e* synowy than fleshy. he was knyght ful Descripcio

hardy *and* Enuyouse; he was newyr*e* aferde ne agryse to begynne Melerij.

thynge in fyght that any man ogh don hym o͞n, * Althyr wyth [*Fol. 19

othyr ymewyd. In euery fyght, he was the fryst to Begynne, and þe ª·]

laste hit to leue; al the boldn*es* that any man myght do, he wolde

Passe, or suffyre dethe. The maystry and Prysce to wyn othyr dye, *inter mor-*

nothynge he ne sette betwen. Of al thynge, both this knyghtes *tis et martis*

wer*e* to Preyse mych wyth-all, ner*e* hit that thay, throgh covetyse, *triumphos, nihil me-*

ofte toke holy church ryghtes; but mor*e* harme is, *and* gretly to *dium ponens.*

morne, that defaute haddyn meste al our knyghtes frome the fryst

begynnynge. / What was Robert Steuenes-sone *and* his Sonnys;

What, Robert de barry, of whom is to-for tolde; What, Morice fiz-

geraud *and* his sonnes; What, Miles de seynte dauy; both Robert

and Morices emys, that wyth the fryst boldely come into Irland;

what, Robert fiz-henry, Meyler-is brodyr; What, Reymonde de

Canteton; What, Robert de barry the yonge; What, Reymond Hues- *Quid alii*

Sone; What, othyr of the same gentil, many *and* y-now, whych hit *generosi-tatis ejus-*

wer*e* stronge to telle by name? for no man ne myght hit be-thynke, *dem quam plurimi,*

but har boldenys ne her good dedys shold neu*er* go out of mynde. *cuibus*

¹ They wer a pepill and a kynred, on both sydys, be kynde, bolde and *insignia singulorum*

hardy; on othyr halue of the kynd*e* of Fraunc*e*, *and* ther-of wel *gesta perennem*

taght in wepyn, of mych nembre, of kynred and kynde bolde, eu*er* *poterant laudis*

more to her ende¹ // Whan Reymonde hadd take the Cite of lymerike², *memoriam*

he ordeynyd̄ *and* Purueyed how the Cite myght be best kepte: he *promereri?*

lette brynge thedyr vytayłł, on eu*er*y halue, grete Plente; *and* lefte ²A. D. 1175.

ther Miles of Seynt dauy, w*ith* fifty knyghtes *and* Squyerys an hors,

and CCC bowmen; *and* wyth the othyr Parte of the hoste, w*ith* Ioy

and gladnys, al harmeles, turned agayn Into leynystr*e*.

[CHAPTER XLI.]

THe londe was than in good Pees vndyr Reymondys kepynge, Cap*itulum*

So that non Irysh̃-man durst not styr hym to mysdone. *Herreius*

Heruey of Mounmorthy, that eu*er* had Enuy to hym, ne lefte not, *de Monte Mauricii.*

---

¹⁻¹ O genus! O gens! gemina natura, a Trojanis animositatem, a Gallis

armorum usum originaliter trahens.—*Op.* v. 326.

ne left nat, for the allyance that was ham betwene, þat he ne
dydde hym al þe harme that he myght, & opynly shewed than
þe felony that he longe hadde I-borne yn hys hert. He sent ouer
to þe kynge by Messagers, [1]& made hym to vnderstond that 4
Reymond was yn yndygnacion of the kynge; & ayeyne hys owne
trouth, so hauteyn I-worth, that he wold al Irland take to hym
& to hys [1]; &, for hys lesynges shold þe bettyr be y-leued, feel
þynges he made hym to vndrestond, & so fayr hyt slyked wyth 8
falsnesse, that hyt somet sothe, al that he seyde. The kynge—as
ofte manere ys that lydder tales ben bettyr I-leued, & lenger
I-thoght, that good—he beleued þe fals mannys talys & wryynge,
& sent yn-to Irland four Messagers, that ys to wytten, Robert 12
the power, Osbern of herford, Wyllyam Berynger, & Adam of
yarnemouth, of whych the twey shold abyde with the Erle yn
Irland, & þe other tweyn shold wende ayeyne ynto England wyth
Reymond, as þe kynge hym hadde COMMAWNDET. 16

[CHAPTER XLII.]

Heruy was a man fayr & lygne, eyghen grey & depe,
ouelyche lokynge, fayr semblaunt, of fayr spech & wordes
wel besete; of body more than methlych, of al lymmes ful
becomly; bot as fayr & as becomly as he was wytout, as lydder 20
& as fals of many maner lastes he was wyt-In; ffor, fro the tyme
that he was chyld, he yaf hymself to lecherye; & nat only to many
sengle wommen; bot he ne synned neþer spousbrych ne syblynges;
he was onful & bakbyter, [2] wreyer, false & traytur, duble of 24
tonge & nothyng stydfaste, butt yn [2] falsnesse hys speche thoght
as thogh hyt wer hony & mylk out of hys mouthe, bot euer hyt
was I-meygnet with attyr at þe ende. Som tym he was stalwarth,
as to knyght longeth; bot aftyr, he yaue hym selue more to 28
cowerdyse than to knyghthode; & more he couth hym maken,
than he was worth [3]; hegh of berynge yn hous, & noght of plente;
of mych speche, & lytel sothnesse.

[1—1] illi sinistre rerum eventum indicarit: asseverans quoque Reimundum,
contra regis honorem, et fidem debitam, non tantum Limericum, verum etiam
Hiberniam totam, sibi suisque jam occupare proculdubio proposuisse.—*Op.* v. 327.

[2—2] These words are in a different hand.   [3] MS. wroth.

for the alyaunce that was ham betwen, that he ne did hym al the *harme* that he myght, and opynly shewed than the felony that he longe thoght in herte. he sende ouer to the kynge by messangerys, *and* did hym to vndyrstonde, that Reymonde was in indignacion of the kynge; *and* agayn his owyn throuth, so Hauteyn I-worth, that he wolde al Irland take to hym *and* to his. And, for his lesyngys sholde the bettyr be belewid, ¹ many lesyngys he made hym to vndyrstonde; and So fayre hit glosyd with lesyngis, that hit Semyd trouth, al that he sayde¹. The kynge,—as ofte maner is, that fals talys ben bettyr belewid, *and* lengyr thoght², than good,—he belewid the fals manes talys and accusynge, And Sende Into Irlan͏d' foure Messagers, that is to wittyn, Robert de Power, Osbern of Herforde, Willam Berynger, And adam of Iarnemouth³; of the whych, two sholde abyde with the Erle in Irland, *and* the othyr two sholde wende agayn in-to England, with reymond, as the kynge hym hadd comandyd.

[margin:] A.D. 1175.

[margin:] Et ut hoc figmentum delator regiis auribus tutius et probabilius praesentaret. ² memoria diuturnior. Nota de aduentu Powerencium in Hiberniam.

[CHAPTER XLII.]

HEruey was a man fayre and lygne, eyghyn grey and depe⁴, lolych lokynge, fayre semblant, of fayre Speche *and* wordys wel besette * of body more than metlych, of al Lymmys wel becomly; But as fayre and as Becomly as he was wyth-out, As wickyd and as fals of many maner lastes he was wyth-In. // Fro the tyme that he was chylde, he yaue hym-Selfe to lechery, *and* not only to many Syngyl Women⁵, but he ne synnyd neuer spousebrich ne siblynges; he was onfull *and* bacbyter, wreyer, fals *and* trechoure, doubill of tonge, and nothynge stydfast but in falsnesse; his spech, as hit were honny *and* mylke out of the mouth, but euer hit was medlid with wenym at the Ende. Sometym he was bolde, as longyth to a knyght; but aftyr, he yafe hym [more] to cowardyse than to knyght-hode; *and* more he made of hym-Selfe than he was worth; hey of beryuge in house, *and* not of plente; of myche speche, *and* lytyl trouth.

[margin:] Capitulum xliij^m. Descripcio Heruei. [*Fol. 19 b.] ⁴ prominentibus aspectu amabili. ⁵ nec incestus ullos, nec adulteriam vitans. Vir invidus, delator, et duplex; vir subdolus, facetus, et fallax.

¹⁻¹ ad votum effectui mancipandum, in Bragmannorum morem conjuratas ad hoc catervas Reimundum asserit composuisse. v. 327.

³ Robertum Poerium, et Osbertum de Herlotera, Gulielmum de Bendinges, et Adam de Gernemes. v. 328.

[CHAPTER XLIII.]

A. D. 1176.

Reimund hears that Donnell O'Brien, King of Limerick, is besieging the English there.

Reymond hym dyght for to wende ynto England, as the kynge hym commandet; & nothynge abode, bot wynd & wedyr at the see : come Messagers, hastyly I-sent from the meygne of lymeryke, & tolden that Obreen, the kynge of thomond, was 4 belyggynge lymeryke with ful grete hostes; &, for þey hadden all the wytaylle þat Reymond ham lefte & eke that thay hadden ther-aftyr I-puchassed yn the wenter-tyme, al I-spendet, me shold ham hastyly send socoure. The Erle was ful anguysshous ham 8 for to socour, & spake þer-of to the meygne, & besoght ham wel yonre (yorne ?) theder to go ; bot thay war so wroth & so sory for Reymondes wendynge awey, that euerychon, with oo mouth, for-soken alout, that, without Reymond, for nothynge theder thay 12 nold wend. The Erle toke consaylle her, of the kynges messagers ;

Reimund marches for Limerick, [*Fol. 20 b.]

&, for the thynge was yn grett perryll, at þe end, throgh bysy besechynge of the erle & eke of ham, Reymond turned ayeyne the baneres toward * lymeryke. And as thay come toward 16 Casshel wyth the hoste,—as myght be, syxty knyghtes, & two hundret squyers & thre hundret bowmen, wythout Iresshe-men

with McMurrough of Okensely and King Donnell of Ossory.

that comen eke wyth ham, as Macmorgh of okensely & dofnild of osserye,—me come to ham, & told ham, fore that þay of 20 thomon hadde I-lefte þe sege of lymeryke, & wer I-comen ayeyns ham, to kepe ham yn the paas of Casshel ; & thegh the paas

The men of Thomond barricade the Pass of Cashel against the English.

was stronge yn hymselfe, thay kesten adoun tren, & made dyches thar towr, & hegges vpon, for noon horsman ne shold ouer wend. 24 Whan thay weren negh to the pas I-comen, Reymond deled the hoste a thre. & downyld, þe kynge of Ossery, that ful mychell hated, & foman was to, ham of thomon, saw þe Englyshe hoste— thegh thay fewe wer—of ful good herte, & wel & semly I-wepned, 28

K. Donnell of Ossory appeals to the Anglo-Irish force to fight bravely.

for thay shold be þe trustyer, & the bettre herte haue to hem, & seyd, "Men, that þys lond wyth stalwarthnesse haue I-wonne, assayleth today styfly your fomen ! ffor yf, ye, as your won ys, ouercometh, & the maystry haue ; our sparthes, forth wyth yowr 32 swerdys, our fomen smertly shulle folowen aftyr ; & yf ye—that god forbede !—ben ouercome, syker be ye that we forth with our fomen wyllen turne vpon yowe. Take hede, knygthtes, & vnderstondeth, your townes & your castels ben welle ferr hennes, & 36

[CHAPTER XLIII.]

REymond made hym redy to go into England as the Capitulum xliij^m.
   kynge hym commaundid and nothynge abode but wynde
and wedyr at the See. Come messagers hastely sende frome A. D. 1176.
the meny of lymerike, and toldyn that Obreen, the kynge of
Thomonde, was besegyn lymerike with ful grete hostis; and, for *quoniam*
thay haddyn al the vytaill that Reymonde with ham had lefte, *omnia ali-*
menta, tam
and also that thay purchasid sithenys, thay had al spende, And *ibi inventa*
quam at-
that thay sholde hastely sende ham Socoure. The Erle was ful *tracta,*
angwyschous ham for-to socoure and Spake therof to the meny *brumali*
tempore
and besoght ham wel ofte thedyr to go, but thay were so wroth *consump-*
serant.
and So sory for Reymondes goynge away, thay euerchone wyth o *se illuc*
woyse forsokyn al, that wyth-out Reymonde for no-thynge thedyr *ituros*
absque
thay wolde goo. / The Erle toke consayl her-of of the kynges *Reimundo*
messangers, and for the thynge was in gret Perel. at the Ende *omnes*
unanimiter
throw besechynge of the Erle and also of ham Reymond turned *contra-*
dicerent.
agayn the baners toward lymerike. And as thay come to-ward
cassel with the hoste—as myght be, Sixti knyghtys and two hundrid ^1 *audivit*
Tuhetmo-
Squyeres and iij^c bowmen, without Iryssh-men that comyn also *nienses,*
obsidione
with ham, as Macmurgh of O-kensley and dofnyld of Ossery—thay *relicta, ei*
come to ham, and tolde ham, ^1 fore that thay of Thomon hadd lefte *in passu*
Cassiliensi
the sege of lymerike, and were comyn agaynes ham, to kepe ham in *obviam*
the Paas of Casshel; and thegh the Paas was stronge in hym-Selfe, *venisse; et*
locum,
thay castyn adoun trees, and made dichis thartowre, and heggys *natura*
difficilem,
vpon, for noone hors-man ne sholde ouer-wende. When thay wer *confragis*
ney to the Paas y-come, Reymond delid the host a thre. And *arborum*
et fossatis
downyld, the kynge of Ossory, that gretly hatid, and enemy was *plurimum*
to ham of Tomonde, Saw the Englyssh host (thegh thay few were) *exaspe-*
rasse;
of ful good herte, and wel semely wepenyd; and for thay sholde be *sepem*
the trustier, and the bettyr herte haue to them; and sayde, " Men, *quoque*
fortissi-
that wyth boldnes this londe haue conquerid, assaylyth this day *mam ex*
styfly youre enemys! For an ye, as youre wone is, ouercomyth, and *transverso*
locasse.
the maystry haue, our Sparrys, forth with youre Swerdys, oure ^2 *in vos cum*
enemys smyrtly shull follow aftyr. And yf ye (that god forbede!) *hostibus*
procul-
ben ouer-come, syckyr be ye ^2 that we forth with oure enemys wil *dubio con-*
turne vpon yow. Take hede, knyghtys, and vndyrstondyth, youre *vertentur.*
* tounys and your castelys Ben wel ferre Hennes, and the flyght ful [*Fol. 20
a.]

A. D. 1176. the flyght ful longe, & our maner ys, to helpe ham that ben omost, & folowe the fleynge. trysteth wel to vs ; bot no lenger than the ouer hand ys your." ❡ Whane thys was yseyd, Meyler, þat was yn the formeste of the host, smertly spronge out, as sparke out of fyr; & al the host aftyr stalwartly com to the pas; & nat wyt-out gret slaght of ham that wythstoden, opened the way, & wentten ouer an estre euen, & a thrydde ester day, that ys to wentten, on a tywesday, as at the other tyme. Also nowe, the host come ynto lymeryk, Reymond lete ryght & arer that, throgh the sege of har fomen, was I-wasted & destrued. & nat lange ther-aftyr, he held parlement wyth the kynge of Connaght & the kynge of Thomon, bot yn oo day bot nat yn o place; ffor the kynge of Connaght held hym yn the watyr of the shynen, yn a myche logh, yn botys, & the kynge of Thomon was thar negh yn a wodde. Reymond was betwene two, at kyldalo, as myght by, syxten myle frome lymeryk. Ther was the parlement so fer forth I-dryuen, that euery of ham delyuered to Reymond good hostages, & othes many-fold sworne hold & trewe, yn good pees for to hold euer efte to the kynge & to hys. Whan thys was I-done, & Reymond turned ayeyne wyth hys hostages to lymeryke, þe prynce of desmond, Dermot Maccarthy, sent by messagers to Reymond, & besoght hym that he ayeyne hy[s] eldeste sone that hete Cormoc Olethan—tha[t] wel negh hym out of hys kynge-dome I-putte—hym, as the kynges trew man, shold helpe ; & large yiftes he byhete, both to Reymond & the meygne, wyth that that thay wold hym helpe. Reymond, as man that had nat loth wynnynges, ne hymself to auaunce, spake her-of to hys falawes, & thay alle graunted to don as he wold, & turned the baners toward the Contreys of Cork. by weyes as thay wentten, thay name many prayes, wher-of the meynge was ful wel apayed, & mych ther-of was oft I-sent to lymeryk, so longe, that throgh help of Reymonde, Dermot recouered al hys kyngedome vpon hys sone —of whyche he was negh I-pute owt :—the sone was I-take & delyuered to the fadyr, & he hym pute yn pryssoun, & nat longe ther-aftyre hym be-lete take out of pryssoun, & smyth of hys hede.

4

8

12

16

20

24

28

32

36

Meiler Fitz-Henry leads the attack, and forces the Pass on Easter Eve April 3. They enter Limerick, and repair it.

Reimund, at

Killaloe,

induces the Irish rebels to swear allegiance to Henry II. He then agrees to help Dermot Mac-Carthy against his son Cormack.

Reimund marches to Cork, and beats Cormack,

who is put in prison, and then beheaded.

Longe. [1] And our*e* man*er* is, to helpe ham that ben omyste, and A. D. 1176. follow the fleyng*e*. trystyth wel to vs; but no longyr than ye haue the ou*er* hande " / Whan this was sayde, Meyler, that was in the formyst of the hoste, smyrtly styrte out, as sparke of fyr*e*; and al the host aftyr, boldely come to the Paas; *and* not wyth-out gret slaght of ham that wythstodyn, openyd the way, *and* wentyn ou*er* an Estre-evyn, and the thyrd Estyr-day, that is to say, on a tyvysday, as at the othyr tyme. also now þe hoste come to lymerik, Reymond lette rere that throw the sege of har enemys was wastid̃ *and* destrued. *and* not lange ther-aftyr, he helde Parlement wyth the kynge of Connaght *and* the kynge of Thomonde, both in oo day, but not in oo Place; For the kynge of Connaght helde hym in the watyr of shynnyn, in a myche logh, in botis, and the kynge of Thomonde was thar negh in a wodd̃. Reymonde was betwen two at kyldalo, as myght by, syxtene mile from lymerik. Ther was the Parlement So fer forth drywen, that eu*er*y of ham delyuerid to Reymond good hostagis, *and* othis manyfolde Sworn, holde and trew, in good Pees forto holde eu*er* aftyr to the kynge and to his. Whan this was don, *and* Reymond turned agayn wi*th* his hostagis to lymerike, the P*ri*nce of Desmonde, Dermot Maccarthy, sende by messagers to Reymonde, and besoght hym that he-agayn his eldyst Sone that hete Cormok Olethan, that wel ney hym out of his kyngdome Putte,—hym, as the kyng*es* trew man, sholde helpe; *and* large yftys he Promysyd, both to Reymond *and* the meny, yf thay wolde hym helpe. Reymond, as man that had no loth wynnynges, ne hym-Selfe to auctorice, Spake herof to his fellowis; and thay al graunted to do as he wolde, and turned the baners toward the contreis of Corke. [2] by weyes as thay wentyn, thay rerid many Prayes, Wherof the meny was ful wel appayed and wel arrayed, *and* mych therof was ofte sende to lymerik. So longe, that by the helpe of Reymond, Dermot recoverid al his kyngdome vpon his sone, of whom he was ney Putt out / the Sone was take, and delyuerid to the Fadyr; and he Putt hym in prysone. and not longe ther-aftyr, hym he lette take out of pryson, *and* smyte of his hede.

Nota quod hibernici non sunt amici nisi quandiu forma faciet.

[1] *Et nos victoribus semper adhae- rentes, solum per- sequimur fugientes. De nobis itaque confidite, sed vic- tores.*

fidelitatem Anglorum regi et suis de cetero inviolabi- liter exhi- bendam sacra- mentis corpora- liter prae- stitis reno- vaverit.

[2] *Multis itaque tum praedis in brevi quam stipendiis, familia in partibus illisabunde refecta, et alimen- torum copia Li- mericum abinde persaepe transmissa.*

A.D. 1176.   [CHAPTER XLIV.]

The whyle that Reymond was in this maner yn
desmon, come a Messager to hym ffrom dyuelyn,
hastyly I-sent, & broght hym a *lettre* from basile, hys wyf; bot
he that hyt broght, wyst nat what hyt was. Reymond hadde 4
wyth hym a clerk that he wel tryst to; he lete hym rede the
lettre priuelych, that thus myche hym seyde: "To hyre leue
lord & hyr spouse Reymond, hys basyle sendeth gretynge. as to
hyr̄ selue, wyt thou, lef man, that the grete chek-toth that so sore 8
me oke, ys I-falle. Wherfore, yf thou any thynge recheste of thy
self, other of me, ne leue nat to come hastyly to me." Whan
Reymond thys herd, he vnderstode that the mych toth that hyr
was I-falle, betokned þe Erles deth; for he lefte hym ful seke at 12
dyuelyne, whan he parted from hym. And thegh he lange ther̄-to-
fore was ded, for̄ drede of Iresshe-men he was for-hold tyl
Reymondes comes, & the meygnees, ynto leynestre. Reymond
turned sone to lymeryke. & þe sorow that was yn hys hert 16
with-yn, he, for al hyt, as myche as he myght, *with* fayr semblant
makynge *with*-out; & ful fewe men, he shewed the aduentur̄ that
so sodeynly was byfalle; & of ham that mooste good kouth, he
besoght consaylle & rede, what was ham to done. Than was 20
comenly har̄ rede such: "what fore the erles deth, what for
Reymondes wendynge out of the lond, that the sytè of lymeryke,
that was so ferr̄, & amonge so many enemyes, me shold leue voyde;
& al the meygne holy led ynto leynestre, þe townes vpon þe see 24
& the castels for to kepe." Reymond, thegh hym loth wer̄,
*gra*unted thys, & stod to har̄ rede; &, for he ne fond none that
aftyr hym wold ther̄ abyde, he betoke Obreen̄, the kynge of
thomon̄, the Cytè to kepe as the kynges baroun, & toke of hym 28
efte newe hostages, & many new othes I-swore, the toun harmles
for to kepe, & the pees trewly for to hold. Vpon̄ thys forward,
thay wentten al out of the Cytè, & lefte Obren̄ & hys men *with*-yn;
& vnnethes thay war̄ I-passed the brygge, that þe tother̄ end nas 32
I-broken̄ anoon ryght behynd ham, & þe toun, that wel & fast was
I-walled, & wel I-byld *with* good housses I-herl erged o wyttaylle
that on euery half þether was I-broght well I-stoffe[1], nat *with*out

[CHAPTER XLIV.]

A.D. 1176.

The whyle that Reymond was in this maner in
desmonde, come a Messager to hym frome deuelyn,
Hastly sende, and broght hym a lettyr frome basyle, his wyfe;
but he that hit broght, wyst not what hit was. Reymond hadd
with hym a clerke that he trust wel to. / He mad him rede the
lettyr priuely, þat thus mych hym sayde: " To hir welbelowid lorde
and Spouse, Reymond, his basylle sendyth gretynge. as to hyre-
Selfe, wit thou, lefe man, that the grete chektoth that so sore me
grewid, is falle; Werfor, yf ye rekyth any-thynge of youre-Selfe,
othyr of me, ne leue not to come hastely to me." When Reymond
this herde, he vndyrstod by the mych toth, that * Hyr was fall,
Betokenyd the Erlys deth; for He Lefte Hym ful seke at deuelyn
when he lefte hym. And thegh he lang therto-for was ded, for
fere of Irysh-men, he was for-holde tyl Reymondes comys and
the menyes, in-to leynystere. Reymond turned sone to lymerike.
and the Sorrow that was in his herte wythin, ¹ he, for al hit, as
mych as he cowthe, made fayre semblant without ¹; and to ful few
men he shewid the aduenture that so sodeynly was byfall; and of
ham that moste good couth, he besoght consayl and rede, what was
ham to done. Than was comynly har consail Such, " what for the
Erlys deth, what for Reymondys ² wendynge out of the londe, that
the Cite of lymerik, that was so ferre, and amonge so many enemys,
that they sholde leue woyde; and al the meny, holy lede Into
leynystere, the tovnes and the castelys vpon the See forto kepe."
Reymond, thegh loth hit was to hym, gravntyd this, and stode to
har rede; and, for he ne found none that aftyr hym wolde byde
there, He yaue Obreyn, the kynge of Thomonde, the Cite to kepe
as the kynges barovne, and toke of hym, fryst, new hostagis, and
many new othys Sware, the touñe harmles forto kepe, and the Pees
trewely forto hold / Vpon thys, thay wentyn al out of the Cite,
and lefte obreen and his men within / and vnnethys thay were
Passyd the brige, that the othyr ende nas brokyn anoone ryght
behynde ham; and the toun, that wel and faste was wallid, ³ and wel
bylid with good houses, I-herbergid of wytalis, that on euery halfe
thedyr was broght wel Stuffid, not wythout gret Sorynys of herte,

² de[parting?] at first written here.

Marginal Latin notes:
Capitulum xliiijᵐ.
nota De morte comitis Richardi.
quod dens ille molaris et magnus, qui tantum mihi dolu- erat, jam cecidit.
[*Fol. 20 b.]
usque ad Reimundi famili- aeque redi- tum.
¹⁻¹ exte- riore vultus hilaritate valde dissi- mulans.
totamque familiam integre.
Duvenaldo Tuhetmo- niae prin- cipi.
³ aedificiis decenter ornatam, alimentis undique congestis plane refertam.

A. D. 1176. grette sorynesse of hert, thay sawe on fourͬ partyes I-sette afyrͬ;

O'Brien burns Limerick. & thys the traytoᵤr Obren shewed openlych how me shal tryst to Iryshemen trouth. ❡ Reymond, with all the meygne, wentt hym

Richard Fitz-Gilbert, Earl of Striguil, is buried. tho to dyuelyɴ; & the Erles body, that by hys byddynge was I-kept 4 vnburyed, [was buryed] yn the modyr-church of þe Trynyte, to-for the swete rode, by procurynge of sent laurence, that was yn that tyme erchebysshoppe of dyuelyɴ.

[CHAPTER XLV.]

Henry II's Commissioners go back to him. Aftyrͬ that þe Erle was dede, the kynges mes- 8 sagers, that wereɴ aftyr Reymond I-come, vpon newe aduenturs toke new consaylle. Thay lefte Reymond keper of Irland, & wentten ham ynto Engeland hastyly to the kynge, &

Nota the goodnesse of Geraud. Henry II sends Wm. de Courcy Fitz-Aude-line and others to Ireland. told hym of the erles deth, & the state of the lond. The kynge 12 sent than ynto Irlande, Wyllyam aldelinessesone, procuratoᵤr of the lond, with x knyghtes of hys owɴ priue meygne; & with hym, Ihoɴ de Courcy with other x; Robert steuenessone & Myles de Cogaɴ, þat al two yerͬ yn engeland & yn gascoyne nobly haddeɴ with the 16 kynge I-be, come þaɴ ynto Irland with xxᵗⁱ knyghtes. Tythynges come to Reymond that thay warͬ arryued; & he anoon-ryght went

[*Fol. 21 b.] Reimund yields all his towns and host-ages. His fine retinue excites Fitz-Aude-line's envy, ayeyns ham with mych gladnesse * & fayr felawshyppe of knyghtes to Weysford. Ther he yeld vp to Wyllyam, as to Seneschal from 20 the kynge I-sent, al the kynges townes, & hys castels, & al the ostages of Irland. Wylliam sawe Reymond wyth so many & so fayr yonglynges bylad, & beheld Meyllerͬ & other knyghtes of hys kyn, fayr & rychely y-wepned of o maner vepne, wel thrytty, vpon 24 ful fayrͬ hors, sheldes about harͬ nekkes, & spers yn hand, pleynge to-geddre ynto al the feldes: he turned hym to hys men, & seyd al soft, "Thys pryd shal be pute In, ar hyt be lange, & þese sheldes to-dreued." Ffro that tyme euer aftyr, these & meste al 28 otherͬ proc[ur]atours yn Irland, as thoght hyt werͬ by on oth togeddre I-swore, throgh ond & enuy ne stynt neuer to besech

and he always works against Reimund and the Geraldines. Reymond & Meillerͬ, Robertes sones, & Moryce, & al that kynrede, al þe enuy that þay myght & durst; for þys ys euermore barͬ 32 wayte & harͬ aduentur: euer whaɴ grete nede byfelle yn tyme of werͬ, thay war lef & derward, & the formeste to I-clepped, & to bataylle, throgh hardynes, formest & fyrst redy: whaɴ non ned was,

thay Saw on foure Parties sette afyre. And thus the tray-toure A.D. 1176.
Obreyn shewid opynly how we sholde trust to Iryssh-men trouth // *corpus*
Reymond, *with* al the meny, went to deuelyn; and the Erlis body *comitis*
that by his byddynge was kepte vnburied [was buried] in þe modyr *quod ...*
church of the trynyte, to-for the Swete Rode, by *procurynge* of *servatum*
Seynt laurance, that was in that tyme Archebyschope of Deuelyn. *... in ec-*
clesia ...
est tumu-

[CHAPTER XLV.]

latum.

Aftyr that the Erle was dede, the kynges mes- *Capitulum*
sangers, that weryn aftyr Reymond come, vpon new *xlvᵐ.*
aduentures toke new consail. Thay lefte Reymond keper of *goodnys*
Irland, *and* thay went into Inglande hastely to the kynge, and tolde *of Geral-*
dynes.
hym of the Erle-is deth, *and* the state of the londe // The kynge *Nota de*
sende than into Irland, Willam Aldelinys Sone, Procuratoure of the *adventu*
Willelmi
londe, x. knyghtis of his owyn Pryue meny; And *with* hym Ihon de *Addellini*
filij, et
Cursi, *with* othyr x; Robert Steuen-es [sone] *and* Miles de cogan, *Iohannis*
that al two yere in England' and in gascoyn nobely haddyn *with* *de Cursi,*
in Hiber-
the kynge be,come than Into Irland *with* xxᵗⁱ. knyghtis. Thythynges *niam.*
come to Reymond that thay ware londid'; *and* he anone-ryght went *¹ Super-*
agaynes ham *with* mych gladnys, *and* fayre felochipp of knyghtes, *biam*
hanc, in
to weysforde. Ther he yaue to Willam, as to Senescal from the *brevi com-*
kynge sende, al the kynges townes, and his castelis, and al the *primam, et*
clipeos
hostages of Irland. Willam Saw Reymond *with* so many and so *istos*
fayre yonglynges * Bylad, And Be-Helde Meyler and Othyr *dispergam.*
Knyghtes of His Kyn, fayre and riche wepenyd of o maner *[*Fol. 21*
a.]
wepyn, wel xxxᵗⁱ, vpon ful fayre hors, sheldys aboute har neckys,
and sperris in honde, Pleyynge to-gadderes in-to al the feldys.
He turned hym to his men, *and* sayde al softe, "This Pryde shal *Nota de*
be Put In¹ ar hit be lange, and this sheldys to-dreued." Fro that *geraldinis.*
Nota
tyme euer aftyr, *and* thes *and* most al othyr procuratoures in *causam*
invidie
Irland, as thegh hit were by one othe to-giddyr Sworne, throgh *inter*
hate and envy ne stynte thay neuer to malyngne agaynys Reymond *aldelini*
filium et
and meyler, Robert-es Sonnes *and* Morices, and al the kynred of *geraldinos*
geraldines, al the envy that thay myght *and* durste; for this is
euer-more har abydynge *and* har aduenture: Euer whan grete *Semper in*
armata
nede bifel in tyme of werre, thay wer lefe *and* derwarde, *and* the *militia*
fryst to be callid for bolnys, *and* to battail fryst redy: whan no *cari.*

A. D. 1176. anooñ thay weꝛ loth, & I-pute abake ; heꝛ felowsʰyp I-left yñ yurne
to harme. Na the wodde of haꝛ gentryce, throgh non enuy ne
myght neuer be I-rotet ; for euer ham spryngyth new spourges, of

Yet the whych the myght yn the lond nys nat lytelle. Who beth that 4
Geraldines
won and kepeth the contreys ? the Geraudynes : Who throgh þurleth the
kept
Ireland. hostes ? the Geraudynes : Who ben that fomen adredeth ? þe
Geraudines : Who ben that enuy bacbyteth ? þe Geraudines.

Had justice Hade thay I-found prynce yn any tyme, that haꝛ stalwarthnesse 8
been done
them, ham had y-yold, as thay worthy weꝛ, yn good pees & stydfast
they 'd
have held hadden I-broght the state of Irland. Bot thegh thay nededen
the land in neuer so well, thay ne hade bot lytele thanke, otheꝛ noon ; haꝛ
peace.
trauaylle yuel I-yold, & ouerthrow yn haꝛ goodnesse, & mysbeleue 12
& bacbyttynge of haꝛ stalwarthnesse ; & to otheꝛ, the prynces
trysten, wyt whych no staluarthnese was I-founde, ne no power
hadde well to done without helpe & socouꝛ of ham. And also

Fitz- Aldelinese-sone, at hys comynge ynto Irland, he wente from toun to 16
Audeline
sought his toun vpoñ þe see, & þrogʰ soght the Cyttes theꝛ plente was of
ease, and mete & drynke ; bot the monteynes, & þe londes with-In, nold he
neuer come negʰ. gold & syluyre, whaꝛ-of mych plente was yn þe

opprest lond, wel hungrylych he gaderede, to helpe-with pledynge & 20
the poor,
not the pullynge of pees men, & nogh of theues ne of reuers. In that
thieves. tyme, about myd-heruest, Moryce fyzt-Geraud deyed, nat without
Maurice
Fitz- gret Sorynesse of al hys, & mych harme & lost to al Irland ; ffor
Gerald dies he was a man methefull, suttell, & stalwarth : treweꝛ man ne 24
about Sept.
1. No stydfaster mañ, ne left he non yn Irland. ⁌ Wyllyam adelinese-
truer man
was left in sone ran Moryce sones to harme anon, & ne stynt neuer tyl he
Ireland.
Fitz-Aude- hadde I-take of hym þe Castel of Wykelowe wyth falsnesse. of
line robs Reymond & Robert steuenesse-sone, he name the londes that thay 28
Maurice's
sons. hadden yn the vale of dyuelyn & yn Ophelayn ; & otheꝛ that
hadden londes yñ pes, he name thay londes to the kynges behoud,
& delyuered ham londes furthyre yñ marche, & yn perryll nexth

No one is haꝛ fomen : al with vnryght, & by hys owne wyll ; ffor theꝛ ys 32
so keen as
an upstart nothynge so bold ne so kene as ys that mañ that ys of noght
set to rule. I-come, Whan he ys an-hegh I-broght, & vnkyndely I-sette yn
maystry. ⁌ Wyllyam was a man mych of body, & of makynge ;

[*Fol. 22 *good met-yeuer ; fre & corteys by semblant ; bot al that he dyde any 36
a.]

nede was anoon they wer*e* hatyd *and* Putte abake, her fellochip A.D. 1176.
left *and* turne to harme. // Na the wodd of har gentryce, throgh Not*a* de
non envy ne myght, neu*er* be y-roted, for eu*er* ham spryngyth geraudynes.
new Spourgis, of whych the myght in the londe is not lytell.
What ben thay that kepyth the contrayes? the Geraudynes. Who *Qui sunt*
throw thurlyth the hostis? the geraudines. Who ben that Enemys *qui penetrant hostis*
dreddyth? the geraudynes. What ben thay that envy bacbityth? *penetralia?*
the geraudines. Hade thay found prynce in any tyme that har Note the
streynth ham wolde yeue, as thay worthy wer to haue / in good harde adventure of
pees *and* stydfast thay haddyn broght the state of Irland. But Geraldines.
thegh thay eu*er* so wel had done, thay hadd but lytyll change,
or noone, for her laboure. But eu*er* thay profited in har goodnys ;
and mysbeleue and bacbitynge, of hare boldnys. And to othyr
the Pryncis trystyn, wyth whych no boldnys was founde, ne
Power had wel to do / wi*th*-out helpe and Socoure of ham //
And also Aldelines Son*n*e, at his comyng*e* into Irland, he went
from tou*n* to tou*n* vpon the See-syde, *and* throw soght the Citteis Nota quo
ther Plente was of mette and drynke; but the montaynys *and* the *tempore mortuus*
londe wi*th*-In, he wolde neu*er* come ney. / golde *and* sylu*er*, wherof *erat ille Mauricius*
mych Plentey was in the lond, wel hungryly he gadderid to-giddyr, *geraldi*
wi*th* pledyng*e* and Pullyng*e* of peese men, *and* not of theuys ne of *filius.*
Robers. In þat tyme about Mid-heruest, Morice fiz-geraud deyed, Descripcio
not wi*th*-out grette Sorrow of al his, *and* mych harme and lost*es* to *Maurici fiz geraud.*
al Irlande // For he was a man meteful, Suttyl *and* bolde: trewer (*See* p. 76.
man, ne stydfastyr man, ne lefte he none in Irlande // Willa*m* 7.)
Aldelinys sone ran Morices sone to harme, *and* styntid neu*er* til he
hadd take of hym the castel of Wickelow wyth falsnes. Of *fraudulenter*
Reymond *and* of Robert Steuenes-sone, he toke the londys that *eripuit.*
thay hadd in the vale of Deuelyn, *and* in Ophelan; *and* othyr that
hadd londis in Pees, he toke thay londys to the kynges be-howe,
and delyuerid ham landys furthyr in Marche, *and* in Peril nexte [1] *Asperius nihil est*
har enemys, al wi*th* vnryght *and* by his owyn will. For ther is *humili,*
nothynge so bolde ne so kene, as is that man that is of noght come, *cum surgit in altum.*
whan he is an-hey broght, *and* vnkyndely sette in Maystry [1] // Claud.
Willam was a man mych of body *and* of makyng*e*, good mete- Eutrop. i.
* yeu*er*, fre and corteyse By Semblant. But ale that He did any 181.
[*Fol. 21 b.]

I

Bad char-
acter of
William
de Fitz-
Audeline.
to wyshype al hyt was yn spyinge, felonye, & trecherye; euer he
shedde attyr vndyr hony.   To-day he wold do the wyrshype,
to-morow he wold the reue & do shendshype; the meke & þe
lotles he vndedde, þe sterne & the hawteyn he plessed; softe with 4
wyld men, & hard with pees men; of fayr spech, soft, fals,
trecheur; argh & enuyous, dronklewe & lecheour.

A. D. 1177.   [CHAPTER XLVI.]

John de
Courci sees
Fitz-
Audeline's
rascality.
Iohan de Courcy saw that al thynge that Willyam
dydde was couetise And trecherye, & that he nas 8
nothynge trewe to ham that vndyr hym wer, ne dredlyche to
the mysdoynge. he chase hym of the meygne of dyuelyn a few,
bot thay wer good & stalwarth & hardy throgh al thynge, so
He gets
troops from
Dublin;
invades
Ulster,
that he hadde xxᵗⁱij knyghtes, fyfty squyers, & fotmen as myght 12
be by ccc, & went hym ynto Vlnester, whare non engeleshe-man
I-wepned to-for hym was I-seye. Than was fulfylled a prophecye
of Merlyn, that thys seyd: "A whyt knyght, syttynge on a
whyt hors, berynge fowles yn hys sheld, shal formest assayll 16
Vlnestre." Thys Ihon was a man ful whyt, & rood þan vpon
a whyt hors, & bar yn hys sheld, ernes I-peynted. he went hym
throgh Myth & throgh Vryel thre dayes goynge; & the forth
and takes
Down.
King Mac
Donlevy
flees.
day erlych, come to doune without any lete of any foman. 20
Vnwyttynge he come; In he wente. dyuelyn, the kynge, was
shorthlych a-fryght of so derne comynge, left the toun & flow; the
meygne, that was myssayse & hungry, fond ther mete & drynke
Inowe, & pylfre of gold & syluer & clothes, & eke whar-wyth thay 24
war wel arrayed, & har hert wel comforted. Into the toun was
The Pope's
Legate,
Vivian,
tries to
get rid of
De Courci,
than I-come a legat of Rome, that hete Vyuyen, & was y-come out
of scotland. Thys legat was youre aboute, pees to make betwene
the kynge & Iohn: myche he spake & mych he hym profred, & 28
more he behete, & trewage to beren euery yer to Englyssh-men, by
so that he wold the lond leue, & turne ayeyne. Myche he spake
ther-of, & mych hym bysoght; bot noght he wold hym hyr, ffor hys
who means
to win or
die.
thoght was al I-turned, the lond for to wyn, or the lyf to forlese. 32
Donleue saw that he, wyth fayr spech ne fayr beheste, noght ne
myght spede; he sent anoon aftyr hys folke, & withyn the viij day
he gadered to-gyddyr an hoste of ten thousand men, stalwarth

to wyrchyppe, al Hit was in Spyinge, felony, and trechery; euer *Descripcio*
he shed Venym vndyr hony. Tho day he wolde do the wyrchipp; *Willelmi Aldelmi.*
to-morrow he wolde the rew, *and* do shenshipp. the meke and the
buxu*m* he vndid; the sterne and hawteyn he Plesyd; Softe wi*th*
wylde men, harde wi*th* Pees men; of fayre spech, Softe, fals
trechoure; feynte *and* Envyous, dronklewe *and* lecherer*e*.

[CHAPTER XLVI.]

A. D. 1177.

I Ohan de Cursy Saw that al thyng*e* that willam did *Capitulum*
was couetyse and trecherye, and that he was nothyng*e* *xlvj*^m. trew to ham that vndyr hym wer*e*, ne dredfull to his enemys.
He chose hym of the meny of Deuelyn a few, but thay wer*e* good
and bolde, and hardy throgh al thyng*e*, So that he hadd xxij^{ti}
knyghtis, fyfty Squyer*es*, *and* footmen as myght be by thre hundri*d*,
and wente hym to vllyster, whar noone Englys*h*-man wepeny*d* to-
for hym was seyn. Than was fulfillid a prophesy of merlyng*e*, that *argent*
thus say*d*: "a whyte knyght, syttyng*e* on a whyte hors, berryng*e* *iij egles*
dysplayed fowlis on his sheld*e*, shal formyst*e* assayle vllyster*e*." This Ihon *gules*
was a man ful whyte, and rode vpon a whyte hors, and bare in his *crowned* *armed and* shelde, ernys y-peyntyd. he went throw myth *and* throw Vriel thre *beaked* *golde.*
dayes goyng*e*; and the fourth day Erlych, come to doune, wythout
any lette of any enemy. Vn-wyttyng*e* he come; In he wente.
Dunleue, the kyng*e*, was schortlych agaste of so suddeyn comyng*e*,
lefte the tou*n* and flow; the mayny, that was myssaysid and
hungry, founde ther mett*e* and drynke y-now, and Pylfre of
golde and Syluyr *and* clothis, *and* also wher-wi*th* thay wer wel
arrayed, and her hert*e* wel confortid. In-to the tou*n* was than
y-come a legate of Rome that was callid Vyuyen and was come *Romanae* out of scotlonde. this legate was besy about, Pees to make *sedis* *legatus.*
be-twen the kyng*e and* Iho*n*. mych he spake, *and* mych he hym *multa*
profer*id*, *and* more he promysyd, *and* trewage to here euery yere to *quidem* *verba sua* Englyss*h*-men, So that he wolde the lond lewe, *and* turne agayn. *soria nec* *persua-* gretly her-of he spoke *and* be-soght; but noght he wolde hym hyr*e*; *soria pro-*
For his thoght was al turned, the lond*e* forto wynn*e*, or his lyfe *ponebat.*
for-sake. Dounleue Saw that he, wyth fayr*e* spech*e* ne fayr*e* [1] *se verbis* promes, nothyng*e* myght sped*e* [1]. he send anoone aftyr his Pepill, *minime* *profecto* and wyth-in viij^o dayes he gaddrid to-giddyr an hoste of x. M^l *enim.*

I 2

Mac Don-
levy be-
sieges De
Courci in
Down.

to fyght, & besegete staluarthly the Cyte of doun þer Iohn̄ was In ;
for yn thys lond, as yn al other, the northeren men̄ ben stordyer &
smerter to fyght than other. Iohn̄ saw thay hostes comynge to
hym-ward : thegh he fewe wer, natheles thay war al hardy & stal- 4
warth he chase ; & leuer hym was, out wend, & with streynth

De Courci
leaves his
corner of
the town,
sallies out,

to assaye the aduenturs of battaylle, than yn the lytel feble fortelet
that he yn & herne of the toun yn so lytel whyle hadde arerede,
amyd hys fomen, beseged & hungrod, deye. He went hym out to 8
hard fyght : & whan thay hadde fyrste, from fer̃, I-suywed har
arowes, thay smytten ther aftyre hertelych to-gydder, sper ayeyne

fights
splendidly,

sper, swerd ayeyne sparth ; & many one the lyf ther forlese. Bot
who hadde y-sey Iohnes dynttes with swerd, how he smote of þat man 12
þe heed from the scholderes, that man the arme & þe shuldre from

[*Fol. 22
b.]

þe body, that man the heed I-clouen fer doun * ynto the body, he
myght wel sygge that hys myght & hys mayn oght wel be I-preysed.

backt well
by Roger
le Poer,

Thegh many war yn thys fyght that stalwarthly dydden, natheles, 16
Roger the power, that ther-aftyr was of grete myght yn Osserye &
yn the Contrey of leghlyn, was the other that best dydde. Aftyr

and at last
wins.

grete fyght & lange, þat ther was of wel vnlyche hostes, at þe laste
the Iresshe host was ouercome & I-scomfyte ; many I-slawe by the 20
see strond whyder-ward they flowen : than was fulfylled a prophecye that Colmkylle seyde of thys fyght : he seyd, ' that so many
men̄ shold be I-slaw yn that place, that har fomen myght waden to

His men
walk up
to their
knees in
Irish blood
on the
slimy
strand
[¹ ? dyn ..]

the knees yn her blode.' & so hyt was than ; ffor as thay flowen to-for 24
ham yn the slyme, thay folweden aftyr & slowen ham ; & as thay
dyueden adoun, the blode of ham that waren̄ I-slawe, & fleted
abouen, toke to þe knee of ham that slowen ham. The same
prophete seyd also, 'that a pouere mane, & as thoght he wer flow or 28
banshed out of other landes, with lytel folk shold come ynto doun¹,
& the toun wynne, wythout soccoure of any herrer '; & other many
fyghtes & aduentures of thynge that yn that contray shold betyde,

De Courci
has his
Victory
written in
Irish.

whych al openly wer fulfylled yn Iohn de Courcy. That same 32
boke, Ihon hadde an Iresshe I-wrytte, & was hym ther-aftyr as
shewer of al hys dedys. In the same boke was eke I-found, that
a man̄ with folke I-wepned shold, with strenynth, the walles of
Waterford to-breken ; & with grette slaght of þe cytȝeynes, the toun 36

men, bolde to fyght / and besegyt boldely the Cite of doun ther
Ihon was In / For in this lond, as in al othyr, the nordryn men
ben sturdier *and* smyrtyr to fyght than othyr. Ihon Saw the
hostys comynge to-wardes hym, *and* chose ; and lewyr was, out wende,
and wyth streynth to assay the aduentures of battayl, than in the *quam exili*
lytel feble fortelet, that he in *and* herne of the toun in so lytel *municipio, quod in*
tyme hadd arrerid, amyd his enemys be be-segid, and to dey wit*h* *urbis angulo*
hungyr. he went out to hard fight. and when thay had fryste, *tenuiter*
frome fer shote her arrowys, thay smytten aftyr hertely to-giddyr, *erexerat.*
sper*e* agaynys sper*e*, Swerde agaynys Spare ; *and* many there the
lyfe loste. But who had y-sey Ihonys strokys wyth Swerd, how
he smote Of that man the hede frome the sholdris, that man the
Arme and the shuldyr * frome the body, Hee myght wel Sey, that [*Fol. 22
His myght and His mayn oght Wel to be Praysid. Thegh many a.]
wer in this fyght that boldely did, Natheles Rohere le Power, that
ther-aftyr was of gret myght in Ossory and in the contrey of
leghlyn, was the othyr that best did. Aftyr grete *and* lange [1] *nimis impari*
fyghtynge of wel vnlych hostis [1], at the last, the Irys*h* hoste was *certamine.*
ouercome *and* scomfited, *and* many slayne by the strondis syde *per mari-namglisim.*
whedyr thay flowe / than was fulfillid a prophesy that colmekyl [2] [2] *Hibernici Kolumbae.*
Sayde of this fyght. He sayde, 'that So many men sholde be slayn *Prae glisis*
in that Place, that har enemys myght wadyn to the knees in her *namque mollitie,*
blode' / And so hit was than. For as thay fleddyn to-for ham in *dum ad ima pene-*
the Slyme, thay folwedyn aftyr and kyllid ham ; and as thay *traret*
dyuedyn done, the blode of ham that weryn slayne, *and* fletid *humana pondero-*
abow, toke to the knees of them that ham Slayn*e*. The same *sitas, terrae*
Prophet sayde also, 'that a pou*ere* man, and as thegh he wer*e* flow *lubricac*
or banshed but of othyr landys, wit*h* lytel folke sholde come to *sanguis profluus*
doune, and the toune wynne wyth-out Soccou*re* of any herrer'; and *superfi-ciem*
othyr many fightes and aduentures of thynge that in that contray *tenens,*
sholde befalle, whych al opynly wer fulfillid in Ihon̄ de Cursy. *genua cruraque*
That same boke, ther-aftyr had Ihon de Cursy on Irys*h* writte, *de focili pertinge-*
and was to hym ther-aftyr as merrowr*e* of al his dedys. In þe *bat.*
sayde boke is also fovnde, that a man wit*h* pepil wepenyd, sholde
wit*h* streynth the wallis of watyrford breke : *and* wit*h* grete slaght

A. D. 1177.
St. Colum-
ba's pro-
phecies
fulfild by
De Courci.

De Courci
had Fights
1. and 2. at
Down;

3. at Fir-
lee, where
he was
beaten;

4. at Uriel;

5. at Newry
Bridge.

Jn. de
Courci
described.

[*Fol. 23
a.]
He loved
fighting,
and often
attackt his
foe in rear.

wyꝺ; & fro thenꝛes, by Weysford, wend to dyuelyn without any
lette; & þe cytè wyn: & al þis ys found fulfylled of the Erl: he
seyd eke 'that the Cytè of lymerykc shold of Englysshe-men shold
be twyes I-lefte, & at the thrydde tyme y-hold': & so hyt was, on 4
tyme of Reymond, another of phylepe de Bruse, as hyt openlyer shal
be I-shewed yn hys own place. Ther-of þe prophecye was thys
y-seyd, 'þe cytè thrise I-soght, at þe thryd tyme shal be I-hold.'
Twey grete fyghtes, Iohꝺ ther ledde & wan at douꝼ; that oon aftyr 8
candelmase, as hyt ys I-told, þat other at mydsomyre, wher he, wyth
fewe men, ouercome the battaylle of fyftene thousand, & slow of ham
ful many. The þrydde was at ferly at a pray-takynge: thar thay
come throgh a narowe pas, and hadde so styf fyght, & so stronge, that 12
hys men was, some y-slawe, & the oþer dele so dyscomfyte ynto
al þe woddes, that vnneth ther be-left hym wyth aleueth
thousande; & he, as man wonderly stalwarth, with so fewe wyth
hym, whan thay hadde har hors I-loste, thay went a-fote al 16
y-wepned: a xxxti myl weye thay helden the fyght of har fomen; &
twey dayes & two nyght thay waꝛ fastynge, tyl thay come to hys
castel. The ferth fyght was yn vryel; ther many of hys weren
I-sley, & the oþer descomfyte, & put ham to flyght: the fyfte at 20
yueres brygge, as he come wyth fewe men out of England;
natheles, ther he ouercome, & slowe ful many, & come hol & sond to
hys owne. Thus yn thre grete fyghtes he wan the ouer-hand;
& yn twey, theghᷓ he harme tholled, he dydde hys fomen mych 24
more. Iohn was a man whyte & fayre; of lymmes bony & synowy;
mych of body; non hardyer than he, stalwarth, & fyghter stronge of
yought; yn euery fyght the fyrst, & the meste perrylle he wold
* euer be In; he was so coueytouse of fyght, & so bernynge whan he 28
hoste lad, & come to fyght, that he neuer wold hym hold as ledeꝛ,
bot wyth the fyrst wold yn smyte, som whyle behynd, theꝛ most
perrylle was, that oft al the oste was the vnredyeꝛ, and thoght that
thay wer ouercome, and al hadden forlore: & theghᷓ he weꝛ yn 32
wepne vnmetly stordy, & sterne, out of wepne natheles, he was
meke and sobre, & mych wyrshypped god & holy chyrche, & yn al
thynge he leuet god and hys seruyce; & al that hym betyd, he
thanked god that hym the grace sent. He spoused Godefreys 36

of the Citteseynes, the toun wyn : And al this fund fulfillid of the A. D. 1177.
Erle. He sayde also that the Cite of lymerike, of Englysh-men *ab Anglo-*
twyes sholde be lefte, and the thyrde tyme sholde be holde. And *run gente*
bis dese-
So hit was, on tyme of Reymonde, a-nothyr of Phylip de bruse, *rendam, et*
tertio reti-
as hit opynlyer shal be shewid in his owyn Place. Therof the *nendam.*
prophesy was thus sayde : " The Cite thryse soght, at the thyrde
tyme shal be holde," Two grete fyghtis, Ihon ther abode, *and* ham
ouercomyd at doun / that oone aftyr candylmasse, as hit is tolde /
that othyr, aftyr mydsomer, wher he, w*ith* few men, did ouercome (Jure 24.)
the battail o xv. M*t*, *and* Slayne of ham ful many. The thyrd was
at ferly, at a pray takyn : thar thay come throw a narrow Paas, and *in praedae*
captione.
had so styfe fyght, that his men was, some slayne, *and* othyr Part so
descomfite in-to al the woddys, that vnneth w*ith* hym was lefte M*t* ;
and he, as man woundyrly bolde, w*ith* so few w*ith* hym, Whan *Ipse vero,*
vir virtutis
thay hadd har hors loste, thay went afoote al wepenyd : xxx*ti* myle *invictae,*
wey thay heldyn the fyght of har ennemys; *and* two dayes and *cum tan-*
tilla
two nyghtes thay wer fastynge, til thay come to his castel. the *suorum*
paucitate.
iiij*e* fyght was in Vriel, ther many of his were slayn, and the othyr
dyscomfite, and Put ham to flyght ; the v. fyght at yuores bryge, as *apud pon-*
tem Ivori.
he come w*ith* few men out of England. natheles, ther he ouercome,
and slayne ful many, and come hole and Sounde to his owyn.
Thus in thre grete fyghtis he had the ouer-hande; *and* in two, Descripcio
Iohann[is]
thegh he loste the ouer-hand, he did his enemys mych mor*e* // de Cur:y.
Ihon was a man whyte *and* fayr*e* ; of lymmes, bony and * Synowy ; [*Fol. 22
b.]
myche of Body ; noone Hardier than Hee ; Bolde, and fyghter *vir fortis*
stronge of youth : in euery fyght the fryst, and the meste peril *et bellator*
ab adoles-
he wolde eue*r* be In / he was So covetouse of fyght, and So *centia.*
bernynge whan he hoste ladd, *and* come to fyght, that he hym
neue*r* wolde holde as leder*e*, but w*ith* the fryste wolde smyte, *ducem*
exuens, et
Sumtyme be-hynnde, ther mor*e* Peril was, that ofte al the hoste *militem*
was the vnredyer, and thoght that thay wer ouercome, and al *induens.*
haddyn for-lore. And thegh he were in wepyn vnmetly sturdy *in armis*
immode-
and Sterne, Out of wepyn natheles he was meke and sobyr, *and* *ratus.*
mych vy:chippid god and holy church, and in al thyng he lowid
god *and* his ser*v*ice ; and all that hym befel, he thankyd good that
hym :he grace sende. He Spousyd Godfredes doghtyr, the kynge

A. D. 1177.
At last, De Courci overcame all foes.

doghter, the kynges of Mane; & aftyr many selcouth battaylles that he dydde, nat wythout grete labour & perrylle of lyf & myche myssayse, at the last he was all aboue, & clenlych hadde ouercomen. He casteled the lond yn couenable places, & such pes made, that non 4 better ne myght be, ne stedfaster. Bot gret wonder ys, & nat bot as god hyt wold, that thay four grete postès of the conquest of Irland, namely, Robert steuenes-sone, heruy of Mountynorthy, Reymon le Gros, and Ihon de Courcy, mythten neuer haue 8 chyldren of her spoused wyues. Thus mych we haue shortly I-told of Ihon de Courcy; & the other parte of hys stalwarth gestes, we leueth to wryte to other that ham wrytte wyllen, & turneth ayeyne ther we afore lefte.

Not one of the 4 great Pillars of the Conquest of Ireland had a child.

12

[CHAPTER XLVII.]

The Legate Vivian holds a Synod at Dublin, March 13, in Henry II's favour,

Wiuyen, that in-to Irlande was legat I-comen, come to dyuelyn; theder he made come to-for hym al the bysshoppes & the clergye of Irland & held hys senne. ther he shewed openly the kynges ryght of Engelond to Irland, 16 & the popes graunt, & hys confyrmacion; &, vp mansynge, forbed lered & lewed, that non neuere so hardy to comen ayeyns the kynges trouth. &, fore the Iresshe-men wer I-woned to don al har vytayllys yn chyrches, he yawe the Englysshe-men leue, that 20 whan me ladde hostes, & myghten nowher elles wytayll fynd, that yn chyrch war I-found, me shold hardyly out take, & yeue the kepers of the chyrch the worth, as ryght wer.

and gives the English leave to take food from churches.

[CHAPTER XLVIII.]

Miles de Cogan with 500 men, invades Con- naught.

Aftyr that, Miles de Cogan, that vnder Aldelinesse- 24 sone was keper & conestable of dyuelyn, wyth fowrty knyghtes, of whych Rolf, Robertes sone, fytz-esteuene, was one, I-sette mayster ouer ham vnder Myles, & two hundret other an hors, & thre hundret bowmen, passeden the water of shynnen, 28 & wentten ynto Connaght, whar Englesshe-men was neuere er comen. The men of Connaght wer I-ware of har comes; thay drowen ham ynto erth-hous many; & al the vytaylle that thay ne myght nat take wyth ham, thay put yn chyrches; & tounnes & 32 chyrches thay setten al afyr & branten. & yn despyte of the En- glesshe-men, & yn hope þat god shold take wrech of ham, thay toke

The Irish take to earth- houses, and burn their buildings.

of man ; *and* aftyr many Selchouth battalys that he did, not A. D. 1177.
wyth-out grete laboure *and* Peril of lyfe *and* mych myssayse, And *tandem in*
at the last he was al abow, *and* clenly hadd ouercome. He *arce vic-* *toriae*
castelid the londe in behowabyll Placys ; and Suche Pes made, *plene*
constitutus.
that noone bettyr ne myght be, ne stydfastyr. But hit is grete
wondyr, and not but as god hit wolde, that thay iiij*e* grete Post*es* *hi grandes*
of the conqueste of Irland, Namely, Robert Steuenes-sone, heruey *expugna-* *tionis*
of Mountmorthy, Reymond le gras / and Ihon de Cursy, myghten *Hibernicae*
postes.
neu*er* haue childe of her Spousyd wyues / Thus mych we haue
Shortely tolde of Ihon de Curcy ; And the othyr Parte of his
bolde gestis, we lewyth to write to othe*res* that ham write wille,
And turnyth agayñe ther we afore lefte.

[CHAPTER XLVII.]

Vluyen, that into Irland was legate, come to deuelyn : *Capitulum*
thedyr he made come to-for hym al the bischopis and *xlvij*ᵐ*.*
convocata
the clergy of Irland, *and* helde his Senne. ther he Shewid opynly the *Dubliniae*
kyngis ryght of England to Irland, and the Popis graunte and *episco-* *porum*
his confirmacion ; *and*, vpon Payn of Cursynge chargid both lerrid *synodo.*
and lewyd, that noone neu*er* so hardy to come agaynys the kyngis
trouthe. And, for the Irysh-men wer wonyd to do al har vitalys *ad ecclesi-*
in churchis, he yaue the Englysh-men leue, that whan thay ladd *arum*
refugia
hostis, *and* myght no vytalis ellys fynde, that that in church were *victualia*
founde, thay sholde hardely out-take, *and* yeue the keper*es* of the *transfer-* *rentur.*
church the worthe, as ryght were.

Capitulum
[CHAPTER XLVIII.] *xlviij*ᵐ*.*
¹⁻¹ *urbibus*
Aftyr that, Miles de Cogan, that vndyr aldelines-sone was *undique et*
keper and constabil of Deuelyn, wit*h* xl. knyghtes, of wych *villis igne* *proprio*
Rolfe, Robert-es sone, fitz-Steuen, was one, y-sette Maystyr ou*er* ham *combustis;*
vndyr Milis, and two C an hors, CCC bowmen, Passyd the watyr of *alimentis* *quoque*
Shynnyñ, *and* went Into Connaght / wher englysh-men was neu*er* *cunctis,*
quae
therto-forne. The men of connaght wer y-ware of har comynge / *hypogeis*
¹ thay drew ham into Erthe-hous many ; and al þ*e* wytalis that thay *subter-* *raneis*
ne myght take wit*h* ham, thay Put in churches ; *and* touñes *and* *abscondere*
churches thay sette afyre and brantyn¹. and in dyspyte of the *non pote-* *rant, simul*
englysh-men, *and* in trust that god wold do vengeance on ham, thay *cum eccle-* *siis igne*
consumptis.

A. D. 1177.
The
English
advance to
Tuam,
but find no
food, and
retreat
safely to
Dublin,
beating
King
Roderic of
Connaught
on the way.

þe rodes crucyfyed, & ymages of haloweᵫ, & kesten to-for ham ynto al the feldes. The Englesshe meygne wentten tyl thay come to tuen, & theꝛ thay abodde viij dayes yn bare lond & blote. And whan thay myght no mane fynd, ne nothynge wher-by thay myght 4 lyue, thay turned ayeyne to the shynnen. ther thay found ayeyns ham, Oconghouꝛ yn a wodde, wyth thre grete hostes. the Engelesshe boldly smytteᵫ vpoᵫ ham, & slowe of ham ful many, passeden oᵫ, & come to dyuelyᵫ al sound, out-tak þre meᵫ, that yn that fyght 8 wereᵫ I-lefte.

[CHAPTER XLIX.]

Fitz-
Audeline
goes back
to England.
He got
Jesus's
Crosier to
Dublin.

[*Fol. 23
b.]
Hugh de
Laci and
Robert le
Poer come
to Ireland.

Miles de
Cogan and
Robert
Fitz-
Stephen
get Cork.
Philip de
Bruse has
Limerick.

Sone theꝛ aftyꝛ, Aldelinessone was I-sent aftiꝛ ynto Engelonde, that no good yn Irland dydde bot oon, that, by procurynge of hym, an holy baghell & of 12 grete vertue, that me cleped Ihesus baghel, was I-broght from Ardmaꝰ to dyuelyᵫ, & yet ys at the chyrch of the Try- nyte : & come * ynto Irland Hugꝰ de Lacy, heye Seneshal of al the lond, & Robert de Poweꝛ wyth hym, Conestable of Water- 16 ford. Myles de Cogaᵫ & Robert steucnessoᵫ wentten also ouer the see ynto Engeland; bot thay comen sone ayeyne, & phylepe de Bruse wyth ham; & hadde the kynge I-yeuen ham thre, al the lond of Desmond. Robert & Myles hadden the south Con- 20 trey, that ys to wytteᵫ, from lysmore al aboute Corke vii Cantredes, saue the kynge the Cytè of Corke, wyth þe next cantrede. Phylype de Bruse, the kynge yaf al the Contrey of lymeryke, saue the Cytè & hys next cantred : these thre I-feffed 24 to-geddeꝛ, come ouer ynto Irland yn o felewshyppe, & arryueden at Waterford, & fro thennes thay wenttcᵫ to Corke al harmlcs. Thay waꝛ thaꝛ fayꝛ receyued of þe Cytteyns, & of a knyght that

They force
peace on
Dermot
Mac-
Carthy,
and divide
the town-
lands near
Cork.

was kepeꝛ of the Cytè, that hete Rychard of Londone. Whaᵫ 28 thay hadde I-broght to pees Demot Mac charthy, prynce of desmone, & otheꝛ many of the contrey of moche power, Robert and myles deled betwen ham the vij cantredes next the Cytè; & felle by lot[1] to Robert, thre on the eeste syde ; Myles, four yn the weste ; 32 mo to the on than to the otheꝛ, for the lond was wors; the kepynge of the Cytè comune to ham bothe; the renth & the trywage

---

[1] MS. bot.

toke the roodys crucyfied, *and* ymagis of Sayntis, *and* kesten to-for A. D. 1177.
ham into al the feldys. The Englis-men wentyn tyl thay come to ¹ *in hostili*
tuem, And ther abode viij dayes in bare * Londe ande Blote ¹. And *terra.*
[*Fol. 23
When thay myght no man fynde, ne nothynge Wherby thay myght a.]
lyue, thay turned agayn to the Shynnyn. ther thay found agaynys *terram*
alimentis
ham / Oconghoure in a wodde, with thre grete hostis. The *vacuam*
englysh boldely smytten vpon ham, *and* Slow of ham ful many, *inveniens.*
tribus
Passyd ouer, and come to Deuelyn al sounde, out-take thre men *tantum*
arcariis
that in that fyght weryn lefte. / *amissis.*

[CHAPTER XLIX.]

SOne theraftyr, aldelines Sone was sende aftyr in-to *Capitulum*
England, that no good in Irland didde but oone, *baculum*
xlix^m.
that, by procurynge of hym, an holy baghel and of grete Vertu, that *virtuosissi-*
mum, quem
is callid *Iesus*² baghel, was broght frome Ardmagh to Deuelyn, and *baculum*
yet is at the Trynyte church // And come Into Irland Hugh de *Jesu*
vocant.
lacy, hey Seneschal of al the londe ³, And Robert de Power *with* hym ³ *generalem*
Hiberniae
Constable of watyrford, Miles de Cogan *and* Robert S[t]euenes-Sone *procura-*
wentyn ouer the See also in-to England ; but thay comyn Sone *torem.*
agayn, and Philip de bruse *with* hame, and the kynge yaue ham
thre al the londe of Desmonde. Robert and Miles haddyn the
South contrey, that is to Say, from Lysmore al aboute Corke, vije
candredes, Saue the kynge the Cite of Corke, *with* the nexte
candrede ; Philip de Bruse the kynge yaue al þe contrey of
lymerik, Saue the Cite and his nexte Candrede : thes thre, feffyd *Trans-*
euntes
to-giddyr, come ouer Into Irland in oo fellochipp, and londyn at *igitur in*
Watyrford, and fro thens thay wenten to Corke al harmeles. Thay *Hiberniam*
mense
wer thar fayre rescewyd of the Citteseynys, and of a knyght that *Novembri,*
was keper of the citte, that was callid Richarde of london. Whan *cum tri-*
plici fa-
thay hadd broght to pees Dermot Maccarthy, Prince of Desmon, and *milia, tres*
othyr many of the contrey of mych Powere, Robert and Miles delid *viri con-*
foedati
betwen ham the vij Candredes nexte the Cite ; and fell by lotte to *simul et*
confoe-
Robert, thre on the Este syde ; Miles foure in the weste : mo to the *derati.*
on than to the othyr, for the londe was wors ; the kepynge of the
Cite comyn to ham both. the rent and the triwage of the othyr

² Ihc, MS.

A Cantred oíf the otheꝛ fouꝛ & xx cantredes, as hyt wold falle, euyn to dele

A Cantred is 100 townlands. betwen ꝛam: & ys a cantrede to sygge, an hundret toꝛꝺ lond.

Robert Fitz-Stephen, Miles de Cogan, and Philip de Bruse go to Limerick. Whaꝺ thys was I-doꝺ, thay wentten wyth Phelype to lymeryke. Robeꝛt hadde wyth hym xxxti knyghtes & lxti sweynes; Myles, xxti 4 knyghtes & fyfty squyers; Phelype, xxti knyghtes & xlti squyers; & fotmen wyth euery of ham ful many: they came to the Cytè,

Philip ought to attack Limerick, but funks it, and retreats: & noght was betweꝺ ham bot the watyre of the shynneꝺ; & Robert & Myles baden Phylepe to wend ouer & assaylle the 8 toun; othyr, yf hym leuer weꝛ, to reꝛ hym a castele vpon the same watyre afor the toun. Phelepe, thegh he knyght wer stalwarth & hardy yn hym selue, natheles, throgh feble consaylle

he has such a set of scamps in his force. of ham that wyth hym, weꝛ he chase; & mych leuer hym was, leue 12 the Contrey, & harmles turne ayeyne to hys owꝺ, Than amonge so many fomeꝺ & so fer londes, yn so grete perrylle to abydde; & that no wonderꝛ nas, thegh hym yn thyke vyage mys byfelle, that so many lydderꝛ men, theues, & manslaghtres of the marche 16 of Wales—& thay to-fore al other—hadde I-chose & I-draw to hys felewshyppe. Noght lange ther-aftyr, Meredus, Robertes sone, yonge knyght & stalwarth, nat wyth-out myche wepynge & sorow

The Council of Lateran, March 1179, 3 eclipses in 3 years of many, deyed yn the Cytè of Corke. That whylle, was I-hold 20 at Rome the consaylle oíf latran, that meꝺ so moche speketh of, vonder the pope Alyxsandyꝛ the thyrdde. & was wyth-yn thre yeꝛ, thre eclypses of the sone. ℭ Whaꝺ Robert steuenessoꝺ &

Miles de Cogan and his son-in-law go to Lismore, Myles of Cogane, wel fyfe yeyr, al desmone yn good pees haddeꝺ 24 to-gyddyꝛ I-holde, Myles & hys Othome Rauíf, Robertes soꝺ, that a lytyll ther-to-fore hadde hys doghteꝛ I-spoused, wentten to the contrey of lysmor, to hold parlement wyth ham of Waterford. & as thay sateꝺ yn the feldes abydynge aftyr ham, 28 Mactyr, that theder was wyth ham I-come, & wyth whom thay

and are treacherously slain, by Mac Tire. sholdeꝺ that nyght[1] be I-herbrowed, vnwyttyngly smoꞇ vpon ham behynd, & ham both, wyth fyue otheꝛ knyghtes, theꝛ slowen wyth sparthes; & otheꝛ fewe that wer wyth ham vnneth escaped. 32

The Irish [* Fol. 24 a.] then rebel. Throgh that thynge, al the contrey forth theꝛ-aftyꝛ worth so I-storbet, that Demot Maccarthy & al the hegh men of * the contray, forth wyth Mactyre, ayeyne har trouth, wyth-droweꝺ ham

[1] MS. myght.

foure *and* xx^{ti} candredes, as hit wolde falle, euen to dele be-twen

ham // And a Candrede is as myche to Say as, an hundrid toun- Quid est

londe // Whan this was don, thay wentyn w*it*h Philip to Lymerike. candreda. *tanta*

Robert had wyth hym xxx^{ti} knyghtes and xl. Squyer*es* ; Miles, xx^{ti} *terrae portio,*

knyghtes, l. Squyer*es*; and Philip, xx. knyghtys *and* xl. Squyer*es*; *and* *quanta centum*

footmen w*it*h euery of ham ful many. Thay came to the Cite, and *villas continere*

noght was betwen ham but the watyr of the Shynnyn. And Robert *solet.*

and Miles badyn Philip wende ou*er*, and assayle the tou*n* ; Othyr,

yf hym leu*er* were, to rere hym a castel vpon the same watyr afor 1—1 *pusilla-*

the tou*n*. Philip, thegh he was knyght bolde and hardy in hym-Selfe, *nimi tamen suorum*

natheles, ¹throgh febil consail of them that wyth hym, wer*e* he chose ; *consilio. potius*

and myche leu*er* hym was, leue the contrey, *and* harmeles turne *indemnis ad sua*

agayn to his owyn, Then amonge so many enemys, *and* in so fere *reverti,*

londys, in So grete Peril to abyde ¹. and that no wondyr nas, thegh *quam in terra tam*

hym in thylke vyage mys-be-felle, that ² So many wyckyd men, con- *hostili tamque*

dicon*es and* manequeller*es* of the marche of Walis (*and* thay to-for *remota fortunae*

al othir) hadd y-chose and y-draw to his fellochipp. Not longe *tentare pericula*

theraftyr, Meredus, Rober[t]es-sone, yonge * Knyght *and* Bolde, not *praeelegit.*

w*it*h-out mych wepynge *and* Sorrow of many, Dyed in the Cite of [* **Fol. 23 b.**]

Corke. That tyme, was holde at Rome ³ the consail of latran, that ² *viros*

men of mych Spekyth, vndyr the Pope Alysandyr the thyrde. *and* *homicidas, seditiosos*

was w*it*hin iije yere, iij^e Eclipsis of the Sonne ⁴. Whan Robert *ac flagi-tiosos.*

Steuenes-Sone and Miles de Cogan, wel v^e yere al Desmond in good ³ *sedit Romae.*

pees hadden to-gaddyr holde, Miles, *and* his Sone-in-law, Raufe, ⁴ *non*

Robert-es Sone, that a lytel thertofor*e* to his doghtyr had spousi*d*, *generales tamen, sed*

wenten to the contrey of lysmor*e*, to holde Parlement w*it*h ham of *partiales.*

watyrforde. and as thay Satyn in the feldys abydynge aftyr ham, Mac-

tyre, that thedyr w*it*h hame was come, *and* w*it*h whome thay sholde A. D. 1182.

be that nyght logide, Vnwyttyngly Smote vpon ham ; and ham both, *improvisis a tergo*

wyth v. othyr knyghtes, thay Slayn wyth Sparr*es*; *and* othyr few that *securium*

wer*e* w*it*h ham, vnneth escapid. Throght that thyng*e*, al the contrey *ictibus sunt interempti.*

was in wer*e*, So that Dermot Maccarthy and al the hey men of the

Contrey forth w*it*h Mactyre, agayn*e* har trouth, w*it*hdrowen al frome

A. D. 1182. al from the Englysshemen, & turned vpon Robert steuenes-sone,

Robert Fitz-Stephen is attackt by Irish rebels. (The North Irish are true, and fight; the South are false, and trick.)

that oft hadde harde happes assayed; & neuer eft, tyl Reymond to hym come, and helpe hym for to wyn the londe & worth to herytage; ffor Robert ne myght nat pees haue, as he rather hadde. 4 As the northren me[n] loueth fyght, also the southren, falsness; thay trusteth to streynth, these to sleghtes; thay to staluarth-nesse, these to traysoune. Whan Reymond herd that Robert was so narow byladde yn the toun of Corke, wyth hys fomen al 8 about beseget, he put hym to shyppe yn the hauen of Watyrford,

Reimund Fitz-Gerald sails to Cork to help him.

wyth xx^{ti} knyghtes & squyers, & bowmen, wel ccc; leftene the lond al on the ryght hond, & wentten about by the see, fort he come to Cork, to gaddre hele to hys frendes, & vnhele to hys 12 fomen. Aftyr many & selcouth camplynges, many of har fomen

They put down the rebellion.

thay slow, & many out of contray thay dryuen, & the moste parte & the beste come to pees; & so the grete tempeste of that weddyr hape, yn lytel whyle was I-queynt & I-stylled.   16

A. D. 1182-3.

[CHAPTER L.]

There come to Ireland, Richard de Cogan in 1182; and in 1183, Philip de Barry, and Giraldus Cambrensis, who wrote 3 books on Ireland.

Nat longe ther aftyr, come into Irland Richard de Cogan, Miles brother, wyth fair meygne from the kynge I-sent; & ther-aftyr, yn the begynnyge of Marce, come Phylype de barry, a man slegh & staluarth, wyth moch 20 folk & fayr, both for to help Robert & Reymond, & for to castely hys lond of Olethane, whych Robert hym hadde I-yeue; and yn the same flot come Maystyr Geraud, that phelypees brother & Robertes neueu, ful good clerk, & a man that al the 24 conqueste, & þe state, & þe wondres of Irland, & the kyndes of pepel from the begynnynge, ful Inly soght & oft greped, & thre bokes ther-of maked wyth grete trauayl, fywe yer that he was

Hervey of Mount-maurice turns monk.

ther. about that tyme, heruy of Mountnorthy yeldet hym monke 28 at crystes chyrch yn cantyrbery, to whych he hadde thar-to-forne I-yeue hys chyrches of hys lond be Waterford & Weys-ford. Wold god that he hadde I-chaunget hys culuertnesse and he dydde hys knyghthode, and trecherye as he dydde hys 32 clothynge [1].

---

[1] Qui utinam sicut habitum, sic et animum, sicut militiam sic et malitiam deposuisset.—Gir. Camb. Op. v. 352.

the Englysh-men, and turned vpon Robert Steuenes-Sone, that ofte A. D. 1182.
had harde Aduenturis assayed ; and neuer efte, til Reymond to hym *donec Rei-*
mundus, in
come *and* helpyd hym forto wyn the londe *and* broght to heritage ; *heredi-*
tatem
For Robert ne myght not pees haue, as he radyr hadd.   As the *patruo Ste-*
northeryn men lowyth fyght, also the Southeryñ, falsnys : ¹ thay *phanidae*
succedens,
trustyth to Streynth, thes to sleghtes ; thay to boldnys, thes to *urbis*
traysone ¹ // When Reymonde herd that Robert was So narrow by- *custodiam*
solus
ladde in the tou*n* of corke, wyth his Ennemys al about besegid, he *obtinuit,*
[nec tunc
Put hym to shipp in the hawyn of watyrword' wit*h* xx. knyghtes and *plene] pris-*
Squyeris *and* bow-men wel CCC, leften the londe al on the ryght *tinam*
pacem
hande *and* wentyn aboute by the See, fort he come to corke, to *recupe-*
ravit.
grette gladnys to his frendis, *and* Sorrow to his ennemys.   Aftyr
many *and* selcouth Camplyngys, many of har enemys thay haue
Slayne, *and* many out of¹ contray thay dryuen ; and the meste Parte
and the beste come to Pees ; and So the grete tempeste of that
weddyr hapid, in lytil whyle was broght to an ² ende. /

[CHAPTER L.]   A. D. 1182.

N Ot longe ther-aftyr, come Into Irland Richard *Capi*t*ul*um
de Cogan, Miles-is brothyr, w*it*h fayre maynny   l.
frome the kynge y-Sende, and ther-aftyr, in the begynnynge of A. D. 1183.
Marce, come Philip de barry, a man sley and bolde, wyth mych
pepill *and* fayre, forto helpe both Robert *and* Reymond, and forto
castel his londe of olethane, whych Robert hym hade yeue.   And *et alius*
Stepha-
in the same flytte come Maystyr Geraude, that Philippes brodyr *nidae*
nepos
and Robert-is Eme, ful good clerke, *and* a man that al the conquest *Philip-*
pique
and the state and the wondris of Irland, and the kynde of Pepill *frater,*
from the begynnynge, ful Inwardly soght, and thre bokys therof *tam avun-*
culum
makyd wyth grette trauayll, v. yere that he was ther-aboute // *quam*
fratrem
About that tyme, Heruey of Montmorthy yeldyd hym monke at *plurimum*
crystes church in cantyr-berry, to whych he had therto-forne yeue *consilio*
juvans.
his churchis of his lond betwen Watyrforde * And Weysforde. [*Fol. 24
Wolde god that he hadd y-chaunged His culuertnesse as he didd a.]
his knyghthode, and his trayson as he didd his clothynge //

¹—¹ Illa laudis, haec fraudis cupida ; illa Martis, haec artis ope confisa ; illa
viribus nititur, hacc versutiis ; illa praeliis, haec proditionibus.—*Op.* v. 350.
² and, MS.

A. D. 1177.
Hugh de
Laci castles
Leinster
and Meath,

The while that this was thus in Desmone I-done,
Hugh de Lassy, as man that queynth was &
staluarth, both leynester & meth [1] nobely casteled, & yn many
places ther other faylled to-for hym ; & fayn was about, to setten 4
yn har londes, Thay that wyth streynth & vnryghtly weren out

and makes
such peace
that men
till their
land.

I-dryue, both englysshe & Iresshe ; so that, yn lytyll stond, was
so good pees that men arreden & tylleden har londes, and the
lond ynto al wel I-stored wyth corne. he drogh to hym 8
slegthlych, wyth wyrsshype doynge, & stydfaste forward makynge,
the heghest of the lond folk; from place to place byled the
lond wyth castel ; & yn lytyll whyll, so good pees made, toke
of other, & auaunced hys owne ryuely, & rych ham maked. 12

He so
attracts
the Irish,
that he is
suspected
of aiming
to be their
King.

The folk of Irland, wyth frenesse & sleghtes, drogh so, & allyed
to hym, that men hadden grete ortrow vpon hym, that he, ayeyne
the kynge & hys owne trouth, wold make hym self kynge I-crouned
of the lond. As thys was, & mych spech yn [   ] [2] of thys 16
thynge, comon ynto Irland twey knyghtes from the kynge I-sent,—
that oon heet Ihon, the conestabel of chestre, & that other,

A. D. 1181.

Rychard of the pek,—for to receyue the kepynge of Irland, & that

John,
Constable
of Chester,
and
Richard de
Pec arrive.
[*Fol. 42
b.]

hugh shold wend ouer ynto Englond to the kynge; both har [3] he 20
ouer went, by comyn red of ham al, thay arrereden yn that
somyr many castells yn leynester; ffor ar that, Myth * was wel
castelled, & leynestre bot lytyl. Thar þay rereden a castel to

Many
castles
are built.

Reymond, yn forthred Onolan; Another to Gryffyne hys brother; 24
the thyrde, yn Omurthy, to Water de rydlesford a kylka ; the ferth,
to Iohn the herford, at Tyllagh yn felmeth, & other many.

Meiler
Fitz-Henry
gets Kil-
dare, but
changes it
for Leix.

Meyller hadde that tyme kyldar of the erles yifte, & the contrey
about ; bot that me toke of hym for oo coste, & yaf hym þe 28
contray of leys as yn chaunge. for hyt was smert lond, woddy,
& of Marche, & ferr, me sette hym thar as man of marche,
that I-nowe couth theron.

[1] MS. moch.

[2] Space left for a word. A later hand has written something which is
illegible. The Latin has only 'fama' : see opp. and Gir. Camb. Op. v. 355.

[3] but ere : Sed antequam.

[CHAPTER LI.]

The Whyle that this was thus dōne in desmond, *Capitulum lj^m.*
Hugh de Lacy, as man that sly was *and* bolde, *Hugo vero*
both leynyster and myth nobely he castelid, and in many Plac*es* *de Laci, summa*
ther othyr falid to-for hym; *and* fayne was aboute to Settyn in har *solicitu- dine, victos*
lond*es*, Thay that wyth Streynth *and* vnryght / were out-drywe, *ab aliis,*
both Englysh and Irysh, So that, in lytel whyle, was So good Pees *et violenter a finibus*
that men Erredyn *and* tilledyn har landys, *and* the lond Into al *ejectos, ad pacem*
wel Storid w*ith* cōrne. he drew to hym Slyly, w*ith* wyrchipp *revocans,*
doynge and Stidfast forward makynge, the heghest of the lond- *eisdem olim*
Pepyll; *and* frome Place to Place byled the lound w*ith* castelis; *deserta*
and in lytyll Whyle, so good Pees made, toke of othyr, *and* *tam armentis*
au*a*unced his owyn ryuely, *and* ryche ham made. The Pepill of *pascua, quam*
Irland, wyth frenes *and* sleghtes, drow So, *and* allied to hym, that *ruricolis*
men haddyn grete exstymacion vpon hym, that he, agayn the kynge *rura restituit.*
and his owyn trouth, wolde make hym-Selfe kynge y-crouned of the
londe. As this was, *and* mych Spech in taale of thys thynge, comen *et prae- notatae*
Into Irland, two knyghtes from the kynge y-sende: that oone was *suspicionis*
callid Ihōn, the Constabill Of cestre, and that othyr, Richarde of the *fama cre- brescente.*
Peke, forto rescew the kepynge of Irland; and that hugh Sholde
wend ou*er* Into Englande, to the kynge. but ar he ou*er* wente, by
comyñ assente of ham all, thay arreredyn in that Som*er* many
castelys in leynyster; For ar that, Mythe was well castelid, and
leynyster but lytell. Thar thay reredyn a castell to Reymond̄ in [¹ The
fothred o nolan ¹; Anothyr to gryffyn his brodyr; the thyrde in ² O'Nolan's barony of
Omurthy, to wat*er* de redelesford at kylka; the iiij^e. to Ihōn the Fothurtu, now Forth,
herford, at Tillagh in felmeth, *and* othyr many. Meyler*e* hadd that in Carlow.]
tyme kyldar*e* of the Erlis yfte, and the contrey about; but that thay *ex parte regis, tan-*
toke of hym for oo Purpos, *and* yaue hym the contray of leys in *quam in excambium*
chaunge. for hit was wille londe *and* woddy, *and* of Marche, *and* *contu-*
ferre, thay sette hym ther*e* as man of Marche, þat y-now kouth *lerunt.*
therōn.

² MS to. Lat.: tertium in Omurethi, Gualtero de Ridenesfordia, apud
Tristerdermoth; quartum Johanni de Clahulla super aquam Beruae, non procul
a Lechlinia: quintum Johanni Herefordensi apud Collacht.—*Op.* v. 355.

K

CHAPTER LII

A. D.
1181–2.

Hugh de
Lacy is sent
back to
rule Ire-
land; and
John of
Salisbury
with him.
He builds
Castles.

Whan this was I-don͝, in the somyr Hugh wente owr in-to Engelande. Ayeyne the wyntter the kynge toke of hym̄ sykernesse, & sent hym sone ayeyne keper of Irland, as he rather was sette ; wyth hym a clerk, Robert of 4 slepsbery[1], that shold hym be an help & consaylle, & wytnes of hys deddes. At thys comynge, hugh arered manye castells : On to Meyller at tachmeho, & than͝ he yaue hym hys nece to wyue; another thar negh, yn Oboy, to Robert de Byga3 ; & 8 other many, both yn leynestre & yn Myth, that longe hyt war to namy al by name.

CHAPTER LIII

Nota de
lupo con-
fitente.

A priest
is askt to
shrive a
sick
woman.

He finds
a sick
wolf,

who talks
to him :

he shrives
her.

For the sins
of the
Irish, God
turnd her
into a
wolf.

About that tyme, befel a wonder aduentur yn a wodde of Myth, of a preste that yede by weyes ; 12 & as he come throgh that wodde, come a man͝ ayeyns hym, & badde hym, for goddys loue, that he shold wend wyth hym for to shryue hys wyf, that lay seke þer negh. The preste turned wyth hym ; & whan͝ he come somdel negh, he herd gronynge 16 and wonynge, as thegh hyt wer of a woman͝ ; & whan͝ he come ryght to, than͝ was hyt a wolfi that lay ther & groned. Þe preste that saw, & was wel sore aferd, & turned hym aweyward : the man͝ and the wolfi both spake to hym, & bad hym that he ne 20 shold nat be adredde, & that he shold turne to shryue hyr. The preste than toke herth to hym, & blessyt hym, & yede sytte besyde hyr : & the wolf spake to hym, & shroue to þe preste. & whan͝ thay hadde þat I-don͝, þe preste bethoght hym, and thoght that 24 thynge that was forshape, & hade gras to spek, that hyt myght also wel haue grace & ynsyght of other thynge. he sette to, & asked of the out-comen͝ men that ynto the lond wer comen, howe hyt shold be of ham. The wolf answard & seyd, that ' for the syn͝ 28 of þe lond-folke, almyghty gode tok wreche of ham, & sent that folk for to brynge ham yn thraldome ; & so thay shold be tyl the same folk war efte encombret whyth[2] syn͝ ; & than thay shold haue power for to done ham the same wrech, for har 32 synnes.'

---

[1] I. e. salopsbery, Salisbury.   [2] MS. whych.

[CHAPTER LII.]

WHan this was done, In the Somer Hugh went *Capitulum* lij^m.
ouer Into England'. agayn the Wyntyr, the
kynge toke of hym Surte, and sende hym Sone agayn kepere of
Irland, as he to-for was. Sende with hym a clerke, Robert of
Slepsbery, that to hym sholde be helpe and consayl, and wytnes of
his dedis. At this comynge, Hugh lette make many castelis. On
to Meyler at tachmeho, and than he yaue hym his deth to rescew [!]
Anothyr thar ney, in Oboy, to Robert de Bigaz ; and Othyr many,
both in leynystere and in Myth, that longe hit were to reherse ham
al by name.

A.D.
1181–2.

Roberto …
Salopes-
buriensi

cui et
neptem
suam tunc
dedit
uxorem.

[CHAPTER LIII.]

About that tyme, befel a merwelos aduenture in
a wodd of Myth, of a Preste that went by weyes.
And as he came throw that wodd, came a man agaynes hym ¹, and
Prayed hym for the lowe of god, that * He sholde go wyth Hym
forto shrywe Hys wyfe, that Lay seke ther-By. The prest turned
wyth hym ; and whan he came Somdel ney, he herde gronynge
and con-Playnynge, as hit were of a woman ; and whan he came
there wher she lay, than was hit a wolfe, that lay there and
gronyd. the prest that Saw, and was sore aferde, and turnyd hym
to goo / the man and the wolfe both spake wyth hym, and bade
hym that he sholde not be afferde, and that he sholde turne to
shryw hyre. The Prest toke herte to hym, and blessid hym, and
wente and satte be-syde hyre. And the Wolfe spake to hym, and
confeste hyr to the preste. and when thay hadd that done, the preste
bethoght hym, and thoght that thynge that was in myse-lyckenys,
And hadd grace to speke, that hit mygh[t] also wel haue grace and
Insyght in othyr thynge. He enquerid of the strangeres that were
come Into londe, how hit sholde be of ham ? The wolfe answerid
and sayde, that ' for the synne of the londe-pepil, almghty god was
displesyd wyth ham, and sende that Pepill to brynge ham in
thraldome ; and So thay sholde be, thil the Same Pepill were aftyr
encombrid' wyth Synne ². And then thay sholde haue Power to do
to ham the Same Wrechydnys, for har Synnes.'

Capitulum liij^m.
N*ota* de lupo con-fitente.
[*Fol. 24 b.]
[See Gir. Camb.'s *Topographia,* ch. 19, *Op.* v. 101 : it gives the story, with different details.]
² *Sin autem,*
quia pro-
clivis est
cursus ad
voluptates,
et imita-
trix natura
vitiorum,
ad nostros
ex convictu
mores forte
descen-
derint,
divinam in
se quoque
procul-
dubio
vindictam
provoca-
bunt.

¹ ecce lupus ad eos accedens. Gir. Camb. *Op.* v. 101.

K 2

[CHAPTER LIV.]

A.D.
1180–6.
Henry II's
sons again
rebel.

Nat longe ther-aftyr, þe yonge kynge henry, the old kynge henryes sone, & his brother Geffrey, the Erl of bretaynge, wyth-out many hegh men of thys half þe see, and yen half that ham weren an help & consaylle, the thyrde tyme 4 ayeyne hys fader began to aryse; bot sone ther-aftyr, as thegh hyt wer throgh wrech of god, thay bothe deyeden, the on about mydsomyr at Marcelle—& þat was the yonge kynge,—& þe erl sone ther-aftyr deyed eke at parys: and thys þe kynges werr 8 ayeynes his[1] sones was y-endet.

Prince
Henry
dies,
11 June
1183:
Geoffrey
dies
19 Aug.
1186.

[CHAPTER LV.]

St. Laur-
ence,
Archbp. of
Dublin,

WNder this, laurence, Erchebisshope of Dyuelyne, (that at the consaylle of the latran hadde I-be, & as me seyde, ther he hadde purchased ayenys the 12 kynge for loue of hys lond-folke, whar-of the kynge hadde grete ortrow vp-on hym, wher-for he lete hym of hys passage ynto

dies at Eu
14 Nov.
1180,
[*Fol. 25
a.]

Irland,) the xviij kalends of december, deyed at Oye yn nor- mandye; a good mane and holy; & þat, gode almyghty sheweth, 16 by many myracles þat he openly doth for hym. Me *rede eke of hym, that he was seke thre dayes ar he thader come;

after
having
prophesied
his death
there.

and whan he sawe our lady-chyrch, that ys the modyr-chyrch of the toun, he seyd thys vers of the psauter, as prophecye, throgh 20 þe holy goste: 'Hec Requies mea in seculum seculi' et cetera: & ys thus mych to sygge an-englysshe, 'Thys ys my reste, world wyth-out end; her I wyll wonne, for I hyt haue I-chose.'

John
Comin is
next Arch-
bishop,
A. D. 1181.
He is con-
secrated at
Velletri,
A. D. 1182.

¶ Aftyr hym, was Erchebysshop of dyuelyne, Ihon comyn, a 24 man of England borne; & yn England, at euesham, of the clergye of dyuelyn (by queyntyse and procurment of the kynge), by on accorde I-chose; & of the pope lucye, at the Cyte of Wellet, ther- aftyr I-hodet & I-sacred; a man, good clerke & ryghtful; & by 28 hys myght, mych ryght laked þe stat of holy chyrch yn Irland.

[CHAPTER LVI.]

Henry II
gives
Ireland to
his son
John.

The kynge henry, as he there-to-fore hadde I-thoght, yaue the Lond of Irland to hys yongeste sone, Iohn by name; & whan he hyt hadde hym I-yeue, 32

[1] overlined later.

[CHAPTER LIV.]

NOt longe ther-aftyr, the yonge kynge henry, the *Capitulum* liiij^m.
olde kynge henryes Sone, and his brodyr Geffery, A.D.
the Erle of brytayne, *with* othyr many hey men of this halfe the see, 1180-6.
and yen half that ham weryn an helpe and consayl, the thyrde tyme *prae-potentes*
agayn his fadyr be-gan to arryse; but Sone ther-aftyr, as hit were *Pictaviae proceres,*
throgh Sentence of god, thay both died, the one aboute Mid- *cum electa*
somyr*e* at Marcelle, *and* that was the yonge kynge; *and* the Erle *Gallicae militiae*
Sone ther-aftyr diede also at Paris: *and* thus the kynges werre *juventute.*
agayn*es* his Sonnes was Endyd̃.

[CHAPTER LV.]

VNdyr this laurance, Archebischope of Deuelyn, *Capitulum* lv^m.
(that at the consail of the Latran hadd I-be, *and* as
thay Sayde, ther he had Purchasid agayn*es* the kynge for loue of
his londe-Pepill, wharof the kynge had grette artrow vpon hym,
Wherfor he lette hym of his passage in-to Irland,) the xviij k*alend*s 14 Nov.
of Decembyr died at Oye in Normandy, a good man and holy, and 1180.
that god almyghty Shewid many Miraclis for / that he opynly
doth for hym.   We rede also of hym, that he was seke iij^e dayes ar
he thadyr came; and whan he Saw our Ladyes churche, that is the
modyr churche of the tou*n*, he sayde this vers of the Sawter,
as *p*rophesy throw the holy goste: "Hec requies mea in *seculum*
*sec*uli: Hic habitabo [1], quoniam elegi eam."   And is thus mych to
Say in Englys̃h, "This is my reste, worlde wythout Ende.   Her
y wyl dwele, for y hit haue chose" // Aftyr hym, was Archebischope A. D. 1181.
of Deuelyn, Ihon Comyn, a man of England borne; and in England,
at euesham, of the clergi of deuelyn (by queyntyse *and* procurment
of the kynge), by oone acorde chose; and of the Pope Lucie, at the [2] *ecclesiae*
Hibernicae
Cite of wellet, ther-aftyr y-hodet *and* y-Sacrid; a man, god clerke, *statum*
and ryghtful, and by his myght / mych ryght lakyd the state of *egregie subli-*
holy churche In Irland̃ [2]. *masset.*

[CHAPTER LVI.]

THe kyng*e* Henry, as he there-tofor hadd thoght, *Capitulum* lvj^m.
yaue the londe of Irland̃ to his yongest Sone, Ihõn by [Fol. 25
Name.   And whan he hit hadde hym yeue, he Sende the Arche- a.]

[1] habitobo, MS.

A. D. 1184. he sent þe Erchebysshope of dyuelyn ouer þe see, to ordeyn ayeyne

Archbp. Comin is sent to Ireland; Hugh de Lacy is recald, and Philip of Worcester takes his place. He took tallage of all, and curses with it.

hys sones comynge. & sone aftyr þat, hugh de lassy was I-sent
aftyr ynto Englond ; and come ynto Irland, Phelype of Wyrcestre,
procurato[ur] of þe lond, wyth fourty knyghtes ; a man that was 4
good knyght, curteys, & good mete-yeuer ; bot oþer good ne dydde
he noon, saue þat he went from contray to contray, & asked,
& wyth streynth toke, both of letred & of lewed, þe cursed
tallages of gold & of syluer. & I wnderstond that he neuer good 8
dydde þerwyth ; ne neuer mane shalle, that so catell gadereth ; for
many crystes curs, & trew mannys & womannes, pouer & ryche,
thay gadereth eke þer-wyth : & wel vnsyker may man be, to do
hys lyf yn aduentur wyth ham that catel so wynnethe.   12

[CHAPTER LVII.]

The fyrst comynge of kynge Iohn ynto Irland.

Whan the kynges sone hadde arayed al dynge
that nede was, for to come yn-to Irland, he
put hym to saylle at Melyford, a ferth estre day. he hadde

He lands at Waterford

good wynd, & a-morow arryued at Waterford, wyth thre hun- 16
dret knyghtys, & other an-hors, & a-fote ful many. he arryued,

25 April,

the yer of hys old .xxij. ; of hys faderes comynge ynto Irland
.xiiij. ; of the Erles comynge .xiiij. ; of Robertes comynge, fytz-

1185.

steuen .xv. ; the yeer of owr lordes Incarnacion .M. C. lxxxv. 20
Steuenes-sone was forman, & opened the wey to þe Erl ; the

Those who conquer the land before him deserve all praise.

Erl to þe kynge ; the kynge to hys sone ; & mych hyt ys to
preyse, & grete thynge he began, that fyrste ynto Irland so
boldly come, the thynge to begyn.   Moch also to preysene, he, that 24
aftyr the begynnynge, so nobely come for to eche thynge that
was begon ; & most of al to preysen, he that al thynge fulle

Nota the kyng his tytyle to Irland.

endet, & the lordshype clenlych wan ouer al other [Hy. II]. Her, men
mowen well vndrestond, that the Englesshy-men ne came nat 28
wyth so mych vnryght yn-to Irland as many folk weneth ; for

Fitz-Stephen and Striguil had good right to come to Ireland.

Robert, steuenes-sone, & þe Erl, wyth good ryght come to
Macmorgh ynto leynester ; the on, hys trouth for to hold, & hym
for to helpe ; that other, for loue of hys doghtre ; nathles, of 32
Waterford, ne of Myth, ne of Desmon, whych the Erl at the
begynnynge name to hym, & conquered out of leynestre, ne sey
I noght that he hadde al fully ryght ther-to.   Bot of the fyft

bischope of Deuelyn ou*er* the see, to ordeyn agayñ his comynge. A. D. 1184.
And Sone aftyr that, hugh de Lacy was Sende [1] into Englandʼ; And
come Into Irland, Philipp of Wircestre, procurato*ur* of the londe, [Philip,
w*ith* fourty knyght*es*; a man that was good knyght / curteys, and in his
expedition
goode mete-yeuer; but othyr good ne did he noone; Saue that he to
Armagh,]
went from cont*ray* to contray, and askyd, and wyth streynth toke, *a clero*
both of lerid *and* lewid, the cursid tollagis of golde and Sylu*er*. *sacro auri*
tributum
And I vndyrstonde that he neu*er* good did ther-w*ith*; ne neu*er* man *execrabile*
tam
shall, that So good gadderid; for many crystis curs, *and* trew manys *exigens*
and womannys, Pou*er* and rych, thay gadderid also ther-wyth : and *quam*
extorquens.
wel vnsur*e* may a man to be, to do his lyfe in aduentur*e* wyth them *—Op.* v.
360.
that So goode doth gette.

[CHAPTER LVII.]

Whan the kynges Sone hadd arrayed al thynge Capit*ul*um
lvij*m*.
that nede was forto come Into Irland, he Putt hym
to Sayl at Millefordʼthe iiij*e* day aftyr Estyr. He had good wynde, The fryst
comyng of
and amorrow londid at Watyrforde, wyth CCC knyghtes, *and* othyr kynge
an-hors and a-foote ful many. he londyd, the yere of his age xxij, Lhoñ Into
Irlande.
Of his faderis comynge Into Irlande xiij, Of the Erlis comynge
xiiij, of Roberes comyng*e* fitz Steuyñ xv, the yer*e* of Our*e* lordys
Incarnacioñ M*t*. Clxxxv. Steuenes Sone was the fryst man, And [*Op.* v.
382]
oppenyd the wey to the Erle : the Erle to the kynge; the kynge to
his Sone ; and gretly he is to Preyse, and grete thyng*e* he began, that *Multum*
ergo con-
fryst in-to Irland So boldely come, the thyng*e* to begyn ; gretly also *tulit qui*
ausu nobili
he is to Preyse, that, aftyr the begynnynge, so nobely come forto *princi-*
execute the thynge that was begon ; And moste of al he is to *pium*
dedit.
Preyse, that al thynge full Endyd, *and* the lorchip clenly conquesyd
ou*er* al othyr // Here men mowen wel vndyrstond, that the Eng- Nota the
kyngys
lysh-men came not wyth so mych vnryght into Irland as many titil to
Irlande.
pepill wenyth. For Robert Steuenes-Sone *and* the Erle come to
Macmurgh into leynystre ; that oon, on his throuth forto holde, and
hym forto helpe, / that othyr, for loue of his doghtyr. Natheles, of
Watyrford, ne of Mythe, nethyr of Desmon, wych the Erle at the
begynnynge toke to hym *and* conquerid out of leynystre, I Sey not [2] *quintae*
portionis
that he hadd ful ryght therto. But of the fryst Parte of the londe [2] *insulae.*

¹ Sende aftyr, MS.

Henry II's fivefold right to Ireland:

1. All the Irish Princes yielded to him.

[*Fol. 25 b.]

2. The Pope of Rome granted Ireland to him.

3. Gurguntius won Ireland.

4. Arthur had truage from Ireland.

5. The Irish came from Bayonne, subject to England.

English kings are, of right, Lords of Ireland.

Nota that Iresshemen bene false of kynd.

parte of the lond that was the Erles throgh hys wyf, The lordshype clenly þe erl yaf the kynge; & al þe prynces of the lond ther-aftyr, by har good wyll, yolden ham to the kynge, to be euermor sugget to hym & to hys. Vp*-on al thys, þe pope of 4 Rome, that ys heede of al crystendome, and that hath a specyall ryght of al the Ilondes of crystendome as wyde as the world ys, he yaf plenerly, and confermed to the kynge, the lordshyp of the lond, as hyt ys to-fore I-told. and of eldre ryght we 8 fyndeth eke I-wrytte, that the kynges of England haue to Irland of Germon, Belynes sone, kynge of Brytaygne, that ys nowe Englond, he come ynto Irland, & whan the lond; & many yer me bar hym truage, and other aftyr hym, ynto brytaygne. 12 Ther-aftyr the kynge Arthur hadde truage eke out of Irland; & Gylmory the kynge, that than was wyth other kynge of the Ilondes, was wyth hym at the grete feste that he held at karlyon. On other halue, the folk of Irland come formeste out of bastles 16 & out of Bayon, that longeth now to gascoyne, wherof the kynges of england ben lordes. And thys me may wel vnderstond, that both by old ryght & by newe, the kynges of Englond owen wel to haue the lordshyp of Irland. And thegh the folk of the lond 20 neuer ne hadde be subyet ther-byfore, hyt oght be I-noght, þat thay al by good wylle yold ham to kynge henry, by othes & by ostages, & al sykernesse that hymself lyked; & þe popes that þer-aftyr hym graunted & confermed the lordshyp of the lond, 24 & accorsed al ham that yn any tyme thar-ayeyn come. And thegh thay, throgh kynd falsnesse & vnstablenesse that yn ham ys, lytyl tel of othes & of mansynge, natheles, thay wer neuer, throgh no man that power hadde, ther-of assoylled ne vnbound. 28 Bot man may bynd hymself wyth such thynge, bot nat so lyghly vnbynd.

[CHAPTER LVIII.]

Giraldus says no more of the Conquest, but explains why it was never completed.

Maystir Geraud ne telleth no forther of the conquest; bot of þe lette where-throgh the lond 32 was [not] clenlych I-conquered, ne the folk fully I-broght yn thedone, he telleth such resons :—Thay that fyrst comen, hadden ful wel I-spedde wyth-out any lette, yif þe kynge ne hadd so astyly

that was the Erlis by hys wyfe, The lorchipp clenly the Erle yaue
to the kynge; and al the Pryncys of the londe ther-aftyr, by har
good-will, yoldyn ham to the kynge to be euer-more subiecte to
hym and to hys. Vpon al this, the pope of Rome, that is hede of al
crystyndome, *and* that hath a Special ryght of al the Ilondys of *qui insulas*
crystyndome, as wid as the worlde is, he yaue Plenerly, *and* con- *omnes sibi speciali*
fermyd to the kynge, the lorchipp of the lond, as hit is to-fore tolde. *quodam jure re-*
And of eldyre ryght we fyndyth also y-writte, that the kynge *spiciunt.*
of Englande haue to Irlande * of Gormon, Pelynes Sone, Kyng of [*Fol. 25
Prytaigne [1], that is now England, he come Into Irland, and toke b.]
the londe ; *and* many a yere thay bare hym truage, *and* othyr aftyr
hym, Into brytaigne. Ther-aftyr also, kynge Artoure hadd truage [2] *Hiber- niae reges*
out of Irland [2]; and Gylmory the kynge, that that tyme was wyth *Tribu- tarios*
othyre kynges of the Ilandis, was w*ith* hym at the grete feste that *habuisse.*
he helde at karlion. On othyr halue, the Pepil of Irlande come *Praeterea urbs*
fryste out of Bascles *and* out of Bayon, that longyth now to gas- *Baonensis,*
coyne, Wherof the kynges of Englande ben lordys. And thus ye *quam hodie nostra*
may wel vndyrstonde that, both by olde ryght and by new, the *continet*
kynges of England owen well to haue the lorchipp of Irland. And *Gasconia, Blasconiae*
thegh the folke of the londe neuer hadd be Subiecte ther-by-fore, hit *caput est,*
oght be y-now, that thay al, by good-will, yaue ham to the kynge *unde Hiber-*
henry by othys and hostag*es*, *and* by al maner Surte that he *nenses pro- uenerant.*
desyrid [3]; and the Popis that ther-aftyr hym gra*u*nted *and* confermyd
the lorchipp of the londe, and acorsyd al them that in any tyme
ther-agayn come. ¶ And thegh thay, by kynde falsnes and *Nota* that
vnstabilnes that in ham is, lytel tell of othys *and* of mansynge, Irysh-men
natheles, thay were neuer, by noo man that Power hadd, therof bene fals of kynde.
assoilled ne vnbound. But a man may bynde hym-Selfe w*ith* Such
thynge, but noght So lyght vn-bynde.

[CHAPTER LVIII.]

Maister geraud ne tellyth no ferdyr the conquest ; Capi*tulum*
but of the lette wherfor the londe was [not] clenlych lviij[m].
I-conquerid, ne the Pepil fully y-broght in theudom, he tellyth
Such resonys :—Thay that fryst comen, haddyn full well y-Spede

---

[1] Brytaytaigne, MS.   [3] firmis fidei sacramentique vinculis : v. 320.

1. Henry II's stopping the coming of the English.

I-sent, & forboden that no man ne shold to ham come; & thay that weꝛ ynto þe lond I-come, shold the lond leue, & turne ayeyne, otheꝛ forlese al that thay helden of the kynge yn otheꝛ londes.   And whaꝓ the kynge was ynto the lond 4

2. His going home so soon after his Invasion of Ireland.

hymself I-come wyth so moch power, hyt had he wel ynoght, naꝛ that he hadd so sone turned ayeyne, throgh the popes heste & þe cardynals, & eke the lyddernesse that hys sones hadden I-purueyed to do hym, the whyll that he was out of lond. ffor 8 the folk that, at the begynnynge of so sodeyne comynge, was so

The Irish, at first frightend, learnt to fight and shoot,

swyth amayed, & aferd & agrysed of the wepned men stalwarth-nesse, and of the derne wondynge of arwes, throgh lange abydynge & sleuyth of Maystres that no stalwarthnesse ne sykernesse was 12 wyth, by lytyll & lytel lerned, wepne to berꝛ, arwes to shote; & so wel woned ham ther-to, that oft ham byfelle wonderly goode

and often beat the English.

happes yn fyght vpoꝓ englysshe-meꝓ; & on thys maner, that at the begynnynge lyghly myght be I-shent & I-broght vnder fote, 16 wortheꝓ bold & staluarth to wythstond, & defend ham-self.   Me may rede & ouerseche the boke of kynges, þe prophetes, al the old rede fro end to otheꝛ, & other tymes that afoor haue I-be;

War comes on folk only for their sins. The Irish sind, but God gave

me shal neuer fynd that werꝛ & hate came vpoꝓ folk, bot for 20 haꝛ synnes; & so hyt may wel be of the folk of Irland, that oft serued wel, for haꝛ synnes, to haue werre & wrak of otheꝛ out-londes men; natheles, god almyghty was nat ham so wengeable wrot, that he tholled ham fully, nether al to be vndone, ne fully 24

[*Fol. 26 a.]

I-broght yn-to theudome, nether * thay clenly forelore grace; ne

no one grace to enslave them.

the other clenlych hadden grace, the Maystrye to hawe, ham fully & preysebly yn theudome for to hold.   Me fynt that þe Iresshe-men haddeꝓ four prophetes, euery yn hys tyme, Patryk, Molynge, 28

The four chief Irish Prophets say that the

Braken, & Colmkylly, whos bokes ben wyth ham an Iresshe I-wrytte; euery of ham spekeꝓ of the fyght of thys conqueste, & seyne that 'lange stryf & oft fyghtynge shal be for thys lond; & oft the lond shal be I-horyed & I-steyned wyth grete slaght of 32

English shan't fully conquer Ireland till Doomsday;

men.'   Bot vnnethe thay beheteth the Englyssh peple fully þe maystrye a lytell aꝛ domesday, & that the lond shal from see to see be I-castelled & fully I-won.   Bot the englysshe-meꝓ sholleꝓ, ar that, oft wel feble be, & myche desayse yn the lond so [? se].   Barcaꝓ 36

wit*h*-out any lette, yf the kynge ne hadd So hastely y-sende *and* *si non*
primis
comandid that no man ne sholde to ham come ; and thay that were *praecur-*
sorum
Into the londe y-come, sholde the londe lewe, *and* turne ayeyn, *adventibus*
othyr to lese al that thay heldyn of the kynge in othyre londys. *regio*
fuisset
And whan the kyng*e* was Into the land hym-Selfe y-come wit*h* So *edicto*
mych Power, hit hadd y-be wel y-now, [1] nar that he hadd So Sone *praecisa*
sequela.
turned agayn, throgh the Popis coman*d*ment and the cardynalis, [1] *si ab*
And also the wickydnys that his Sones haddyn y-Purueyed to do͞ne *ausu nobili*
tam prae-
hym, the whyle that he was out of londe. For the Pepil that, at *mature*
the begynnyng*e* of So Sodeyn comyng*e*, was So gretly aferde *and* *intestina*
conspi-
agrisid the wepynnyd-men boldenys, *and* of the cruel woundyng*e* of *ratio non*
arowes, throw longe abydynge and Sleuth of Maysters, that no *revocasset.*
boldnys ne Sickyrnys was wyth, by lytell and lytell lernyd wepyn͂
to berr*e*, Arrowes to shote ; *and* So wel vsyd ham therto, that
many tymys ham by-fell wondyrly good happys in fyght vpon
englysh͂-men ; and on this maner*e*, that at the begynnyng*e* lygh[t]ly *confundi*
poterat.
myght be shente *and* broght vndyrfoote, Weryn bolde and hardy
to Wythstonde *and* defende ham-Selfe / We may rede and ou*er*-
seche the boke of kynges, the p*ro*phetis, al the olde rede fro ende to *totam . .*
Veteris
o*p*er, *and* othyr tymys that to-for haue y-be, We shal neu*er* *Testamenti*
fynde that wer*e* ne hate came vpon Pepill, but for har Synnes. *seriem.*
And So hit may wel be of the Pepil of Irland, that ofte seru*ed*
wel, for har Synnes, to haue werr*e* * and wrake of othyr strange [*Fol. 26
a.]
comen men. Natheles, god almyghty was not ham so wengeabil
wroth that he wolde fully ham Putte out of londe, nethyr*e* al to be *rel omnino*
subjici
vndone, ne fully broght Into traldome, nethyr thay clenly forlorne *meruit vel*
grace. Nethyr ne othyr hadd not fully grace, the Maystry to haue, *deleri.*
and ham fully *and* Pesabilly in thraldome to holde / ¶ We Nota de
prophetis
fyndyth that the Irysh͂-men haddyn iiij*e* p*ro*phetis euery in his Hibernie.
tyme, **Patrike, Molynge, Brakan and Colmkylle**, Whos bokis ben
wyth ham in Irysh͂ writte. Euery of ham Spekyth of the fyght of
this conqueste, And Sayne that ' lange stryfe *and* of fyghtynge shal
be for this londe ; *and* ofte the lond shal be defowlid *and* y-steynyd
wyth grete Slaght of men.' But vnnethe thay g*ra*untyth that the
Englysh͂ pepil fully the maystry, a lytel ar the day of Dome, *and* that [2] *ex toto*
subacta et
the lond shal from See to See / be castelid *and* fully Enhabited [2] / *incas-*
But þe Englysh͂-men shal, ar that, ofte wel febil be, *and* mych *tellata.*

but they shall be troubled by a King from St. Patrick's Mountains.

seyth, that 'throgh a kynge that shal come out of the wyl mon-
tayngnes of seynt patrykes þat me cleppeth slesto (slesco?),
& on a soneday-nyght[1], a castel yn the wodd contreys of Offalye
shal to-brek, most what al the Englysshe-men of Irland shullen 4
be I-stourbet' / /

[CHAPTER LIX.]

I'll tell you why Prince John didn't succeed in Ireland.

Now and for whych thynge hit was, that the
kynges sonnes trauaille, and har mochel costes,
at thys tyme ne sped nat as tham ogh, hyt ys non harme 8
thegh me her sette; for thegh of thynge that ys I-past ne be no
remedy, natheles, of thynge that ys to come, me may be war
by ensample of har dede.   Whan the kynges sone was Icome

When he landed, rich men welcomd him, but had their beards pulld by his young Normans.

to lond at Waterford, theder come to hym Iresshe-men of the 12
contray, rych men, and of pees trew hym besoght, & made hym
grete gladnesshe as hare lord, & profred hym to kyssen.   Thay
anoon ryght of tho new men, & namely of the Normannes, weren
shame-fully receyued, & lothly I-hokred, & by the berdes—whych, 16
yn the maner of the contrey, they hadden grete & long—some of
ham shamly weren I-shaken & I-draw.   As sone as thay comen to

The Irish went off disgusted, and told their countrymen.

har owne, wyth al that thay hadden thay wyth-drowen ham, & left
the contrey & wenten to the kynge of Thomon, and hym [told], & 20
also the kynge of desmon & the kynge of Connaght, what thay
hadd receyued & found wyth the kynges sone. ❡ A yonglynge al
wyth yonglynges gouerned ; & by yonge men rede, al he wroght; no
wytte ne no staluarthnesse wyth hym was found ; no sekernese ne 24
trouth to Iresshemen, thayr south nat behete.   Whan tythynges

The three chiefs of Ireland (of Limerick, Connaught, and Cork,)

her-of was I-spronge, thay thre cheftayns of Irland that wer ther
redy to come to the kynges sone, & ham to hym, & do hym homage,
thay thogthten that, aftyr thay smal harmes, wolden come more ; & 28
whan me such thynge dydde to good men & meke, wel wors

swore they'd fight for their freedom to the death.

me wold do the prouth & the vnbuxum.   Thay toke ham to
rede, & swor to-gedder that thay wolden vpon har lynes wythstond
the ryghtes of har old fredomes, & defende, for to be al to-hewen. 32
And for that thay shold [2] th[is] th[yng] the better to end brynge, thay

---

[1] MS. sone myght.   [2] From this line to the end of the page, the ends
of the lines are missing, the corner of the page being torn off.

myssayse haue in the londe. So **Brakan Seyth**, that 'throgh[1] a kynge that shal come of the wylde Montaignes of Seynte Patrickes, that is callid Selfco, and on a soneday-nyght[2], a castel in the wode contreies of Ofelanye shal breke, most what al the Englysh-men of Irland shal be strobyd.'

Slefto, alias Ofaley.

[Chapter LIX.]

Ow and for wyche thyng*e* hit was, that the kynges Sones travayll, *and* his grete costes, at this tyme sped noght as tham oght, Hit is none harme thegh I her reherse. Forto speke of thyng*e* that is Paste, is no remedy ; Nevyrthelasse, of thyng*e* that is to come, we may be-ware by ensampil of har ded*es* //

¶ Whan the kynges Sone was come to londe at Watyrforde, thedyr come to hym Irysh-men of the contray, rych men[3], and of trew Pees hym be-soght / and made hym grete gladnys as har lorde, *and* proferid to kysse hym. Than ancone ryght / of two new men, [4]*and* namely of the Normanes, waryn shamefully rescewid, *and* lewidly Pullid ham by the Berdys, whych, in the man*er* of the contrey, thay haddyn grete *and* longe. Some of them wer Shamefully shaken *and* ydrawen. As Sone as thay comen to har owyn, wyth all that thay hadde, thay wythdrowen ham *and* lefte the contrey, *and* wente to the kynge of Thomonde, *and* tolde hym, *and* also the kynge of Desmonde and the kynge of Connaght, what thay hadd rescewyd *and* found with the kynges sone. ¶ A yonglynge al wyth yonglynges gouernyd, *and* by yonge men consayl al didd; And no witte ne boldnys wyth hym was founde; ne Surte, ne trouth, to yrysh-men thay couth not promyse[5]. ¶ Whan tythyngys herof was spronge, thay iij*e* captaynys of Irland[6] that was that tyme redy to come to the kynges sone, *and* yelde ham to hym, *and* to do hym homage, thay thoghten, that aftyr thay smale harmys, wolde come mor*e* ; and whan thay Such thynge did to good men *and* meke, Wel wors thay wolde do to the Prute *and* the vnbuxum. Thay toke hame to * consail, and Sware to-gadder*es* that thay woldyn vpon Har Lywes wythstond the ryghtes of har olde fredomys, *and* defende til thay were al hewyde. And for thay sholde this thynge the bettyr brynge to

*Capitulum lix*m.
[3] *viri non infirmi, fideles hactenus Anglis, et pacifici, tanquam domino congratu-lantes, et eum in osculo pacis sus-cipientes.*
[4] *a novis nostris et Normannis.*
[5] *nullam Hibernicis securi-tatem pro-mittentes.*
[6] *tres prin-cipales tunc temporis Hiberniae postes, Limeri-censis, Connac-tensis, et Corga-giensis. Ihesus.*
[*Fol. 26 b.]
antiquae libertatis sub capitum discrimine jura tuendum.

---

[1] per quemdam regem, de desertis Patricii montibus venturum, et nocte Dominica, castrum quoddam in nemorosis Ophelanie partibus irrupturum, omnes fere Anglici ab Hibernia turbabuntur.—*Op.* v. 385.

[2] MS. sone myght (the same mistake, as before, in both MSS.).

The Irish rebels make friends with their foes. Tho' false themselves, they object to others being false to them.

sentteñ about ynto al the lond, & allyed h . . . & maden frendes of ham that weř byfore fome[n], & thus throgh ham that th . . -nyge putte (þrogħ pryde) from ham, both thaye & al other most dele were . . . . þys folke, as euery otheř wyld folk, thegh thay no 4 wyrshype ne couthe . . . . me shold do ham wyrshype & manshype.   And thegh thay nat be . . . . . . wyth falsnesse, natheles thay shonneth that otheř do ham [any falshede;] & thus the good that thay loueth yn otheř, thay rech. . . . . ham 8 to-gyddeř thay . . . . *Euery wysman vnderstond hym

[*Fol. 26 b.] John's failure is explaind by Re-hoboam's, whose following of young men's advice, lost him ten Tribes of Israel.

by Roboam, Salomones sone, how mych harme falleth of pryde & ouertrowshype. whañ he, aftyř hys fadyř, was made kynge of Israel, þe folk come to hym, & bysoght hym that he shold ham somwhat 12 allegge of þe seruyces that thay weř I-woned to do hys fadyr. He was yonge ; and by yonge meñ consaylle, answard & seyd, 'My fyngyř ys gretteř thañ was my faders ryggebone ; & yf he yow bette wyth yardes, y wyl yow bette wyth breres.' ❡ Throgh that 16 answař, the ten kynredes hym lefteñ, & maden ham kynge of Ieroboam, & neuer aftyř weren vnder hym ne nooñ of hys : of al

John gave the lands of faithful Irish, to new men.

So these Irish turnd against him.

þe folk of Israel, non wyth hym abode, bot twey kynredes. Vpon thys, þe Iresshe-men londes, that, fro the tyme that Robert steuenes- 20 sone fyrst come ynto þe lond, trewly wyth englysshe-men haddeñ I-be, weř I-take fro ham, & yeuen to the newe meñ. And thay anooñ turned to the Iresshe-men, & aspyed al the harme that thay myght do to þe Englysshe ; & werř, so mych the more harme dydde, 24 that thay so pryue werř wyth ham ther-byfore

[CHAPTER LX.]

The coast towns and castles were given to rebels, who only gatherd gold, and did harm to peace-men, not to foes.

The tounes vp-on the see, and the castels, wyth the londes that to ham belonget, & the truages & the rentes that shold be I-spende yn comyn nede of the 28 lond, & to ham, of rebelles thay wař I-sette to such that wel fayne gadered gold & syluer wyth-yn wowes, eten wel & drynkeñ, and laddeñ Idel lyf, & al thynge vnprofytably wastedeñ, to harme of pees-meñ, & nat of fomeñ. Amonge otheř harmes betydde yit 32 more, that yn lond so smert & so kene, & folk so weyward & so vnredy, & so mych harme doynge, The kepynge & the maystry toke

Ende, thay Sende about into al the londe, and allied ham togad-
deris, *and* madyn frendys of tham that wer*e* enemys. And thus throw
ham, that thay at the begynnynge Putte (throw Pryde) from them,
both thay and al other*es* for the more parte was fro them stirrid.
¶ This Pepyll, as euery othyr wylde Pepill, thegh thay no wyrchipp
kowth not, Natheles thay wolde that hy sholde do ham wyrchippe
and manship. And thegh thay be not aferde ne ashamyd to be
founde wyth falsnesse, Natheles, thay Shonnyth that any othyr
sholde do ham any falshede : and thay lowyth trouth; and thus
good that thay lowyth in othe*res*, thay thynke no fors whow lytill
be found in ham-Selfe therof. Euery vysman vndyrstond hym by
Roboam, Salomones Sone, how mych harym fallyth of Pryde.
Whan he, aftyr his fadyr, was made kynge of Israel, the Pepil
come to hym, *and* besoght hym that he sholde ham Somewhate
allegge of the Servyces that thay wer*e* wonyd to do to his fadyr.
He was yonge ; and, by yonge men consayl, answerid and Sayde,
¶ " My fyngyr is mor*e* *and* grettyr then was my Fadyris bake-bone;
And yf he bette yow wyth yard*es*, y will bette you w*ith* breris " /
¶ And for that answere, al the tene kynr*edes* lefte hym / *and*
made ham a kynge of Ieroboam ; *and* neu*er* aftyr weryn vndyr
hym, ne noone of his. Of al the Pepil of Israel, none w*ith* hym
abode, but two kynredis. Vpon this, the Irysħ-men londes that
fro the tyme that Robert Steuenes Sone fryste come Into the londe,
trewely wyth englysħ-men haddyn, wer take fro ham, *and* yewyn
to two new men [1]. And thay anoone turnyd to the Irysħ-men, *and*
aspied al the harme that thay myght do to þe Englysħ ; and
werre, so mych the mor*e* harme didde, that thay were so Pryue
wyth ham therto-fore [2].

[CHAPTER LX.]

The tounes vpon the See, *and* the castelis, wyth
the londys that to ham Partenyd, and the truages
and the rentes that sholde be I-Spend in the comyn Profite of the
londe, *and* yaue hit to Rebellys [3], *and* to suche that well fayne
gaderid golde and Sylu*er* wyth-In wowes, etten wel, and drounken,
and laddyn ydill lyfe, and al thynge vnprofytably wastyne, to grete
harme of Pees men, *and* noght to enemys. Amonge al othyr harmys
befell yit mor*e*, that in the londe So Smyrte *and* So kene, *and*
Pepil So weywar d̓ and So vnredy, *and* So mych harme doynge,

Marginalia:

Quia
primos a
nobis inso-
lenter re-
pulimus...
tam illos
quam
majores
universos
eo exemplo
procul
absterrui-
mus bonum
quod in
aliis
diligunt,
minus in
se reperiri
non
erubescunt.
ego vos
caedam
scorpio-
nibus.
[1] novis
nostris,
contra
promissa
contu-
limus.
[2] tanto
quidem ad
nocendum
efficaciores,
quanto
prius
fuerant
fami-
liariores.
[3] talibus
est
assignata,
qui aurum
Cap*itulum*
lxm.
assidue
intra
muros
aucupantes
... cum
civium, non
hostium
damno
cuncta in-
utilitercon-
sumebant.

The English Governors were cowards, and liked women better than war.

an hand, that leuer[1] hadde har rych robes, than ham to wepne; leuer to sytte at borde, þan hoste to lede; redyer to fle þan to fyght; leuer to hold a fayr mayd by the womb, than sper & sheld to ber an hand; nether trewe to har vnderlynges, ne dredful to har 4 enemyes. Thay had nat that good herte, ne of ky[nde] yt com to ham, for to spar the meke, & wreke ham on the prout; bot al ayeyne that, thay sp[arid &[2]] lykled wyth the sterne, & pulled & strope

The Irish now burnt, slew, and stole. The English of the coast stuck to wine and women. The inland was plun-derd by the Irish.

ham that non harme dydde. Vnder whych gouernours, the 8 Iresshe-men begon to pryde & take ouer-hand of the englysshe, branten and slowen, robbeden And stellen; for the maystres wyth har meygne, helden ham alwey yn the cytees vpon the see, þer plente was of wyn & of women, to whych they weren al clenlych 12 I-yeue to. Bot the lond wyth-In, & the marches next har enemyes, & the castles & the tounes that weren amyd, weren I-lefte & I-brant, the men I-robbed & I-sleyn, wyth-out any lette. The good knyghtes & the eldre folk of the lond, as men that me 16 noght told-by that whyle, wyth-drow ham al sleghtly, & held ham al stylle, for to awayty al soft, what endynge such hyddous stormes

Every-where was wailing; every day fresh news of fire and slaughter.

wold ham. That whyle, þe state of the lond was such, In al places was weylynge & wonynge, yollynge & crynge; Al þe weyes forlete; 20 no man ne trust to mete wyth other; euery day come newe tythynges of bernynge & sleynge, robbynge & revyng[3] yn the out londes: vnneth a lytel shadow of pees was yn þe bourgh tounes, þer the wyn quenched al þe sorowe; the gold & the syluer, al oþer 24 harmes; thar me shold yn so lydder world wend from contray to

Judges

contray wyth folk I-wepned, and chasty ham that mysdeden. Thay setten Iustyces of bench yn har robes of scarlet & menyuer: men

ruind good men and true, [*Fol. 27 a.] worse than Irish foes did.

wyth swerdes & battes ham for to kepe, ther no nede was. Than 28 was þe motynge, the pledynge and reynnynge of good men and trewe that * non harme dydden: wors ham dydde the harme & the ten that þay ther-throgh hadden, þan the robbynge & reuynge that thar enemyes ham dydde. ⟨ Another thynge that mych was to 32

[1] MS. leuer.   [2] Torn out.
[3] The corner of p. 26 b was torn off before being written upon, so that there are no words missing, and the lines follow each other as usual.

The kepynge[1], *and* the men that was Maysteres to kepe the lande, he A. D. 1185.
had lewer his rych clothis to were, than wepyn to berre; *and* lowid [1] *Stipen-diaria*
bettyr to sitte at borde, than hoste to lede; and more redyer to fle *quippe*
than to fyght; leuer to holde a fayre mayde by the wombe, than *familia, suos*
spere and Shelde to ber an honde. And also they wer not trewe *imitata magistros,*
to har Subiectis, ne dredfull to har enemys. Thay had not that *suisque*
* good Herte, ne of good Kynde Hit come to Ham, forto Spare the *majoribus morem*
meke, *and* wreke Ham on the Prowte; but al the contrary thay did. *gerens.*
Thay Sparid *and* fikyllid wyth the sterne, and toke *and* Pullid the [*Fol. 27 a.]
meke, *and* them that noone harme did // Vndyr whych gouernors,
the Irysh-men begon to be Prowde, and to haue the Maystry of the
Englysh-men, *and* branten, *and* Slayne, *and* Stellen / For thay
Maysteris, wyth har meny, heldyn[2] ham at al tymys in the Citteis [2] [heldym MS.]
vpon the see-syde, ther Plente was of wyne and of women, to the *vino veneri-*
wyche thay yaue ham clenly to. But the lond wyth-In, *and* the *que data, maritimis*
marchis nexte har enemys, and the castelis *and* the tounes that *in urbibus*
weryn a-myde, weryn lefte and brante, the men robyd and Slayn, *moram assidue*
wyth-out any resistence. The good knyghtes *and* the eldyr Pepill *faciebat.*
of the londe, as men that noght is tolde by, that tyme wythdrow *Antiqua vero*
ham al Slyly, *and* held ham al stylle, for-to witte al Softe what *militia*
Ende Suche grete Stormys sholde haue. That tyme, the state of *novorum ingruente*
the londe was Suche, In al Placis was wepynge and cryenge, and *malitia, tanquam*
myche Sorrow. All the weyes was lefte, that no man trustid not *vilis et*
to mete with anothyr; euery day come newe tythyngis of brennynge *reprobata, latuit*
and Sleynge, robbynge and rewynge in the out-landis. Vnneth a *interim et siluit.*
lytyll Sadow of Pees was in the burgage tounes[3], ther the wyne [3] *sed solum*
quenchid al the Sorrow; the golde and the syluere, al the harmys. *in urbibus pacis*
Thar thay Sholde, in so wyckyd a tyme, goo from contray to *ut cumque*
contray wyth Pepill y-wepenyd, *and* correcte ham that did amys; *servari umbra vi-*
Thay Syttyn Iustices of benche in hare Roobis of Scarlete *and* *debatur.*
menywere; men with Swerdis *and* battis forto kepe ham, ther [See the Latin
no nede was. Than was the motynge, the pledynge, *and* reyuynge below,
of goode men and trew, that noone harme didde. Wors hame didd P. 152.]
the harme and the angyr that thay ther throgh haddyn / than the
robbynge and reuynge that har enemys ham dide // Anothyr
thynge that gretly is to mowrne, be-felle also, wher-of god was

L

A. D. 1185. rewe byfelle also, whar̃-of gode was worste I-quemed: Ther prince cometh newly to londe hyt becometh welle that he wyrshype god & holy chyrch, mayntenynge the ryghtes, & yeue more there-to.

Prince John spoild the Irish Church. Bot þe newe prynce nat only held hym from that for to eche the 4 good of holy chyrch, bot londes & rentes & pryuyleges that thay of old world hadde & vsed, at hys fyrst comynge yn many places he bename al clene ; yñ other̃ places he chaunged, & yaue wors & lasse thar̃ for̃ ; & hyt may wel be, þat hys spede yn othere thynges was 8

The Irish began to rebel. euer the wors & noght þe bettyr̃. On thys maner the englysshe wereñ both argh & woke to assayllen and to fyght, þe Iresshe stronge & bold to wythstonde, tyl that þe new prynce saue openly that al thynge vnder̃ hys newe meñ yede to loste ; he chaunget 12 ham & renued, as meñ that nothynge couth, & drogĥ to hym the

So John de Courci was made Ruler, and at once mended matters. old knyghtes & the good meñ that wareñ ther-to-for̃ Ivsed to fyght yn the maner of þe lond, & sette Ioĥn de Curcy maystre & cheffeteyne of al thynge that was to done ; vnder whoñ þe state & 16 þe pees of the lond, by as mych began anooñ ryght to amend, as Ioĥn, of hert & of staluarthnesshe, passed al other̃, passynge & throgh sechynge the Inlondes, as Desmone, Thomone, Mounester̃, Connaght ; & let nat the meygne vndo hamself wyth oft harme & 20 lostes, doynge to hys fomen, & oft to hym-self & to hys, as he that noght was adredde to assaye þe vnsyker̃ aduentures of fyght & of baret.

[CHAPTER LXI.]

Prince John had three sets of men : 1. Normans, the worst, whom he trusted most ; 2. the English he brought with him ; 3. the English in Ireland, the best, whom he trusted least. [1]The yonge prynce at the begynnynge hadde wyth 24 hym thre manere of meygne, Normannes, Englysshe, & þe Englysshe that he found yn the lond. In wyrshype, gret frenshype, & loue, he hold the fyrst & the worst ; In lasse, the mydmest & the better ; In allerleste, the latest & þe 28 beste. The fyrst ne myght nat lyue wyth-out wyn, yn whyche thay wereñ fostred ; & for-thy thay forsokeñ on al wyse to beñ yn marches & yn castels fer̃ from the see I-sette ; no-wher̃ bot about the kynges sone & hys body, kepe thay myght nat be, & hym fulwen, 32 & negh hym be, wyth-out any departynge. fer̃ from the weste &

---

[1] The usual large initial letter is omitted here, a space being left for it in which a small t is put.

moste dysplesyd.   Ther Prynce comyth newely to londe, hit A.D. 1185. becomyth that he wirchippe god and holy churche, mayntenynge *nihil de* the ryghtes, *and* yeue more therto.   But the new Prynce, not oonly *novo con-ferentes . .* helde hym frome that, forto eche the good of hooly church ; but *quinimmo* londis and rentis *and* Pryuylegis that thay of olde Worlde hadde *terris statim sub-* *and* vsyd / At his fryst comynge, in many Placis he toke al clene, *latis et* and in othyr Placis he chaungid, *and* yaue Wors and lasse therfor. *possessioni-bus . .* And hit may wel be, that his Spede in othyr thyngis was eu*er* the wors, *and* noght the bettyr.   On this man*er* the Englysh-men wer both febill and feynte to assaylen and to fyght, and the Irysh-men *hostibus* bolde *and* stronge to wythstonde, till that the new Prynce opynly *autem ad rebellan-* Saw that al thynge vndyr his new men yede to loste.   he chaunged *dum auda-* ham, *and* remewid as men that nothynge kowth, *and* drewe to hym *cissimis.* the olde knyghtes, and the good men that weryn therto-for y-vsyd *summam rerum* to fyght in the maner of the londe, And Sette Ihon de Curcy, *geren-* Maystyr and captayn of al thynge that was to dou*n*, Vndyr Whom *darum curam* the State and the Pees of the londe, by as-mych began anoone *commisit.* ryght to amende, as Iho͞n, of herte *and of Boldnys, Passid all [*Fol. 27 othyr, Passynge *and* throw shechynge the In-Londys, As Des- b.] monde, Thomon, Mownyster, Connaght, *and* lette not the meny *penitimas terrae* Vndo ham-Selfe wyth ofte harme *and* lostis, doynge to his ennemys *partes.* *and* ofte to hym-Selfe *and* to his, as he that noght was adrede *incertam* to assay the vnsure aduentures of fyght And of battaylle. *bellici certaminis aleam.*

[CHAPTER LXI.]

The yonge Prynce at the begynnynge hadd wit*h* *Capitulum* hym thre maner of men*n*y, Normanes, Englyssh, *lxj{jn}.* and the Englyssh that he founde in the londe / In grete wyrchipp, *In summa* frendshipp and loue, he helde the fryste and the worste.   In lasse, *familiari-tate primos* the Secounde and the bettyr.   And in alltherleste, the latyste and *habuimus.* the beste.   The fryste myght not lyue wyth-out wyn, in whych they 2 *solum* weryn fosterid ; And therfor thay forsoke to be in marchis and in *filii regis* castelis ferre frome the See ysette¹ / and² myght not be in no *latera stipare,* Place but aboute the kyngis Sone, (*and* [from] his body, kepe thay *solum filio* myght not be,) and hym followyn, *and* ney to hym be, wit*h*-out any *regis in-separa-* departynge.   ferre from the Weste, and ney to the Eeste ; Fer from *biliter assistere*

¹ Primi vino, quo nutriti fuerant, carere non volentes, in remotis marchiis, et castris procul a mari constructis, moram facere modis omnibus recusabant. — *Op.* v. 394–5.

A. D. 1185. negh al eeste ; fer from myssayse, & negh ayse, thay wyllet euer to
be sette. ❡ Ianglers & bosters, & of grette othes, and stronge
lyers, foderes, whybelers, Moch told by ham-self throgh pryde, &
lytel by other ; yiftes & wyrshype to receyue, thay wer the fyrst ; 4
dout & perrylle to receyue, thay war euer the laste.   The lytel good
that thay dydde that wyth hym comen, that was throgh the
englysshe that he wyth hym broght ; bot thay was no thynge
derward wyth hym ayeyns the other, that no good ne couth do. 8
And for the good knyghtes & the men throgh whych the wey ynto
the lond was fyrst I-opened, wer wyth ham bot as forsaken &
forlete ; non I-cleppeth to conssaylle bot the newe ; to non trusted
he bot to the newe ; to non was wyrshype I-do bot to the newe. 12
Hyt byfelle, that whan thay other wythdrowe ham for such thynge,
& lete ham I-worth, yn al thynge that thay dydde, lytel or noght
thay sp[ed]de.   Such gyltes & so many, thegh thay both wer myche
to wite, yong old & yonge rede, natheles þe yonge lydder rede was 16
more gylty ; ffore boustyous lond and vnredy, hadde al nede to be
Irotet and I-kept throgh wyse men & redy.

John's young men were boasters, liars, bribe-takers.

He forsook the good old Eng-lishmen,

the wise whom the rebels needed.

[Chapter LXII.]

¹ **A**ftyr that the kynges sone hadde the lordshype
of Irland, & ynto the lond was y-come, Aduentures byfelle 20
that maystyr Gerot shortly toucheth.   Of thre castels that he
anon ryght lete rere, on at Ardfynan, another at lysmore, the
thyrd at Tybraghnych.   Of thre staluarth * knyghtes that throgh
grete mesaduentur weren I-slawe, Robert de Barry at Lysmore ; 24
Reymond, hughes sone, at Olethan ; Reymon of Canteton yn
Osserye.   Of a partye of the meygne of Ardfynan that the kynge
of Thomon descomfyted yn a wod þer negh on a mydsomyr day,
And four knyghtes that ther wer y-slaw ; & thay of Tothmon the 28
sam day wer dyscomfyt to-for Tybragh ; & a grete Iresshe-man,
Ograde, was ther I-slawe, wyth many other of the meygne of
Ardfynan, that sone aftyr, yn a prey-takynge toward lymeryke
weyes dyscomfyte, & xix knyghtes I-slawe.   Of the prynce Of 32
Desmon, Dermot Maccarthy, that with many other yn a parlement

John builds three Castles, at Ardfinan, Lismore, Tibragh.

[*Fol. 7 b.]

Three Knights are slain. R. Fitz-Hugh, &c.

Men of Thomond, or Lim-erick, slain ; and O'Grady (?)

Dermot, King of Desmond dies.

---

¹ The usual large initial letter is omitted, space being left for it.

myssayse, *and* nygh to ayse, thay wolde eue*r* to be sette. // Iangleris, A. D. 1185. bosteris, and of grete othis, stronge lyeris, lycheres, Why-beleres, *verbosi, jactatores,* Moche sette by ham-selfe for Pride, *and* lytill by othere*s* : yiftis *enormium* and wyrchipp to rescewe, thay were the fryst ; Dowte and Peril *juramentorum* to rescewe, thay wer eue*r* the laste.   The lytill good that thay *auctores.* didd' that wyth hym comyn, that was throgh the Englyssh that 1 *solum* he wyth hym broght.   But thay was nothynge Derward wyth hym *novis fidem habentes,* agaynys the othyr, that no good ne couth do / And for the *solum* good knyghtes and the men, throw whych the wey into the lond *novos dignos* was fryste oppenyd, wer wyth ham but as forsakyn *and* forlete / *honore putavimus.* non callid to consaill, but the newe ; to noone trustid he¹, but to the new ; to noone was wirchipp do͞ne, but to the newe.   ² Hit ² *effectum est ut illis* befel that, whan thay othyr wythdrow hame for Suche thynge, *se retrahen-* and lette ham alone, wyth al thynge that thay did, Lytell or *tibus, et invitis* noght thay Spede.   Such gyltes and So many, thegh thay both *operas non ingerenti-* wer mych to witte, yonge elde *and* yonge rede, natheles the yonge *bus, in* lewid consaylle was mor gylty ; For bostious, loude *and* vnredy, *cunctis agendis* hadd grete nede to be y-rotid and y-kepete throgh wysmen and *parum isti profecis-* redy. *sent.*

[CHAPTER LXII.]

Aftyr that tyme that the kynges Sone hadde the lordshipp of Irland', and into the londe was come, ad- *Capitulum lxijm.* uentures befell that Maystyr geraude Sortely touchyth.   Of th[r]e castelis that he anoone ryght lette rere, oone at ardfynan, anothyr at lysmore, the thyrde at Tybraght.   Of thre bolde and hardy knyghtes, that throw gret mysaduenture weryn slayne, Robert *falls adversis et* de Barry at lysmore, Reymond Hughes-sone at Olethan, Reymond *aversis.* of Canteton in Ossory.   Of a party of the meny of ardfynan, that *De parte quadam* the kynge of Thomo͞n descomfited in a wodde ther neygh, On a *Archphi-nensis* Mydsome*r* day, And four knyghtes that were Slayn ; and thay of *familia.* Thomonde the same day wer discomfite to-*for tybraght ; and a [*Fol. 28 a.]* grete Irysh-man, Odrade, Was ther Slayn, wyth ma*n*y othyr Of the *De .. * meny of ardfynan, that Sone aftyr in a pray-takynge toward *Oggravi interemp-* lymerike weies Discomfite³, and xix knyghtes wer Slayn.   Of the *tione.* Prynce of Desmonde, Dermot Maccarthy, that w*ith* many othyr in

³ in praedae captione versus Limericum confectis.—*Op.* v. 386.

A.D. 1185. besyde Corke, throgh Tybaud waut*er* & the meygne of Corke, was

Ulstermen slain. I-slawe. Of the meñ of kenalayne, that to boldely wentteñ ynto Mythe to preyeñ, & ther wereñ I-slawe throgh Wyllyam le petyt,

Saints' bodies found. & an hundert heedes of ham I-broght to dyuelyñ. Of othe͞r holy 4 bodyes, patryke, Bryde, &, Colmekyl, at dou*n* I-found, & by Ioħn de

Hugh de Laci slain, A.D. 1186. Courcy we͞r *tra*nslated ; of hugh de lacy, that to trysty was vpon hys Iresshe-meñ, & by traysoñ of ham was I-heded at dernagħ.

❡ Of thretteñ knyghtes, that vnde͞r Iħon de Courcy weren I-slawe 8 at a comynge out of Connaght. Of the staluarth yonge knyght

Roger le Poer slain. Roger the powe͞r, that wyth many of hys, throgh traysone, yn Osserye was I-slawe ; & throgħ that thynge, al the Iresshe of the

The Irish silently conspire, destroy castles, and kill men. lond stylly sworne ham to-gyddy͞r ayeyns the Englysshe; whe͞r 12 throgh that, [1]castels yn many places wereñ I-cast adou*n*, many meñ I-slawe, to grete p*er*rylle to al the lond; & of many othe͞r

aduentures that betyddeñ aftyr that the kynges sone was lord of Irland, of whyche maysty͞r Geraud, ham & ha͞r gestes leueth to 16 other that ham wrytte wold, & lust haddeñ the͞r-to [1]. And as thys An end maked of thys boke.

[1-1] destructis castris pluribus, gravi insulae universae perturbatione : non indigna memoratu singula, translato in filium regis jam regni dominio, sua suorumque gesta suis assignando scriptoribus, ad ulteriora simul et utiliora festinamus.—*Op.* v. 387–8.

The unenglisht last Chapters.

Thus ends Ch. 35 of Giraldus's 2nd Book of his *Expugnacio.* His Ch. 36 is our 60, pp. 142–7, with an added Vision of ' Prince John marking out the foundations of a church, with a large nave and a very small chancel.' His Ch. 37 is our 61, pp. 146–9. In his Ch. 38, he states how the Irish are to be conquerd: in Ch. 39, how they are to be governd. Mr. Dimock's side-notes to these two Chapters are :

Ch. 38.   " In every expedition, the counsel of those ought to be followed, who are best acquainted with the country and manners a parlement besyde Corke, throgh Tybaud Wauter and the meny A. D. 1185. of Corke, was y-Slayn. Of the men of kynnaleyn, that So boldely *in colloquio prope Cor- cagiam, a Corcagien- sibus* wentyn Into Myth, ther to take a pray, and ther weryn Slayn throgh Willam le Petyte, and an C. hedys of ham broght to Deuelyn // Of othyr hooly bodies, Patrike, Bryde, and Colmekil / *et Theo- baldi* at doun y-found, and by Ihou de Curcy were translated. Of *Gualteri familia ferro* Hugh de lacy, that to trysty was vpon his Irysh-men, And by traysone of ham was hedid at Dernagh // Of xiij^e knyghtes, *peremptis.* that vndyr Ihou de Curcy weryn Slayn at a comynge out of *Dernagh in fercall.* connaght; of the bolde yonge knyght, Roger the Powere, that wyth many of his, throw trayson, in Ossory was Slayn; And *et ejusdem casus occa- sione,* Throw that thynge, all the Irysh-men of the londe Pryuely Sworne ham to-giddyr ayeynes the Englyssh-men; Wherthrow that, castellis *clandestina quoque* in many Places weryn caste dovne, and many men Slayn, in Peril *totius Hibernici* of al the londe. And of many othyr aduentures that by chanse *populi in Anglos con- juratione.* fell, aftyr that the kynges sonne was lorde of Irlande, the whych Maystyr Geraud, ham and har gestis lewyth to othyr that ham write wille, and luste haw therto; And as thus an ende makyth of this boke.

Et Sic finis est istius Libri.
Laus deo clementissimo.

of the people. The great difference between French warfare, and that of Ireland and Wales [is]: In these countries, light-armed troops [are] more especially necessary. In any expedition into Ireland or Wales, the troops of the Welsh Marches [are] by far the best. In Irish warfare, archers [ought] to be united with the cavalry. The three parts of the island on this side the Shannon [ought] to be well incastellated; the other part won by degrees.

Ch. 39. The necessity of firm, severe, but moderate rulers. In time of peace, castles [ought] to be built, and roads to be improved. The Irish, once fully subjected, [ought] to be forbidden the use of arms; [and] meanwhile not to be allowed to bear the axe. [They ought] to pay an annual tribute in gold or birds."

Giraldus's Third Book tells how he found and translated the Prophecies of Merlin of Celidon.

When John became King of England, Giraldus sent him a copy of his *Topographia* and *Expugnacio*, with a Proem or Dedicatory Letter printed in the Rolls edition, v. 405–411. It reminds John of Ireland, exhorts him not to forget *it*, the Golden Isle, in favour of England, the Silver one; says it will form a kingdom for one of his sons; warns him that he must leave no danger behind him in Ireland when he goes to recover the foreign possessions he has lost; calls on him to fulfil Henry II's pledges to Pope Adrian, that is, to exalt the Church in Ireland and pay Peter's pence; instances God's vengeance on the non-keeping of these pledges; says how miserable the state of the Irish Church is; and advises John to take an annual tribute of gold, birds, or trees, from the Irish in token of subjection. Lastly, Giraldus asks that a scholar may translate his books into French; gives Walter Map's opinion on his own talk and Giraldus's writings; and says that he (Giraldus) is now old, and 'desires only God's favour and the appreciation of his labours by posterity.'

---

pp. 144–5, lines 9–2 from foot. The side-note and Latin in the Rolls edition, v. 392, are:

Prevalence of law-suits.   Praeterea, quamquam hostilitatis instante procella, armatae militiae tempus ingruerit, non togatae, tanta tamen civilium causarum urgebat importunitas, ut miles veteranus non tam hoste foris, quam intus foro vexaretur.

As to the state of Ireland in 1515, see the document printed in my *Ballads from MSS.* (Ballad Soc.), p. 38–40.

GLOSSARY

(MAINLY)

BY THOMAS AUSTIN.

———•———

& (and), an, a, 2/3, 116/7 ; & noon, anon, 72/18.

A, *prep.* on, 12/17, 16/35 ; in, 44/8 ; by, 66/2.

Abate, *vb.* flutter the wings, 56/32. Used like *Bate.*

Aboue, *adv.* above, he was all a., had the upper hand, 120/3 ; abouen, 116/27 ; abow, 117/26, 121/3.

Abydynge, *sb.* expectation, 111/33.

Abydynge, *vb.* a. aftyr ham, waiting for them, 124/28.

Adde, *vb.* had, 68/2.

A-fryght, *pp.* frightened, afraid, 114/22.

Agryse, *pp.* terrified, 100/2.

Agylte, *vb.* sin, 88/1.

Aleueth, *num. adj.* eleven, 118/14. See opposite page.

Allerformest, foremost of all, 50/24 ; alther-formyst, 51/24.

Allerleste, least of all, 146/28 ; alltherleste, 147/28.

Aller-next, next of all, 12/33 ; althernexte, 13/34.

Allience, *sb.* alliance, allies, 73/27, 87/8.

Allyees, *sb.* allies, 72/27. Fr. *alliés.*

Alonge, *adv.* always, 54/29.

Alout, *adv.* all out, or ? aloud, 104/12.

Althyr, 101/3, ? either.

Aly, *adj.* holy, 42/36.

Amaied, *pp.* amayed, dismayed, 12/16 ; amayed, 16/31, 20/33, 56/5.

Amonneschyd, *vb.* admonished, warned, 57/13 ; amonessed, 93/10 ; amonested, 56/13, 92/10.

An, *prep.* on : an-heghe, on high, 112/34, an-hey, 113/34 ; an-hond, in hand, 74/17 ; an-hors, on horseback, 58/25, 100/28 ; an Iresshe, in Irish, 116/33.

Anguysshes, *sb.* anguishes, anxieties, 96/13 ; angwyschis, 97/13.

Anguysshous, *adj.* anxious, 104/8. O.Fr. *anguissus.*

Anone ryght, *adv.* straightway, 148/22 ; anoone-ryght, 82/2.

Aplesid, *pp.* a. of, pleased with, 37/35.

Ar, *pron.* their, 8/17. See *Har.*

Ar, *conj.* ere, 8/9, 22/23, 74/34 ; are, before, 9/10 ; before, 58/10.

Ared, *vb.* tell, declare, 97/25 ; arede, 96/26.

Arere, *vb.* lift up, stir up, 22/1 ; set right, heal, restore, 44/5 ; restore, rebuild, 106/9 ; areren, raise, 44/15 ; arered, raised, 30/16 ; arere, 23/1.

Arew, arow, in a row, 71/13 ; a rewe, 70/13.

Argh, *adj.* timid, cowardly, 16/30, 114/6 (feinte, 115/6) [1].

Argly, *adv.* timidly, in a cowardly way, 16/23 (fently, 17/23) [1].

Arreden, *vb.* eared, ploughed, cultivated, 128/7 ; Erredyn, 129/7.

Artrow, *sb.* overtrow, mistrust, suspicion, 133/13 ; ortrow, 132/14.

---

[1] In all old words like *argh, arghly,* the reader should look on the opposite page for the Rawlinson MS. equivalent, which is generally later, tho' for the Dublin *ar[y]vcd,* 24/34, the Rawlinson has *londide.*

Aryse, *vb.* arise, rebel, 132/5 ; arryse, 133.

Aryued, *vb.* arrived, landed, 24/34.

As, *conj.* for *ac,* but, 4/2.

Asquynt, *adv.* asquint, aslant, obliquely, 94/20.

Assemble, *vb.* join battle, 24/15, 30/26.

Assembly, *vb.* assemble, 64/5.

Asseth, *sb.* satisfaction, penance, 86/23.

Astage, *sb.* hostage, 24/23.

Astryf, *adv.* astrife, emulously, with rivalry, 50/26.

Atene, *vb.* vex, irritate, 38/24.

Ather, *conj.* either, or, 100/3. Note pronunciation.

A thre, in three parts, 104/26 ; at thre, 67/19.

Attyre, *sb.* venom, 20/23, 102/27, 114/2.

Auctorice, *vb.* legalise, set in authority, 107/27 (avaunce, 106/27).

Aurel, *sb.* April, 77/28 ; auril, 76/28.

A-waitede, *vb.* watcht, expected, 2/19.

Aweyward, *adv.* awayward, off the land, *i. e.* westwardly, 66/33 ; away, 130/19.

Awreke, *vb.* a. hym, awreak himself, avenge himself, 4/5.

A yere, *adv.* yearly, 66/2.

Ayeyne, *prep.* against, on the approach of, 130/2 ; *adv.* again, 130/3.

Ayeyns, *prep.* against, to meet, 54/13.

Ayse, *sb.* ease, 148/1.

Bad, *vb.* prayed, 28/11.

Baghel, *sb.* bagle, crosier, 122/13, 123/12 ; baghell, 122/12. L. *baculum.*

Bale, *sb.* sorrow, evil, 20/24.

Baret, *sb.* barrat, strife, battle, 146/23.

Barnen, *vb.* burnt, 54/4.

Battes, *sb.* bats, sticks, staves, 144/28 ; battis, 145/31.

Becomlyche, *adj.* becoming, comely, 76/14 ; becomly, 102/20 ; becumliche, 54/24.

Becryed, *vb.* cryed to, called on, 30/32, 46/20.

Begetes, *sb.* begets, gains, 81/15 ; beyetes, 80/15.

Begynnyge, *vb.* begin, 54/21.

Be-heght, *pp.* promised, 40/9 ; be-het,

vb. promised, 18/34 ; behete, 28/19, 114/29.

Behoud, *sb.* behoof, benefit, 112/30.

Behowaybyll, *adj.* behovable, needful, suitable, 121/4 ; covenable, D.

Belad, *pp.* narrow b., treated them straitly or hardly, 40/21 ; bilad' hym, led him, lived, 2/9 ; hard' biladde, *vb.* treated hardly, 2/6 ; bylad, 41/22 ; by-ladde, conducted, bore, 54/12.

Beleft, *vb.* remained, 118/14 ; *pp.* remaining, left, 58/10.

Belokene, *pp.* shut in, 50/12 ; belokken, 51/12. See *Belouke,* N. E. D.

Belyggynge, *vb.* beleaguing, beleaguering, 104/5.

Be-name, *vb.* forbad, 31/9 ; be-nomen, *pp.* taken away, 60/34 ; byname, deprive of, 100/9.

Berewid, *vb.* bereft of, 45/5 ; berewys, bereave, *imper.,* 35/10.

Berre, *vb.* bear, 145/2.

Besech, *vb.* beseek, try to get, cast at, show to, 110/30 (malyngne agaynys, 111/30).

Besete, *vb.* beset, blockade, 48/16 : *pp.* set, possest, 102/19 ; besette, 103/19.

Be-taght, *vb.* betook, gave, committed, entrusted, 86/14.

Be-tak, *vb.* accompanyed, 20/18 ; betake, 21/18 ; betaken, settled, arranged, 72/31 ; betoke, entrusted to, 108/27.

Betheght, *vb.* betook, gave to, 92/11 ; betoke, 93/11.

Bethwene, *prep.* between, 10/12.

Blote, *adj.* soft, marshy, wet, 122/3.

Blywe, *adv.* belive, quickly, 29/30.

Bolnys, *sb.* boldness, 111/35.

Bolthenys, *sb.* boldness, 75/15.

Bostious, *adj.* rough, boisterous, 149/17 ; boustyous, 148/17.

Bot, *adj.* both, 106/12.

Bot, *conj.* but, unless, 68/13, 106/12 ; bot yf, unless, 78/30.

Both, *conj.* but, 14/34, 22/7, 32/25, 50/4 ; bott, 22/32 ; bot, 106/12.

Boxome, *adj.* obedient, loyal, nonrebellious, 32/29.

Boxom-fastines, *sb.* buxomfastness

firm obedience, 62/18; buxumfast-nys, 63/18.

Branden, *vb.* burnt, 14/24; brandyn, 15; branten, 120/33.

Brouken, *vb.* brook, enjoy, hold, 34/13.

Buryles, *sb.* buryels, burials, graves, 37/21; (pute, pits, 36/18).

Buttellerie, *sb.* butlery, buttery, 62/27. O. Fr. *bouteillerie.*

By, *vb.* be, 106/15.

By, *prep.* about, near, 15/6; by so, on these terms, 24/23; by forward, by agreement, 74/9; by-halues, besides, aside, 74/24; by so that, on the terms that, 24/23.

Bygger, *sb.* buyer, 40/2, 7.

Byled, *vb.* built, 128/10.

Bynyn, *vb.* benime, take away, 68/22.

Byssy, *adj.* busy, 99/18.

Byth, *vb.* beeth, are, 33/26.

Cabilys, *sb.* cables, 13/12.

Calange, *sb.* challenge, claim, 21/1. O. Fr. *Calanger.*

Campled, *vb.* wrangled, contended, fought, 74/33; camplid, 75/33.

Camplynges, *sb.* wranglings, contests, battles, 126/13.

Candrede, *sb.* cantred, hundred, 56/21; cantred, 8/19, 12/33; a Cantrede is ' an hundret toun lond' (100 town-lands or townships), 124/2.

Castel, *vb.* castle, fortify, 127/22; castely, 126/22; casteled, 128/3.

Cee, *sb.* see: Cee churche, Cathedral, 37/31.

Chamfaste, *adj.* shamefast, 76/13.

Chase, *pp.* chosen, 124/12.

Cheffar, *sb.* trade, 12/7.

Chek-toth, *sb.* cheek-tooth, grinder, double tooth, 108/8.

Chepmen, *sb.* chapmen, 38/33.

Cheuetayn, *sb.* chieftain, 26/11.

Chippe, *sb.* ship, 13/13; chippis, ships, 13/6.

Chippmen, *sb.* shipmen, 13/10.

Churchey, *sb.* churchyard, 71/26; church-hay, 63/32.

Clene, *adv.* clean, quite, entirely, 146/7.

Clenly, *adv.* cleanly, quite, wholly, 121/3, 145/15; clenlych, 120/3.

Clepynge, *sb.* calling, call, 76/2.

Clewe, *vb.* cleft, clave, 31/34, 71/32.

Clos, *sb.* close, enclosed land, 10/5.

Come, *sb.* arrival, coming, 108/15, 120/30; comys, 109/15.

Comerous, *adj.* cumbrous, difficult to pass, 54/8.

Comynly, *adv.* in common, together, 34/33, 38/30.

Condicones, *sb.* 125/15; theves, 124/15.

Conquestre, *sb.* conquest, 56/22. O. Fr.

Constytucions, *sb.* constitutions, laws, 64/26.

Cornelis, *sb.* crenelles, battlements, 16/31.

Corpus domini, *sb.* mass-wafer, 52/23.

Coste, *sb.* purpose (R.), 68/4, 74/17.

Costes, *sb.* coasting-vessels?, 80/5.

Croice, *sb.* cross, 36/29; cros, 37/29. O. Fr. *crois.*

Croun, *sb.* crown of the head, 42/27; croune, 42/24.

Culuertnesse, *sb.* falseness, villainy, 126/31.

Cytteyns, *sb.* citizens, 122/27. O. Fr. *citeien; citayn.*

Dawes, *sb.* days, out of d. = out of life, 34/10, 76/4.

Defended, *vb.* = defendeth, let us defend, *imper.*, 20/28.

Defeuly, *vb.* defoul, tread under foot, 35/29; defouly, 34/29.

Dele, *sb.* deal, part, 62/21.

Deled, *vb.* dealt, divided, 104/25.

Delycion, ? *sb.* daintiness, 98/13.

Delycious, *adj.* delicate, dainty, 99/14.

Demyd, *pp.* deemed, doomed, sentenced, 35/15.

Dennysh, 46/17; Danish.

Derne, *adj.* hidden, 18/30, 114/22.

Dernely, *adv.* secretly, privily, 78/8.

Derward, *adj.* dearworth, precious, 110/34; derwarthest, most valuable, 36/25.

Destrued, *pp.* destroyed, 106/10.

Deue, *adj.* deaf, 44/13.

Deynously, *adv.* disdainfully, 72/3.

Didden, dydde, *vb.* See *Do.*

Do, *vb.* put, 30/6, 38/34, 94/16; turn, 76/6; done hym on, set him on, 100/3; didde, *past t.* turned, 16/31; didden, set, 10/1; dydde, set, 70/7.

Dobbe, *vb.* dub, 94/13.

Dome, *sb.* judgment, 34/14.

Dotous, *adj.* doubtful, uncertain, 86/17 ; doutos, 87/17 ; doutouse, 24/13.

Doute, *vb.* fear, 24/15.

Drawen, *vb.* protract, lead, 50/4.

Dredlyche, *adj.* dreadly, dreadful, terrible, 114/9.

Drent, *vb.* drowned, 32/5.

Durke, *adj.* dark, 50/9.

Durknesse, *sb.* darkness, 50/10.

Durre, *sb.* door, 42/22.

Dyd, *vb.* set, placed, 74/29. See *Do.*

Dynt, *sb.* dint, stroke, 46/17.

Dysheryted, *vb.* 40/20 ; disinherited. D for th, 16/34.

Day, *pron.* they, 10/19, 12/21, 24/10.

Droğñ, *prep.* through, 12/24, 14/8, 18/9, 22/7.

I-Drow, *pp.* thrown, 18/1.

Dynge, *sb.* thing, 88/27.

Eche, *vb.* increase, 146/4.

Edwyte, *vb.* reproved, twitted, rebuked, 60/9.

Eft, *adv.* after, 82/13, 88/26, 90/1 efte, 108/29.

Elde, *sb.* eld, age, 58/30.

Eldren, (*adj.*) ? *sb.* forefathers' (or ancestral), 38/17 ; eldryñ, 39/17.

Eldrene, *sb.* ancestors, 28/6, 7 ; eldryn, 29/6, 7.

Elf (fare), 17/13 ; helf (fare), 16/14 ; elves' doings.

Eme, *sb.* eam, nephew, 31/14, 73/35 ; emys, 15/33, 101/15.

Enchesoun, *sb.* occasion, cause, 88/2, 20/16.

Encombrement, *sb.* encumberment, obstruction, annoyance, harm, 22/13.

Eneche, *vb.* (? increase) ineche, implant, 92/1.

Engyn, *sb.* art, contrivance, 18/28.

Ense, *sb.* ends, 80/29.

Entre, *sb.* entry, 54/6 ; entrest, 55/7.

Entredyte, *vb.* interdict, lay under interdict, 68/15.

Enuy, *sb.* envy, 20/19.

Enuyouse, *adj.* envyous, 114/6 ; envyouse, emulous, 100/2.

Er, *adv.* ere, before, 120/29.

Erne, *vb.* earn, mourn, 34/28.

Erne, *sb.* eagle, 114/18.

Ers, *sb.* ears, 15/24.

Erthe-weyes, *sb.* ways under ground, 19/30.

Erth-hous, *sb.* underground dwelling, 120/31.

Estren, *adj.* eastern, east, 28/27.

Ette, *vb.* ate, 89/22.

Eunynge, *sb.* evening, equal, peer, 54/19.

Evyncrystyñ, *sb.* fellow - christian, 39/11, 67/14.

Exstymacioun, *sb.* suspicion, 129/14. O. Fr. *exstimation.*

Eygne, *sb.* eyes, 97/17.

Facon, *sb.* falcon, 58/4 ; faucoun gentel, 56/30.

Fale, *adj.* fele, many, 74/10, 86/4.

Falthyr, *sb.* fautors, favorers, partisans, 79/7. Fr. *fauteur.*

Fantstones, *sb.* fontstones, stone fonts, 64/33 ; fantstonys, 65.

Farcostes, *sb.* far-coasters?, 80/5, 81/5.

Fawes, *sb.* falls?, heavy, things dropt, 96/2 ; fawis, 97/2.

Febelier, *adj.* more feeble, 69/5.

Fele, *adj.* many, 16/10.

Felony, *sb.* villany, 102/3.

ffer, *adv.* f. within-yn nyght, far into the night, 16/9.

Ferd, *sb.* host, army, 14/5.

Ferde, *sb.* fear, 17/14.

Ferdnesse, *sb.* fear, fright, 20/29, 38/27.

Ferly, *adj.* strange, 16/29.

Ferly, *adv.* wonderfully?, 16/12.

Fersly, *adv.* fiercely, 17/11.

Ferth, *num. adj.* fourth, 118/19.

Festnen, *vb.* make firm, restore, 44/14.

Feynte, *adj.* faint, idle, 115/6.

Feyre, *adv.* far, 50/34.

Fikyllid, *vb.* temporised, 145/9.

Fleted, *vb.* floated, 116/26.

Fletes, *sb.* fleets, 80/9 ; flittes, 81/9 ; flot, 126/23 ; flytte, 127/23.

Fleysly, *adj.* fleshly, fleshy, 100/1.

Flittes, *sb.* See *Fletes.*

Flote, *sb.* fleet, herd of swine, 74/1.

Flowen, *vb.* fled, 96/21.

Fobler, *adj.* feebler, 68/6.

Foderes, *sb.* deceivers, 148/3.

Folk, *adj.* ? for foble, feeble, 50/15.

Folke-mele, indiscriminately, 36/3.

Foolrede, *sb.* fool's counsel, foolery, folly, 68/20 ; fooly, 69.

Foot-falle, *vb.* prostrate oneself, 62/18.

For, *conj.* in order that, 104/24.

Forcleue, *vb.* cleft, 58/2 ; for-clew, 59/2.

Fore-lete, *vb.* let go, 68/29.

For-hold, *pp.* withheld, kept unburied, 108/14.

Forlese, *vb.* forelost, lost, 54/11.

Formane, *sb.* leader, 36/1 ; formene, front ranks, 30/33.

Forme, *adj.* first, 64/15 ; formest, *super.*, 50/28 ; formyst, 51.

Forshape, *pp.* misshapen, 130/25.

Forsoke, *vb.* renounce, refuse, decline, 4/13, 78/17 ; for-sok, 72/16.

Forsoken, *vb.* declined, 104/12.

Forswely, *vb.* swallow up, 58/27.

Fort, *conj.* till, 84/27, 126/11.

Fortelet, *sb.* fortlet, 116/6.

Forth, (before ' with ') *adv.* forthwith, 20/5, 90/20, 104/32.

For-þane, *conj.* Nat f. notwithstanding, 4/1.

For-they, *conj.* therefore, 73/22 ; ffor-thy, 72/23.

Forthmost, *adj.* foremost, 16/4.

Forume, *sb.* form, 39/12.

Forwarde, *sb.* bargain, 10/12 ; agreement, 74/9, 108/30 ; forward-makynge, m. of agreements, 128/9.

Fourdyr, *adv.* further, 15/25.

Franchise, *sb.* freedom, 20/15.

Fresly, *adv.* fiercely, 14/12, 35/34 ; fressely, 81/9.

Frightnes, *sb.* fright, 16/15, 26.

Fryst, *num.* first, 17/4, 31/33.

Fyf, *num. adj.* five, 62/21 ; fywe, 63/21.

Fylthed(e), *sb.* filthhead, filthiness, 64/6, 65/6.

Fyne, *sb.* fine, 66/10.

Galosis, *sb.* gallows, 35/16.

Galyotz, *sb.* pirates ?, 22/32.

Garnesyd, *pp.* garnished, fortified, 51/1. Fr. *garnir.*

Gentil, *sb.* gentry, set, 101/17.

Gentryce, *sb.* set, clan, 112/2.

Gentrye, *sb.* gentry, 100/18.

Gestes, *sb.* deeds, 120/10.

Gettynges, *sb.* gettings, gain, plunder, 26/34.

Girsliche, *adv.* terribly, 14/22 (? *adj.*).

Good, *sb.* goods, 54/5.

Grad, *vb.* cried out, 4/1.

Greped, *vb.* griped, gripped, 126/26.

Grewid, *vb.* grieved, pained, 109/9; grewid, *pp.* 39/25.

Grymly, *adj.* dreadful, terrible, 59/13.

Gylte, *sb.* fault, 40/8.

Gyued, *vb.* gyved, fettered, 60/10 ; gywid, 61/10.

Half, *sb.* side ; ethere h., either side, 8/19 ; euerich h., every side, 4/16 ; euche h., each side, 5/18 ; hys h., his side, 24/32 ; oon h., one side, 22/25 ; a south h., on the south side, 30/16 ; on his moþer half, on his mother's side, 8/15 ; halue, *pl.* 100/21.

Halte, *vb.* held, 64/10 ; holte, hold, 64/11.

Halowene, *sb.* saints, 122/1 ; halwene, 44/11.

Hame, *pron.* them, 4/12.

Hamlynge, *adj.* ambling, 89/21.

Hand, *sb.* other h., second hand, 78/17.

Har, *pron.* their, 9/17, 10/20, 74/31, 120/30; hare, 31/14 ; theirs, 32/15.

Har, *adv.* ere, sooner.

Hard, *pp.* heard, 29/32.

Hardynes, *sb.* hardiness, boldness, 110/35.

Haris, *pron.* theirs, 49/33 ; hars, 48/34.

Hauteyne, *adj.* haughty, 76/16. O. Fr. *hautain.*

Haw, *vb.* have, 34/7 ; hawydyn, had, 27/7.

Haye, *sb.* hay, haw, churchyard, 63/32 ; 62/32.

Hedid, *pp.* headed, beheaded, 151/8.

Heed, *sb.* ? head, 78/33 ; heeddes, heads, princes ?, 34/28.

Heere, *sb.* hair, hair-cloth, 42/5 ; here, 43/5.

Hegh, *vb.* hight (' was callid '), 92/23.

Hegheste, *adj.* highest (' host ' 12/33), 13/33.

Heghlygh, *adv.* highly, 90/25.

Helf far, 16/14, *sb.* elves' doing.

Hell*e*, *vb.* helde, 2/24.

Hellen, *vb.* conceal, hide, 78/1.

Hent, *vb.* received, 10/35; henten, grasp, seize, 56/33, 80/26.

Herbrowe, *vb.* harbour, seek shelter, 66/6.

Her*e*, *pron.* their, 18/29.

Her*e*, *adv.* here, 32/10.

Herly, *adv.* early, 70/7.

Herne, *sb.* nook, corner, 116/7.

Herrer, *sb.* herre, lord, 116/30.

Herth, *sb.* heart, 2/8, 22/28, 50/20.

Herthly, *adj.* earthly, 66/4.

Hertly, *adv.* heartily, courageously, 52/2; hertely, 53/2.

Het, *vb.* was named, 2/3.

Heudes, *sb.* heads, 14/17.

Hey, *adj.* high, 57/29.

Heye, *sb.* 70/27. See *Church-hey*.

Heyth, *adj.* high, noble, 22/32.

Hite, *pron.* it, 25/20.

Hoft-sithes, *adv.* oftentimes, 16/14.

Hold, *adj.* whole, faithful, 60/14; holde, whole, healthy, 59/24.

Homward, *adv.* take h., go home, 86/3.

Hoped, *vb.* looked to, trusted in, had confidence in, 70/22.

Horynesse, *sb.* filthiness, 66/27. Comp. *horowe*, foul, used by Chaucer, pronounced *horry* in Devon. H.

Host, *sb.* army, 16/10, 11, 104/26, 144/2.

Host, *adj.*? hest, hext, highest, largest, 12/32.

Hostyngis, *sb.* expeditions, armies, 17/14.

Hungrod, *adj.* hungered, hungry, 116/8.

Hurtyng, *sb.* hurting, hurt, 16/34.

Hym, *pron.* him; hym þriddesom, comp. Gr. αὐτὸς τρίτος, 14/1, 32/20.

Hyryng*e*, *adj.* hireling, waged, 22/31.

Iappyng*e*, *sb.* japing, jesting, 54/26; Iaypyng*e*, 55/27.

I-bansheth, *pp.* banished, 24/1; y-banshet, 25/1.

I-bydde, *pp.* abided, stayd, 62/8.

I-corne, *pp.* chosen, 22/18.

I-deleth, *pp.* dealt, divided, 66/19.

I-destrued, *pp.* destroyed, 84/32.

I-dobbed, *pp.* dubbed, 94/13.

I-drow, *pp.* thrown, d = th, 18/1.

I-dyght, *pp.* prepared, 58/19.

I-endeth, *pp.* ended, 22/16.

I-flow, *pp.* fled, 46/27.

I-fulled, *pp.* baptized, 64/33; yfullid, 65/33.

I-garnset, *pp.* garnished, fortified, 50/1.

I-hard, *pp.* heard, 28/32.

I-heded, *pp.* beheaded, 150/7.

I-helled, *pp.* iheled, covered, 10/21.

I-herberged, *pp.* filled, stowed, 108/34; I-herbergide, 109/34.

I-herberowid*e*, *pp.* harboured, sheltered, 63/31; I-horberowed, 62/31.

I-hodet, *pp.* hooded, 132/28.

I-hokred, *pp.* insulted, 140/16.

I-horied, *pp.* defiled, 138/32.

I-hosted, *pp.* hosted, quartered, 16/9.

I-lacet, *pp.* laced, 10/17.

Illy, *adv.* in an ill way, 78/7.

Ilyche, *adv.* alike, 66/19.

I-meygnet, *pp.* mingled, 102/27.

Inamliche, *adv.* namely, especially, 16/28.

In-leyde, *pp.* laid in, 37/21.

I-primseined, *pp.* catechized, 64/32, 65/32.

I-quenytea, *pp.* pleased, 36/35.

I-retted, *pp.* charged with, 68/26.

I-roted, *pp.* rooted, 20/27, 112/3, 148/18.

I-sacred, *pp.* sacred, consecrated, 132/28.

I-scomfyte, *pp.* discomfited, 116/20.

I-shent, *pp.* ruined, 68/28, 38/16.

I-shwerne, *pp.* sworn, 24/26.

I-slawe, *pp.* slain, 80/13.

I-stablet, *pp.* established, 64/27.

I-storbet, *pp.* disturbed, 124/34.

I-suywed, *pp.* issued, shot, 116/9.

I-swewed, *pp.* showed, 64/12.

I-told, *pp.* reckoned, 2/4.

I-wepned, *pp.* armed, 80/11.

I-worth, *pp.* become, 102/6, 148/14.

I-wyted, *pp.* blamed, 8/13.

Kappe, *sb.* 46/17; lappe, R. 47/17.

Karue, *vb.* k. of, cut off, 14/23.

Kene, *adj.* keen, fierce, sharp, 112/33.

Kepyng*e*, *sb.* keeping, watch, guard, 53/10; kypyng*e*, 52/9.

Kernel, *sb.* battlement, 10/28.

Knyghten, *sb.* knights', 92/15.

Kynde, *sb.* kind, nature; of k., by nature, naturally, 18/27; Throgh k. of Troy, Through our Trojan origin, 22/26.

Kynde, *adj.* natural, own, 6/27.

Kyndly, *adj.* kindly, natural, 76/16.

Kyndly, *adv.* kindly, naturally, by birth, 22/28; kyndlych, 22/24.

Kynly, *adv.* by kin, by birth, 23/24. See *Kyndly.*

Laked, *vb.* enjoyd, 132/29; lakyd, 133/29.

Large, *adj.* bounteous, generous, 25/2; largh, 24/1.

Laser, *sb.* lazar, leper, 44/13.

Lastes, *sb.* faults, deceits, 102/21.

Latest, *adj.* last in place, 52/1.

Lede, *adj.* folk, 4/24; leed, 64/18.

Lef, *adj.* dear, 108/8; lefe, 111/34.

Lered, *adj.* learned, 42/2; lerid, 43/2.

Leth, *vb.* let, hindered, 52/7; leth, allowed, causd, 64/5.

Lette, *sb.* let, hindrance, 94/5.

Leue, *adj.* dear, 108/6.

Leue, *vb.* leave, omit, 108/10.

Leuet, *vb.* loved, 118/35.

Lewed, *adj.* lewd, uneducated, vulgar, 42/2; lewid, 43/2.

Lewidly, *adv.* lewdly, wickedly, 47/30.

Leyden, *vb.* leyden on, laid on, attacked, 96/2; leydyn, 97/2.

Lif, *adj.* lief, pleasing, 8/22.

Lodderly, *adv.* wickedly, 22/33.

Lodesmane, *sb.* pilot, leader, 22/21; 36/28.

Loge, *sb.* lodge, wattled hut, 10/3.

Loghe, *adj.* low, short, 88/10.

Loly, *adj.* grim, terrible, 40/8, 58/12.

Lolych, *adj.* lovely, affable, 103/18; louelyche, 102/18.

Lome, *adv.* often, frequently, 44/36.

Lost, *sb.* loss, 112/23; loste, 146/12; lostes, 8/2; lostis, 97/24; Lostys, 9/2.

Loth, *adj.* hateful, unpleasant, 14/6, 30/19.

Lotles, *adj.* buxom, obedient, 114/4.

Lout, *vb.* l. ham, lout themselves, do obeisance, 44/26.

Lowe, *sb.* love, 131/14.

Lych, *sb.* like, body, 88/26; lyche, 89.

Lyddere, *adj.* lither, bad, wicked, 44/6, 68/7; lyder, 32/14.

Lyddyrly, *adv.* litherly, wickedly, 46/30.

Lyddernysse, *sb.* litherness, wickednesse, 76/29.

Lygne, *adj.* gentle?, 102/17.

Lyket, *vb.* was liked, pleasd, 34/14.

Lyme, *sb.* limit, bond?, 62/18.

Lyue, *sb.* life, 82/32.

Manequelleres, *sb.* mankillers, 125/16.

Maner, *sb.* manner; many m. metes, many kind of meats, 62/28; manners, politeness, 22/10.

Mane-shipe, *sb.* manship, courtesy, 4/33; manshype, 70/12.

Manly, *adv.* in a manly way, 24/6.

Manred, *sb.* homage, 56/20.

Man-shyply, *adv.* worshipfully, reverently, 66/22.

Manslaghtres, *sb.* manslaughterers, 124/16.

Mansynge, *sb.* cursing, excommunication, 120/17.

Marche, *sb.* march, border, 72/18; 146/31.

Mayny, *sb.* 115/22. See *Meignè.*

Me, *pron.* men (comp. German *man*), one, they, 16/5, 24/14, 32/27, 42/10, 70/33.

Meet-yeuer, *sb.* meat-giver, 54/25; met-yeuer, 112/36. Comp. *mete-gavel.*

Meignè, *sb.* household troops, 22/18; menny, 79/28; mennye, 79/13; meny, 115/10; meygnees, 66/5; meyne, 26/8; meynne, 39/5; meyngne, 27/9. O. Fr. *meignee, meyne.*

Mekely, *adv.* humbly, kindly, 48/2.

Membres, *sb.* manly m., manly members, privy parts, 44/18.

Merres, *sb.* meres, boundaries, 38/17.

Meste, *adv.* most, 42/7.

Mesury, *sb.* misery, 43/15.

Meteful, *adj.* moderate, 113/24. See *Methefull.*

Methe, *sb.* moderation, 98/12.

Methefull, *adj.* moderate, 112/24.

Methelyche, *adj.* moderate, 70/18;

methlych, 98/28 ; metlych, 76/15 ; metlyche, 98/10 ; middle-sized.

Mich, *adj.* much, large, 34/27 ; mich yuell, much or great evil, leprosy, 32/7.

Modelyng, *sb.* meddling, 56/18.

Mone, *sb.* moan, complaint, 28/23.

Morowenynge, *sb.* morning, 82/21.

Most, *vb.* must, could, 40/22.

Mostdele, *adv.* mostdeal, mostly, 16/1.

Mostwhat, *adv.* mostly, for the most part, 88/17.

Mother-church, *sb.* cathedral, 36/29.

Motynge, *sb.* mooting, pleading, disputing, 144/29.

Mych, *adj.* large, 56/29, 74/1 ; myche, 74/2.

Myght & mayn, might & main, 116/15.

Mynyed, *vb.* reminded, warned, 74/29, 84/25.

Mys-byfelle, *vb.* misbefell, fell amiss, 124/15 ; mys-be-felle, 125/16.

Mysdone, *vb.* misdo, 101/32.

Myse-lyckenys, *sb.* mislikeness, strange shape (a wolf-woman), 131/25.

Myssayse, *sb.* misease, 40/5. O. Fr. *mesaise.*

Myssayse, *adj.* miseased, 114/23 ; myssaysid, 115/22.

Na, *adv.* not, 112/2.

Name, *sb.* name, 6/33.

Name, *vb.* took, 6/12 ; name, 2/22, 23 ; n. an hand, 72/24 ; namen, 80/4 ; n. sekernesse, took surety, 74/8.

Namely, *adv.* especially, 52/17, 66/4.

Namy, *vb.* name, 130/10.

Narow, *adv.* narrowly, closely, 40/21 ; narowe, 4/19 ; narrow, 41/22, 97/10.

Naroweis, narrow ways, 81/26.

Nas, *vb.* ne was, was not, 16/21, 26/21, 72/16, 114/8.

Nat forthy, *conj.* notwithstanding, nevertheless, 76/20, 77/22.

Nathales, *conj.* nevertheless, 78/10.

Neb, *sb.* (? nose). face, *vultus*, 98/11.

Neght, *adv.* nigh, nearly, 26/13.

Nembre, *sb.* number, 101/22 ; nenbre, 100/23.

Ner, *vb.* ne were, were not, 30/31, 100/8.

Neue, *sb.* nephew, 14/33. See *eme.*

Neuer (ne were), *vb.* should never be, 121/18 ; neuere, 120/18.

Never no more, 48/31.

Neyght, *adv.* nigh, near, 74/16.

Nobelych, noblych, *adv.* nobly, 35/29, 34/29.

Noon-dayes, *sb.* noonday, 50/32.

North, by n., to the north of, 70/26.

Nuy, *sb.* noy, vexation, affliction, 90/7. Comp. *noxia.*

Nyst, ne wist, knew not, 4/29.

Nythe, *sb.* a nythe = at night, 72/33.

O, *num.* one, 106/12 ; oo, 89/26, 106/12.

O, *prep.* of, 108/34.

Of, *adv.* off, 12/11, 14/23, 32/4, 74/32.

Oftere, *adv.* oftener, 54/22.

Oke, *vb.* ached, paind, 108/9.

Omost, omyste, *adv.* overmost, uppermost, 106/1, 107/1.

Ond, *sb.* hatred, malice, 110/30 ; onde, 111/30.

Onful, *adj.* ondfull, malicious, 102/24 ; onfull, 103/24.

Onþer, *prep.* under, 6/31.

Opyn, *adj.* open, uncovered, 42/22.

Ordeynly, *adv.* well o. = in good order, 46/12.

Ortrow, *sb.* overtrow, mistrust, suspicion, 128/14, 132/14 ; artrow, 133.

Ost, *adj.* burnt ?, 50/2.

Ostmen, *sb.* hostmen, soldiers, 82/23.

Ostynge, *sb.* hosting, expedition, 16/14 ; see *Hostyngis.*

Oþer, *conj.* other, or, 24/6.

Other, *adj.* second, 50/29, 76/12, 88/8.

Ouerd[r]ede, *vb.* ouerdrede, overdreaded, 14/20.

Ouergoste, *vb.* goest beyond, 38/17.

Ouer-hand, *sb.* upperhand, superiority, 34/6, 50/11, 106/3, 118/23.

Ouersaille, *vb.* sail over, upset ?, 16/12.

Ouerthrowen, *vb. pass.* be prostrated, 62/21.

Ouer-truste, *sb.* overboldness, presumption, 22/10. Comp. *Overhope.*

Oure, *pron.* ours, 24/7, 96/15.

Out-chese, *vb.* choose out, 34/8.

Out-commyn, *adj.* come from foreign parts, 12/29 ; out-comen, 18/5.

Out-tak, *pp.* outtaken, except, 122/8.

Owne, *adj.* = own house, tent, 62/31.
Owre, *prep.* over, 130/2.
Ows, *pron.* us, 22/3, 30.

Paas, *sb.* pass, 104/22 ; pas, 104/25 ;
paace, 55/9.
Panetrye, *sb.* pantry, 62/27. Fr.
paneterie.
Pany, *sb.* penny, 92/5.
Paralys, *adj.* paralysed folk, 44/14.
Parlement, *sb.* conference, 6/21, 18/11,
72/31. O. Fr. *parlement.*
Party, *sb.* part, side, 110/1.
Party arms, arms vertically divided,
10/4.
Pelfre, *sb.* pilfer, plunder, 52/8. O. Fr.
pelfrer.
Pledynge, *sb.* suing, 112/20.
Plenary, *adv.* fully, openly, 31/27.
Pleneden, *vb.* sported, 74/18 ; pleydyn,
75.
Plente, *sb.* generosity, 102/31.
Plete, *sb.* plate, 46/10.
Poere, *sb.* power, O. Fr. 48/11.
Postes, *sb.* pillars, supports, 120/6.
Powere, *sb.* forces, 2/22, 4/17.
Prayes, *sb.* preys, booty, 80/1.
Prayes-takynge, *sb.* taking of booty,
78/27 ; pray-takynge, 118/11.
Praye, *vb.* prey, plunder, 80/3, 23 ;
preedyn, plundered, 81/3.
Presons, *sb.* prisoners, 54/5, 15.
Primseine, *vb.* 'sign with the cross,
make a catechumen,' 64/32.
Priuisant, *adj.* foreseeing ?, 80/28.
Prout, prowt, *adj.* proud, 22/5, 38/20.
Prow, *vb.* prove, 85/5.
Prutter, *adj.* prouder, 56/7.
Pullid, *vb.* plundered, robbed, 145/9.
Pullynge, *sb.* pilling, plundering, 112/
21.
Purueynge, *adj.* provident, prudent,
98/21.
Pute, *sb.* pit, 36/18.
Pylfre, *sb.* pilfer, plunder, pillage, 80/4,
114/24. O. Fr. *pelfrer.*
Pynsynge, *sb.* affliction, 88/6.

Queller, *sb.* killer, 44/5.
Queme, *vb.* please, satisfy, 54/30, 98/15.
Quenyntyse, queyntyse, *sb.* cunning,
craft, 98/22, 99/22. O. Fr. *quointise.*

Quethene, *vb.* overcome R., 44/15.
Queynt, *adj.* cunning, sly, wily, 26/1,
98/21 ; quent, 27/1 ; queynth, 128/2.
Quyte, *adj.* quit, clear, free, 96/20.
Quytten, *pp.* free, clean away, 80/
27.

Raas, *sb.* race, rush, 16/12.
Radyr, *adv.* rather, more willingly,
7/13 ; earlier, before, 91/20.
Raght, *vb.* raught, recked, 32/9.
Ran, *vb.* r. to harme, 112/26.
Rascayll, *sb.* rascal, rabble, 50/21.
O. Fr. *rascayle.*
Rathe, *adv.* soon, 24/29, 84/1 ; rather,
sooner, 28/23, 68/14 ; before, 90/20,
130/4.
Rather, *adj.* earlier, previous, original,
86/4, 88/2.
Raunceoun, *sb.* ransom, 46/29.
Rebuked, *vb.* repulsed, checked, 34/34.
Recet, *sb.* refuge, harbour, 18/29,
30/28, 56/5 ; recette, 19/29, 31/28.
Recheste, *vb.* reckest, 108/9.
Rede, *sb.* counsel, 10/18, 68/33.
Remewid, *vb.* removed, 147/13.
Rere, *vb.* rear, raise, exalt, 46/2 ; rerid,
took, captured, lifted, 107/30.
Rescewyd, *vb.* received, 123/27.
Reue, *vb.* rob, 114/3 ; rew, 115/3.
Reuer, *sb.* riever, robber, 112/21.
Reut, *sb.* ruth, pity, 8/1 ; reuth, 22/34,
54/18.
Reuthful, *adj.* ruthful, 32/23.
Reuynge, *sb.* rieving, plundering, 144/
31 ; rewynge, 145/25 ; reyuynge,
145/32.
Rewe, *vb.* rue, regret, 146/1.
Robbed, *vb.* plundered, 80/23.
Rodes, *sb.* r. crucyfyed, crucifixes,
122/1.
Roghly, *adv.* r. lokynge, rough looking,
88/9.
Row, *adv.* r. lokynge, rough looking,
89/9. A. S. *ráw.*
Ruthlynge, *sb.* rattling, 16/13.
Rychesshe, *sb.* riches, 96/24. Fr.
richesse.
Rygge, *sb.* back, 58/2.
Ryght, *vb.* r. vp, raise up, 44/3 ; set
up again, restore, 86/4.
Ryuely, *adv.* especially ?, 128/12.

Salletis, *sb.* sallets, light helmets, 11/24.

Sam-crysp, *adj.* somewhat curled, 98/11; **sam-roed,** *adj.* somewhat ruddy, 54/27; same rede, 89/8; saun-rede, 88/8. A. S. *sam,* half.

Saue, *vb.* saw, 49/6, 146/11.

Sawe, *prep.* save, except, 18/21, 54/10.

Sawe, *vb.* save, 73/6; sawit, saved, 4/23.

Schavnge, *sb.* change, 51/6.

Scomflted, *pp.* discomfited, 117/19.

Screwid, *adj.* shrewd, cursed, bad, evil, 69/6.

See way, seaway (comp. highway, road-way), 80/3.

Seke, *adj.* sick, 66/13.

Sekernesse, *sb.* security, 74/8; syke[r]-nesse, 50/7.

Sekiritesse, *sb.* securities, bonds, 6/22.

Selcouth, *adj.* various, 28/33; wonderful, 44/11, 120/1, 126/13.

Selth, *sb.* happiness, benefit, 50/8, 92/18; success, 98/23.

Selue, *adj.* same, 100/18.

Selyly, *adv.* happily, 42/32.

Semblant, glad s., 98/12; sterne s., 98/27; fayr s., 102/18; semblant, 112/36; look, countenance.

Senne, *sb.* synod, 120/15.

Senthe, *adj.* seventh, 58/30; Senfte, 59/29.

Seysyne, *sb.* seisin, possession, 82/12.

Sheldrun, *sb.* shields, 31/29.

Shendshype, *sb.* injury, harm, 114/3; shenshipp, 115/3.

Sho, *pron.* she, 4/1.

Shorthlych, *adv.* shortly, presently, 114/22.

Shroue, *vb. int.* confessed, 130/23.

Shyrth, *sb.* shirt, 42/5.

Sill, *vb.* sell, 39/34. See *Syllene.*

Sitè, *sb.* city, 32/17, 18.

Sithe, *sb.* times, 26/6.

Skyer, *sb.* squire, 8/32, 33.

Slaght, *sb.* slaughter, 14/16, 20/28, 116/36, 138/32.

Slaked, *vb.* slacked, failed, 48/24.

Sleghly, *adv.* slily, 68/3.

Sleghtes, *sb.* contrivances, 128/13.

Slegthlych, *adv.* craftily, 128/9; sleghtly, 144/17.

Slouedyne, *vb.* slew, 39/8.

Smert, *adj.* smart, sharp, rough; smert lond, rough wild land, 128/29.

Smertly, *adv.* smartly, vigorously, 104/33; smyrtly, 105/33.

Smyth, *vb.* smite, 24/12; *pt.* smote, 106/35.

Snel, *adj.* quick, active, 74/27.

Snellych, *adv.* quickly, 82/3.

Soine, *adv.* soon, 60/11.

Soldrys, *sb.* shoulders, 89/11.

Solempnelych, *adv.* solemnly, 90/25.

Soth, *adj.* sooth, true, 54/1.

Sortelych, *adv.* shortly, 93/14; Sortely, *adv.* shortly, 149/22.

Sorynesse, *sb.* sorriness, soreness, sorrow, 110/1, 112/23.

Spares, *sb.* battle-axe, 83/7; sparris, 17/12. See *Sparth.*

Sparth, *sb.* battle-axe, 74/11, 26, 33; sparthes, 16/13.

Spendynge, *sb.* spending, money, 78/27.

Spourges, *sb.* spurge, thing to get rid of, scourge, 112/3. Comp. O. Fr. *espourger.*

Spousbrych, *sb.* spousebreach, adultery, 102/23.

Spousehede, spoushode, *sb.* wedded state, 64/30.

Sproty, *adj.* thin, small, 54/28. Comp. *Sprot,* sprout, splinter.

Stabil, *vb.* establish, confirm, 69/29; stable, 68/30.

Staluarthly, *adv.* stalwartly, sturdily, 116/1.

Stalwardnesse, *sb.* stalwartness, strength, sturdiness, 52/2; stalwarthnesse, 54/20.

Sted, *sb.* stead, place, state, 22/35; 'state,' 23/35.

Stordy, *adj.* sturdy, 118/33; stordyer, 116/2.

Storkes, *sb.* storks, 28/24.

Strange, *adj.* strong, 54/8.

Streynth, *vb.* strength, strengthen, 68/30.

Streynth, *sb.* strength, force, meaning, 90/29, 96/14.

Streyntnesse, *sb.* strongness, strength, 94/24; streyntnys, 95/24.

Stronge, *adj.* strong, stormy, 66/33.

Stronge, *adv.* strongly, greatly, 4/3.

Stryffly, *adv.* strivingly (? for 'styffly'), 26/29. See *Styfly.*

Styd, *sb.* stead, place, 42/5 ; stydde, 42/6 ; styddes, places, 50/11.

Styfly, *adv.* strongly, valiantly, 80/8, 104/31.

Stylly, *adv.* stilly, in secret, 46/19, 150/12.

Stynte, *vb.* stopped, 111/30; stynt, 112/30.

Suget, *adj.* subject, 24/21 ; subyect, 26/33 ; subyett, 26/21. O. Fr. *Suget.*

Surnesse, *sb.* sureness, security, 51/7.

Surtey, swrte, *sb.* surety, 75/9. Fr. *Sûreté.*

Sybbe, *sb.* relation, 64/29.

Syblynges, *adv.* kinwise, with relatives, 102/23.

Sybrede, *sb.* relationship, 42/11.

Sydlynge, *adv.* sidling, obliquely, 94/19.

Sygge, *vb.* say, 54/18, 98/20.

Sykernesse, *sb.* security, 50/7. See *Sekernesse.*

Sykyrlychest, *adv.* most securely, 68/34.

Syllene, *vb.* sell, 38/32, 40/5.

Syller, *sb.* seller, 40/1.

Talent, *sb.* desire, wish, 6/25.

Tanked, *pp.* thanked, 14/19.

Tene, *sb.* tene, hatred, 4/12.

Tened, *pp.* grieved, vexed, 4/3.

Tethynges, *sb.* tithings, tithes, 66/1.

Thare, *conj.* there = where, 82/18.

Tharmes, *sb.* entrails, intestines, 88/4.

That, *adv.?* read *thar*, 2/24, 65/5.

Thay, *dem.* those, 80/12, 14, 90/26, 116/3 ; they, the, 97/14.

Theghe, *conj.* though, 18/27, 32/9.

Ther, *conj.* where, 32/8, 57/30, 128/4 ; ther-to-for, *adr.* before, 63/29.

Thewes, *sb.* qualities, 16/28, 90/34.

Thewis, *sb.* thieves, 81/30.

Thedynge, *sb.* tiding, 10/7 ; thythyngis, 11/7, 35/31 ; tythynge, 6/15.

this, *adj.* these, 21/29.

Tho, *conj.* when, 4/9.

Tho, *prep.* to, 62/19.

Thoght, *conj.* though, 15/31, 32/7.

Tholle, *vb.* thole, endure, suffer, 4/20 ; þolled, 42/3, 118/24 ; tholleth, sufferd, 38/15 ; tholy, *infin.* 40/5.

Tholmode, *adj.* forbearing, 98/15.

Thondred, *sb.* thunder, 58/28.

þorwe, ? go through with it, 28/12.

Thre, *num.* a thre, in three parts, 66/20 ; at thre, 67/20; tre, 14/5.

Thretynge, *sb.* threatening, 60/9 ; tretynge, 70/9.

þriddesum, *adj.* third, 14/1 ; thrydsome, 32/20 ; thyrdesum, 15/2.

þurleth, *vb.* thirleth, pierceth, 112/5.

Thus, from t. = from this, thence, 60/15.

Thwey, *num.* two, 12/35.

To, *adv.* too, 54/26, 82/3.

To, *art.* the, 10/27.

Toght, *vb.* thought, 16/25, 18/7.

To-hakked, *vb.* hackt to pieces, 82/2.

Toke, *vb.* reacht (to the knee), 116/27.

Told, *vb.* reckoned, 60/8; Moch told by ham-self, thought much of themselves, 148/3 ; tolde, thought, 94/1, 96/25, 97/24.

Tollid, *pp.* sufferd, 39/15.

Ton, *sb.* town, 12/33 ; ton land, townland, division of parish, 124/2.

Toun londe, *sb.* townland, township, division of parish, 125/2.

Tre, *adj.* three, 14/5.

Trewage, *sb.* tribute, 114/29 ; truage, 60/15. O. Fr. *treuage.*

Trogh, *prep.* through, 22/6, 26/1, 62/18 ; troghe, 20/24 ; troght, 28/29.

Trukked, *vb.* trucked, was bartered ?, 48/9.

Trywyly, *adv.* truly, 12/27.

Turnet to, *vb.* turn to, 78/32.

Turues, *sb.* turves, turfs, 30/17.

Twonty, *num.* twenty, 50/28.

Tynge, *sb.* things, 24/14 ; thing, 28/8 ; notynge, nothing, 16/5, 20/9.

Tynke, *vb.* think, 6/26 ; tynken, 22/4.

Tywesday, tywesdaye, tyvysday, tywysday, *sb.* Tuesday, 98/1, 99/1, 2.

Vanhope, *sb.* wanhope, despair, 57/5.

Vend, *vb.* wend, 54/15.

Vepne, *sb.* weapon, 110/24.

Vickydly, *adv.* wickedly, 53/35.

Vncharged, *vb.* unloaded, 10/2.

Vndedde, *vb.* undid, ruined, 114/4 ; vndid, 115/4. See *Vndo*.

Vnderfonge, *vb.* receive, 62/19 ; vndrefynge, 4/32, 8/1 ; vndyrfonge, received, 9/1.

Vndo, *vb.* destroy, ruin, 20/6, 22/4, 84/11, 94/32.

Vndrestondeth, *vb.* understand ye, *imper.* 20/15.

Vneuenly, *adj.* uneven, unequal, inferior, 30/25.

Vnhap, *sb.* mishap, 56/5.

Vnhele, *sb.* misfortune, 126/12.

Vnkede, *adj.* strange, 20/20, 24/28 ; vnkyde, 31/6, 35/2.

Vnkyndely, *adv.* unnaturally, 87/18.

Vnmercyably, *adv.* unmerciably, mercilessly, 55/1. Comp. O. Fr. *merciable*.

Vnmesurable, *adv.* unmeasurably, beyond measure, 54/26 ; vnmeasurably, 55/26.

Vnmetly, *adv.* unmeetly, immoderately, 118/33.

Vnnowmmerabill, *adj.* innumerable, 19/15.

Vnryght, *sb.* wrong, injustice, 86/18 ; vnryght, 112/32.

Vnsikere, *adj.* unsure, 10/2.

Vnsurnes, *sb.* unsureness, insecurity, 51/8.

Vnwardly, *adj.* unwary, ignorant, 52/14.

Vnwarly, *adv.* unwarely, unexpectedly, 78/9.

Vnwemmed, *pp.* unstained, undefiled, 44/7, 92/4 ; vnwemyd, 93/3.

Vpon, *prep.* from, against, 106/32.

Vp-rerid, *pp.* raisd up, 13/2.

Vptake, *vb.* succour, help, support, 92/3.

Vreke, *vb.* wreak, avenge, 145/8.

Vs-self, ourselves, 22/1.

Vyrchip, *vb.* worship, 43/20.

Vyrchipp, *sb.* worship, 5/32.

Wanhope, *sb.* despair, 17/29, 32/12.

Wanhoply, *adj.* desperate, 88/6.

Warliere, *adv.* more warily, 12/19.

Waryr, *adv.* more cautiously, 13/19.

Warytres, *sb.* cursed trees, gallows, 34/16 ; 'galosis,' 35/16.

Wax, *vb.* grew, turnd, became, 2/7 ; arose, grew up, 26/22.

Wayte, *sb.* wait, expectation, 110/33.

Wecchene, *vb.* move, take, 36/31. A.S. *wecgan* : comp. weigh anchor.

Wel, *adv.* well, quite, 52/13 ; frankly, 78/30 ; much, 78/32 ; very, 2/11.

Wenttene, *vb.* think, say ?, 106/8.

Wenynge, *sb.* whining, mourning, 54/17.

Wepne, *sb.* weapon, out of w. = out of harness, when not fighting, 54/31 ; wepyn, 55/31.

Wepne, *vb.* weapon, arm, 50/27 ; weppen, 16/32 ; wepyn, 17/30.

Wer, *vb.* war, 'wer the fight,' 10/27 ; were, 11/28 ; weren, *inf.* 82/16 ; werret, 3/6 ; werry, *inf.* 8/11 ; werryn, 83/16.

Were, *sb.* war, 125/32.

Weued, *sb.* altar, 42/26. A. S.

Whan, *vb.* won, 136/11.

Whan-hopefully, *adv.* unhopefully, despairingly, 16/30.

What for, on account of, 108/21.

Whodyreso, *adv.* whithersoever, 40/11.

Whybelers, *sb.* quibblers ?, 148/3.

Whyle, *sb.* the w. = at that time ?, 82/13 ; = *conj.* while, 82/15 ; That whylle = at that time, 124/20.

Whyth, *prep.* with, 130/31.

Wille, *adj.* wild, rough, 129/29.

Willych, *adv.* vilely, 54/1.

Wndre, *prep.* under, 28/7.

Wnneth, *conj.* unneth, scarcely, 88/15.

Wnselth, *sb.* disadvantage, 50/8.

Wo, *adj.* sorry, 4/35.

Wode, *adv.* wildly, madly, 94/34.

Wodere, *adj.* wilder, madder, 42/27.'

Woke, *adj.* weak, 146/10.

Wolf, woman turned into a, 130.

Wombe, *sb.* belly, 88/4.

Wonder, *adj.* wonderful, 130/11.

Wone, *sb.* custom, usage, 34/15.

Wonet, *pp.* wont, accustomed, 38/33.

Wonne, *sb.* custom, 66/29. See *Wone*.

Wood, *adj.* mad, wild, 42/27.

Worth, *vb.* happened, existed, was, 38/26 ; became, 124/33.

Worthly, (worthy, R.) *vb.* honor, 92/3.

Worthy, *vb.* honor, 93/2.

Wrech, *sb.* wreak, vengeance, 120/34; wreche, 130/29.

Wrechydnys, *sb.* vengeance, 131/33.

Wrethe, *sb.* wrath, 74/22.

Wreyer, *sb.* wrayer, betrayer, 102/24.

Wryttes, *sb.* writs, writings, letters, 56/13; yne wrytte, in writing, 64/7.

Wryynge, *sb.* distorting, falsifying, 102/11.

Wsyd, *pp.* used, accustomed, practist, skilful, 23/27.

Wyage, *sb.* voyage, 62/7.

Wylle, *sb.* at w. = as he wished, 58/22.

Wynd abydynge, wind-bound, waiting for wind, 80/6.

Wyrchiply, *adv.* worshiply, worshipfully, 67/22.

Wyssed, *vb.* directed, guided, 94/19; wissede, 95/19.

Wyt, *prep.* with, 50/15.

Wytht, *prep.* with, 46/17.

Wyttaylle, *sb.* victual, 104/6.

Wyttynge, *sb.* witting, knowledge, 27/3.

-y, *infin.*: See—assembly, castely, de-

fouly, forswely, namy, tholy, werry, 8/11.

Yardes, *sb.* boughs, sticks, 30/17.

Yarne, *vb.* rushed, ran, 82/3.

Y-cast, *pp.* purposed, 68/30.

Y-douted hym, was afraid, 86/1.

Y-dene, *pp.* done, 28/29.

Y-dropesie, *sb.* dropsy, 44/14.

Yern, *vb.* rush, hasten, 74/1, 76/2.

Yernynge, *vb.* running, rushing, 94/34.

Yew, *vb.* yeve, give, 55/32; yewyn, *pp.* 81/9.

Y-lacet, *pp.* laced, 52/11.

Y-leued, *pp.* believed, 102/10.

Ymeuyd, *pp.* moved, 101/4.

Yold, *sb.* yule, Christmas, 42/34; yolde, 43/34.

Yolowe, *adj.* yellow, 98/10.

Yorne, *adv.* gerne, eagerly, 92/21; yonre, 104/10.

Yought, *sb.* youth, 68/20, 118/27.

Youre, *adj.* yare, active, 114/27.

Yoy, *sb.* joy, 100/29.

Yroked, *pp.* rocked, 42/9.

Y-rotid, *pp.* rooted, 149/17.

Yuel, mich, much evil, leprosy, 32/7.

Yurne, *sb.* eagerness?, 112/1.

INDEX

(MAINLY)

BY THOMAS AUSTIN.

—◆—

(For a completer Index, see Mr. Dimock's, *Gir. Camb. Op.* v. 440–60.)